Khalid Mohamed started as revie
his teenage years, for *Close-Up,*
magazine. He then covered crime
The Times of India, Mumbai, from the mid-1970s, engaged in daily reporting and film criticism.

Appointed Media Editor of the paper, he went on to serve as editor of *Filmfare* magazine, while continuing as the daily's film critic for 27 years. He reviewed television for *The Economic Times* besides contributing articles to *The Illustrated Weekly of India* and *Femina.* His writing has also been featured in *India Today, The Indian Express, The Telegraph,* the international film weekly, *Variety,* and in the *Sunday Observer,* London.

He was film critic for *Mid-day,* Senior Editor of *DNA* newspaper, and National Culture Editor and film critic for the *Hindustan Times.*

A post-graduate in Political Science from Mumbai's St Xavier's College, he has translated eminent painter M.F. Husain's autobiography – *Where Art Thou?* – from Hindustani to English.

He has written the original stories and screenplays for three films by Shyam Benegal: *Mammo, Sardari Begum* and *Zubeidaa.* He wrote the original stories and screenplays for the films, *Fiza, Tehzeeb* and *Silsiilay* and also directed them.

He was playwright and director of the stage play *Kennedy Bridge.* His documentaries *The Last Irani Chai, Little Big People* on Mumbai's street children, and *The Master: Shyam Benegal,* have been widely screened at international film festivals and on television.

He has written two short story collections – *Two Mothers and Other Stories* and *Faction: Short Stories by 22 Film Personalities.*

... and co-editor during
... a film society quarterly
... politics and the arts for

THE ALADIA SISTERS

KHALID MOHAMED

Om Books International

First published in 2020 by

Om Books International

Corporate & Editorial Office
A-12, Sector 64, Noida 201 301
Uttar Pradesh, India
Phone: +91 120 477 4100
Email: editorial@ombooks.com
Website: www.ombooksinternational.com

Sales Office
107, Darya Ganj, New Delhi 110 002, India
Phone: +91 11 4000 9000
Fax: +91 11 2327 8091
Email: sales@ombooks.com
Website: www.ombooks.com

Disclaimer: This is a work of fiction. Names, characters, businesses, places, events, locales, and incidents are either the products of the author's imagination or used in a fictitious manner. Any resemblance to actual persons, living or dead, or actual events is purely coincidental.

ISBN: 978-93-5276-631-4

Printed in India

10 9 8 7 6 5 4 3 2 1

For all the grandmothers of the world

Contents

1.	In the Abode of the Gods	9
2.	Alif-Be-Pe, Alphabet Unknown	23
3.	On a Jagged Beat	31
4.	Train to Nowhere	41
5.	On the Couch	58
6.	Emotional Rescue	67
7.	Fragments and Shards	83
8.	The Embroidered Brothel	96
9.	Negotiations	105
10.	On Camera	111
11.	Just Don't Mean A Thing	133
12.	Over the Parcelled Lunch	139
13.	Songs of Love and Longing	153
14.	Still Voices, Distant Lives	161
15.	The Weight of Postcards	174
16.	The Blue Cat, The Laughing Buddha	189
17.	In the Realm of Anxiety	216
18.	Woman in the Box	224

19. Of Our Fathers 230
20. "What can we do for you today?" 236
21. God of all Tragedies 246
22. The Little Shop 253
23. Fall Among the Pigeons 258
24. She's Gone 270
25. Ameena, Eye, Ferozi, Short 281
26. The Prodigal Sisters 295
27. Monday 305
28. Tuesday 311
29. Wednesday 314
30. A Novel 318
31. Ashes and Diamonds 321
32. "Your place is not here…not among us Musalmans" 335
33. The Last Call 343
34. *Epilogue* 347
Acknowledgements 349

1

In the Abode of the Gods

Qalayat, pronounced 'Qaleth', hasn't been mapped yet. A cross between a village and township in the Jind district of Haryana, it's an enclosure empty of monuments and landmarks.

The state of Haryana, in northern India, was formed following the Punjab Reorganisation Act in 1966, much after the opening chapter of the story of the six Aladia sisters.

The name 'Punjab', signifying a confluence of five rivers, had been coined centuries ago by the Central Asian Turkish conquerors, and popularised by the Mughals. But that's for the history books.

In 1966, the state was sub-divided on the criterion of the languages spoken by the inhabitants in its diverse seams and folds.

The sub-districts of Jind and Narwana in the Sangrur province, home to Qalayat, were subsumed into the neo-demarcated state of Haryana, denoting Abode of the Gods. Implacably to date, the administration has been quick to playing the game of divide and govern.

The ongoing division of states in post-independent India has been largely benign. No tragic upheavals. At most, the lines drawn were akin to fleeting worry wrinkles.

The Punjab-Haryana divide wasn't comparable at all to the British barrister Sir Cyril Radcliffe's line of partition in 1947, splicing a sub-continent into India and Pakistan.

Poet W.H. Auden had written about Sir Cyril, describing him wryly as "unbiased". Or "at least he was when he arrived on his mission / Having never set eyes on this land he was called to partition / Between two peoples fanatically at odds /...(given) four judges, two Moslems and two Hindus, to consult with."

The epochal split was red-inked by the clueless British barrister. He had never been east of Paris. India couldn't have been more than an enormous canvas of a colony which had to be tinted in bewildering, separatist shades of brown.

During the near two centuries-long British Raj, territorial lines were unthinkable. Whether under subjugation or after Independence, the Aladia sisters had come to regard themselves as a fusion of Punjab and Haryana. The sisters' spoken dialect was polyglot, their vocabulary a zingy mix of Urdu and Punjabi. Their accents were thickly Haryanvi, the n's spiky, the vowels abbreviated, and the syllables stretched.

The state rupture confused the next generation of the Aladias. They couldn't pinpoint whether they were Haryanvi Jats or Punjabis. Regional identification was kept at bay, with the rejoinder, "We are Haryanvi-Punjabis, both!" or more generically, "We're from somewhere in north India."

Today Qalayat, a fractious acreage, kindles images of water-pumps irrigating wheat, millet and paddy fields. Filigreed tumbledown fast-holds have been fabricated into squat cement-block homes. Doppelganger brick kilns abound. A moss-cloaked mosque topped by a marble dome racked with indigo stone veins, co-exists with the burgeoning Hanuman temples sculpted into the tired trunks of peepul trees – kin to the Bodhi under which between the fourth and sixth centuries B.C., Gautam Buddha is lored to have attained Enlightenment.

Crows peckish as they are anywhere, lounge in the grass pockets toasted by the sun to a tobacco brown. Eagles, kites and vultures soar, on the lookout for a landing point for carrion. Matronly sows grunt, fearing clawed attacks. The cattle, some skeletal, others well proportioned, graze peaceably at dry bushes and tufts. They are protected as much by celestial beings as by crucified scarecrows, and children wielding stone catapults in case the eagles transgress the rules. Dogs of no recognisable breed bark raucously whenever the predatory birds flap too close for comfort.

The term 'village' – or its first cousin 'township' – is anachronistic. Yet, it's handy for annotating the yawning tracts of land dotted with ridges, rivulets and dugouts. On this 21st-century rural scape, collective rejoicing still erupts with the introduction of electricity. The benediction of machine-generated power is celebrated, even though the lights in the areas of darkness come on and go off coquettishly. Rustics can't be choosers. Relief and gratitude are writ large on the rarely expressive faces, transiently. Deep, focused attention is accorded to the let-there-be-light – battiyan jalao – ceremony a month before the quinquennial general elections.

Votes count, manipulated by money-in-cash allurements and orations about an improved life. Primeval amenities attached to row houses, stucco two-storeyed blocks and retail shops are contracted to the most up-to-snuff spokesmen of the constituency, who change as swiftly as their political affiliations, motivated by considerations of caste and creed, of the inclusive and the exclusive. Rancour behind the rejoicing simmers.

Qalayat is prototypical. Electoral promises and pay-offs transmute into terminal deprivation. Enough is never enough. Between 1857 and 1948, administrators of the British Raj didn't deign to go there. They made no promises. That would have meant thankless effort. Presumption: the natives wouldn't have submitted to the kindness of the sola-hatted strangers.

Endemically, the priorities of the British authorities precluded chunky slices of India: the villages were conjectured to be as barren as the kilns. No Governor General had heard of Qalayat.

The Marquesse of Willingdon, Freeman Freeman-Thomas, during his governor generalship, *had* heard of the Aladia sisters in passing, of the six child-women who were in the process of formulating a pact to take a city, any city, by its balls, the balls of a city kept under perpetual surveillance by the British, if need be. Through an illegibly scrawled postcard, the sisters had sought audience with the lord. Bemused, Freeman-Thomas had blinked, "What?"

Audience wasn't granted. The girls – or were they women? – were dismissed as nubile harlots, conniving a clearance to hobnob with the goras.

***

The Aladia sisters were born in rapid succession, 1920 onwards. The Declaration of the Independence of India was promulgated circa 1929 by the Indian National Congress, igniting a fight-to-the-finish for independence from the shackles of the British Empire. Not that this affected the lives of the consecutive newborns in any way.

Informal firmans – do-this, don't-do-that – were issued at home, as they were, are, at every home by Qalayat's cast-in-stone patriarchy. The Aladia parents – Saundha Bhai and Iddanbi – harnessed by a nikaah, had their own meme: to introduce as many children to the world as they could, unknowingly adhering to the misplaced Malthusian theory: more numbers add up to a clockwork everyday life. Their children would carry out chores – they would bring home a day's wage from the farm stretches; they would cook, clean, serve as a support system for their abba and ammi when advanced age would wreak its toll. More the happier – a miscalculation.

Saundha Bhai and Iddanbi Aladia were not scripted to taste happiness. That nectar was exclusively fermented by the gods for others; anyone but them. Love, in the Aladias' unspoken vocabulary, was toxic, as colourless as cyanide.

Or their perseverance could have been a curse. Steadily, Saundha Bhai was convinced that a male child had been denied to them by Allah on purpose. Quixotic were the parvardigar's ways. The Almighty would come around, reconsider. Allah did.

Mashallah, at long last, a son was born to them faster than the midwife could come sprinting, sapped by the couple's serial breeding. The yearned-for boy, flawless and healthy, was named Murad - the desired one. A belated beatitude. The infant's lasting smiles, his brown balletic eyes, his stubby fingers slicing the air like a music conductor's, his dove-like coo-oo-oos, didn't soften the sisters. They boycotted the heaven-consigned ambassador of hope. He couldn't be on their abacus; he was an intruder.

Besides, they had already begun to grow up to the rhythm of their instincts. If Murad was their brother, the sisters computed, he could fend for himself. They wouldn't permit themselves a closer look. They would turn stone-deaf whenever he gurgled for a feed from their mother's breasts. The sisters regarded themselves as Humshira, the Arabic short form for siblings weaned on their mother's milk. 'Hum' encapsulated 'we', 'shira', 'their mother's milk'. The plurality made them singular. For all the Humshira cared, Saundha Bhai and Iddanbi could dote on Murad, cuddle him, shower the infant with plenary adulation. The parents' pride was their daughters' revulsion.

Seven children had to be fed, washed, leashed and reprimanded. Iddanbi complained on loop. So did Saundha Bhai when he was laid off as a supervisor at Zamindar

Harveer Malik's grain cellars. Summoned, if at all, during the harvest season, he would transfer his frustration to Iddanbi, whingeing, "Woman, you're a whore in bed, you tempt me to mount you. Some devil takes a hold of you. Correct yourself or it will be dozakh for you on qayamat day."

Hell and Judgment Day could wait. The good woman wouldn't retaliate – her fail-safe weapon to fend off conjugal warfare. Sexually, she chose to be aggressive, arching her back athletically when her breasts were kneaded.

His incessant admonishments, and seven children, had morphed Saundha Bhai into a beast. He had to devour flesh, his Iddanbi every night. Age didn't matter. He didn't know his birth date anyway. He had mounted a few women. But he was not a sexual predator.

Nishat Mandi, the closest bazaar for sex (bread, fruit, flour and millet would be accepted in lieu of money) teemed with derelict women born to give rather than to gain pleasure and die in Qalayat. With them, Saundha Bhai could get no satisfaction, reach orgasm. He wouldn't come. A girl in her fledgling teenage years had mocked him, "Go somewhere else if you can't get it up. Tchah, you are not man enough." He had become a subject of ridicule in the mandi. "There he comes, a cloud which never rains," the mandi's women would titter, smug with the metaphor.

In the twilight of the bazaar's alleyways, flanked by bleeding, crusted gutters, Saundha Bhai would ruminate, "Iddan is superior to these women on sale...but I could be mistaken. They aren't inferior. I'm at fault; I'm contrite about sinning. It's anxiety which prevents me from satisfying other women and myself. What else could it be? I'm man enough."

Saundha Bhai and Iddanbi were like grandparents to their son Murad, and shamelessly partial. Towards his daughters, Saundha Bhai could be aloof to the point of sadism. He seldom spoke to them, least of all to Mumtaz, the first-born who had been gifted a name implying feminine grace and authority. A name of Arabic origin, it means 'distinguished'.

Unequivocally Saundha Bhai had longed for sons after Mumtaz. Any man would have, he consoled himself. The selection of the sisters' names was a brusque one-letter extension of names favoured for males – with a stroke of a syllable, Jameel became Jameela, Allarakha Allarakhi, Fayaz Fayazi. Feroz who became Ferozi and Ameen Ameena were twins who, apart from their diminutive size, didn't resemble each other.

Amina's right eye was damaged at birth; the retina resembled a black raisin dissolved in milk. Ferozi's eyes were perfect, her height wasn't. She could be mistaken for a dwarf unless she, so mushroom-like, bean-stalked by magic. She did somewhat on reaching puberty. The sisters were relieved. Ferozi was petite, not a freak.

All uniformly the complexion of milk tea, except for the stunted, copper-toned Ferozi, the sisters were as large-framed as the windows of their house built of bumpy, grey stones. The walls inside were as sombre as sorrow, meshed with pebbly cement. The roof was precariously straw-and-reed thatched. The house, without a name or number, was large, the furnishings minimal. A slender, paisley-patterned rug was thrown at the room's centre-point. In a corner, close to the entrance door was a kitchen, a mud-stove revived with lumps of coal which were counted by Iddanbi on her left hand's fingers every morning.

At the distance of a sneeze, Saunda Bhai and Iddanbi occupied a smaller room, an outhouse furnished with narrow conjoined rope charpoys. For the sisters, the cotton-stuffed bedding arranged on a stone platform, would be disinfected of bugs by placing them under the harsh yet healing summer sun. Toilets then were unimaginable. The Aladia brood and their parents had to make do with the privacy of the clusters of shrubbery a tedious walk away from where they would return, carrying back empty, dented water cans, their noses covered by rags to mitigate the stink.

The girls were moon-faced, their jaws chiseled into V-shapes. "Allah created my girls in His spare time," Iddanbi would expostulate to herself, "but forgot to give them a penis. I must have committed unpardonable crimes in my previous birth – there *has* to be a before and after life – to be burdened with girls. They don't obey me, they don't help me. I tell you, Iddan, they should be horsewhipped in the public square."

By dint of being the first-born, Mumtaz was the bully of the pack. Jameela detested the stewardship, but the all-knowing one was Badi Aapa after all. Mumtaz would hum, dance giddily, sing tunelessly, stringing words together – khuda, aapa, abba, ammi, taqdeer – as soon as she could pronounce them. Taqdeer, destiny, became the sisters' marker for all things inopportune or propitious.

Jameela was observant, watchful, rarely speaking but with her unblinking gaze. Allarakhi was dim. She was born, it would have seemed, to be a mute follower. Her inborn talent was to be a listener. She would have flung herself into a river of no return if Badi Aapa Mumtaz had demanded that of her. Fayazi was the gnostic one, oftentimes arguing about why they had to go along with Badi Aapa, and not with the parents, their raison d'être. All the pros and cons considered, the sisters gave in to the leader with reservations. "Why don't you trust me?" Mumtaz would berate the sisters, whenever they demurred. There would be second thoughts but no rejoinders. It made sense to be one of the Humshira herd.

Ferozi and the one-eyed Ameena resided in their exclusory world, sharing wild berries, tamarind and raw mangoes stolen from fenced-off farms. The twins would chatter on deliriously with stray cats, tweaking their whiskers, manicuring the cut of their claws, smoothening and massaging their spotty coats to a sheen

"These two are soft in the head. Let them be. None of those billis stay for long," Badi Aapa Mumtaz would permit the twins to twaddle on, an incovenience as transitory as a passing itch. The ditzy duo was harmless, as long as they didn't pick up black cats associated with bad luck since the dawn of civilisation. Iddanbi also swore by the superstition that a twitch in the right eye was auspicious for men. A twitch in the left eye was a prelude to beneficial news for women.

Murad was a harbinger of ill luck, a contretemps for the sisters. The brother was a twitch in the wrong eye, a black cat who couldn't cross their path. Never.

Without exception, the Humshira giggled whenever Mumtaz said 'uzu-i-tanasul' – penis – instead of the euphemism 'popat ki chonch' – a parrot's beak. The size and shape of their father's beak fascinated them whenever they saw him bathing in water colder than night dew in winter at the shallow mud well in their home's backyard. "That's such a dark, fat chonch. Is he abnormal?" Fayazi would ask of Mumtaz, the key to all mysteries.

"You're so silly, Fejji," Mumtaz would slap Fayazi lightly across the cheek. "We haven't seen anyone else's uzu-i-tanasul yet. So who knows?"

If Mumtaz didn't know, no one else could.

Her word was law, Badi Aapa was an empress in the works. The sisters' eyes would turn from crescents into full moons whenever Mumtaz bathed them in the fount of wisdom. She wouldn't disclose a jot of pride in the fact that their father was rugged, cleft-chinned, symmetrically sculpted. His uncombed hair fell on his forehead, and covered the nape of his neck. His eyes were deep set like a hawk's, his voice as commanding as a soldier's. A tall, hirsute man, his daughters' chins would rise to size him up from head to toe.

Mumtaz longed to consolidate her authority. She had to be sharper, wiser, irrefutable. Wisdom was a stronger suit than curiosity. She didn't know or didn't wish to know why Allah had chosen to place them in Qalayat. Intermittently, she supposed that the Man Above There Somewhere must have drafted a plan for her, for her sisters. It had to be a Man unarguably, the creator of the universe. A Woman? No chance. Their destinies would be His munificence. For the Humshira, He could not rewrite the story of Saundha Bhai and Iddanbi whose kismats were a cipher, ordained to be married off by their parents.

A nikaah in sync with the tenets of Islam must have earned the parents of Saundha Bhai and Iddanbi brownie points, a reserved passage to heaven. Mumtaz couldn't conjure up images of her grandparents, whoever, wherever they may have been, whenever. No memories had lasted of either parents' brothers, sisters, cousins, if there had been any, or any of consequence. Chances are that Iddanbi was 12, Saundha Bhai 13, when they were manacled by the nikaah which no one remembered. In all probability, the rites conducted by a maulvi, were rapidly rendered. No ostentation. The villagers addressed Saundha as Saundha Bhai, a brother to the community, and Iddan as Iddanbi, an elder. Such suffixes were required to circumvent familiarity, malice.

Qalayat was an agrarian order established by zamindars, the landowners. Wheat, millet, rice, and mustard seeds were the principal produce of the region. A panchayat of physically enfeebled, turbanned farmers, selected by the zamindars, served as firefighters for the populace. Of them, Muslims formed a minority, tolerated with caution. The Hindu chief was Mukhiya. The Muslim leader was Maulana, the local head-priest.

To all appearances, Saundha Bhai and Iddanbi were integral to the societal order. For the Humshira, their parents were novitiates though. The sisters weren't ever fed on back stories. They weren't treated to those-were-the-day anecdotes.

The Aladia family tree was a stump. No tales, brief or elaborate, with locations and timelines were recapitulated. At most, there was this broad assertion: Niyaz and Aasoo, parents of Iddanbi, were pious souls. Attempts to convert them to Christianity by Jesuit missionary priests had been rebuffed vehemently. Saundha Bhai's parents were a blank. No surnames, no recall. Where the name Aladia originated from was nebulous.

The sisters left the family stump there. They were into namaaz and rozas. Their faith wasn't frippery; it demanded austerity, penance and adab. Mumtaz couldn't ever be accused of inconsistency, or of harbouring self-doubts. The initiator as naturally as sunrise is to a day, she must have been 14 when she bunched her troupe towards the railway tracks, within visible distance from their home.

The twins, Ameena and Ferozi, were still aged eight or ten. Steam engines belching clouds of smoke clanged past angrily. Transporting coal from Bengal's mines in the east to the factories of the industrialised northern belt, the oxidised doors of the goods trains were clamped shut. The automaton-like engine drivers fixed their sights on the tracks ahead. Impotent pricks, namarads. Mumtaz agonised over the futility of catching an engine driver's eye. She could seduce them but none of the men with soot-smeared faces spared half a glance. Their loss, she sneered. They didn't know what they were missing out on – the blooms in the boscage.

They wouldn't have, if she or her sisters had flung themselves on the tracks. An audacious plan but too risky. Badi Aapa Mumtaz could foresee blood on the tracks, a mass burial.

Seized by another plan, she contacted the gnomish post-office clerk who manned a barely functional post-office, which also served as his home close to the railway tracks. On a slack afternoon, Mumtaz and her sisters badgered the clerk to write, promising to pay him whenever able. The post-card was addressed in rudimentary English calligraphy to the Governor General. No reply.

The forgetful clerk on the anvil of retirement lived alone, didn't expect payment. He looked forward to the company of the sisters; they made him feel wanted. Whenever they asked him about the response to the card, he would smile, "It will come when the last of my teeth fall off. How my gums ache."

2

Alif-Be-Pe, Alphabet Unknown

Alert to the signs of insurgency, Iddanbi's hostility towards her daughters was as irreducible as their poverty. She would boil over, "So many wide-open mouths to feed. May Allah remove you from the face of this earth. See my boy, doesn't even wake up at nights for his feed. He's content with so little. Murad is our angel, our real farishta."

Such slights didn't affect the Humshira. They were immersed in the sport of mutual dependence, typified by the everyday ritual of oiling and braiding their hair which would not be trimmed.

The sisters shared frugal meals – turnips, beets, dry rotis and stringy lamb shorba, bequeathing their raggedy clothes – white muslin kurtas, baggy salwars and dupattas of vivid but fast-fading colours – to the next one in the chain. The sisters didn't know there could be another home, an alternate world which foxy Mumtaz was self-appointed to reveal to them. As the eldest sister, by birthright she had taken charge of her province, an open-air cloister.

Qalayat was as tenacious as the endless nights. There wasn't a peep of electricity. No school for induction in the Urdu alphabet of alif-be-pe. Elementary education wasn't a given of the time, still isn't. No information either about the rat-borne plague which had killed over 2,800 people in the sorcerous city of Bombay. No knowledge about the might of the British Empire, or of the historical visit of King George V and Queen Mary in 1911 to the Delhi Durbar, or of the belated construction of the Gateway of India to commemorate their visit. For Mumtaz and her gang, as for the rest of Qalayat, ignorance of significant events was salvation.

There was nothing within or without Qalayat but the undulating plains relieved by farms and the railway track. Their home was sunlit during summer. It plunged into raven darkness during winter. There would be rain in lashes and drizzles, an adequate amount, which would be welcomed by Saundha Bhai. He could cop a month or two of odd jobs – managing the nullahs from overflowing, repairing roofs, rushing the infirm hakim to the homes of the ailing, all without specifiying a fixed wage. He'd bring home a palm full of coins and wet currency notes of small denomination.

Iddanbi would mew in a feeble jab at humour, "Janaab, I hope you didn't pickpocket anyone in the public square." Then, she would backtrack, "I know you can commit the worst sins but never thieve." This exchange was another yearly custom condoned by the sisters petulantly. Granted a wish, they would have tossed their mother into the murkiest nullah. Not their father. Never mind his aberrations and apathy, they adored him, even if they didn't respect him. Respect wasn't a factor in Qalayat. Survival was, survival which would be the route to the realisation of dreams. Mumtaz was the dictator of dreams.

"Munta! You sleep and sleep, grinning like an idiot," Iddanbi, the seasoned insomniac would shake Mumtaz out of her stupor. Under the starless darkness of nights, the mother would survey her litter. She construed their self-absorption as naïveté. If at least two, even one daughter had discerned that their mother didn't mean what she uttered – that she could kill for them – Iddanbi could have slept for more than a few stolen hours a night or day. There would have been no need to harass Mumtaz out of her sleepfests either.

When any one of her daughters was ill – mostly out of malnutrition – Iddanbi nursed the gosling back to life, concocting herb syrups concocting herb syrups and crushing cinnamon sticks into powder. "Let them die," Mumtaz often heard her father say, tempered by the admission, "we are incapable of keeping all of them alive. I've been a worthless father. I can only beg to be forgiven before seeking entry at heaven's door. I have done my best." Next, he would loudly recite the kalima, "Laahe laaha iliilha Muhammad rasool illah", to beget forgiveness. This paranoia about a tortuous afterlife afflicts all devout Muslims. He wasn't alone.

Allah was the only do-gooder, Iddanbi's only friend who understood, who cared. She would pray five times a day. Some day, her plea for orderliness, for security, would be heard. Presumably, Iddanbi's mother, Aasoo, had taught her a few dohas. Presumably, her father, Niyaz, had rocked the infant Iddan, in his arms. The rest of the prayer which she had invented, was conducted on a namaaz rug – a woven purple chenille – a hand-woven marvel even after all these years. Astagfirullah, forgive me, she would chant a hundred times over. Allah was renowned for lenience.

Iddanbi's heart was lucent. The Almighty would look at his creation with mercy, a sturdy, amenable woman in her mid-30s…or was she in her 40s? She couldn't be sure. Head covered with a sparsely sequined dupatta, she would mutter and mumble her bespoke prayer, appealing dutifully for the well-being of Murad, of her daughters, of her husband, in that order. She wouldn't omit herself from the safekeeping appeal. She wasn't that noble; she longed to live.

The daughters too trusted Allah unconditionally. Ammi and Abba would mend their ways, they would have to. Right at this moment, they were necessary evils. Ever the pragmatic Mumtaz had to concede – if Iddanbi carried out the scutwork, cooking a breakfast of baked rotis with a gruel of leftovers, if she breast-fed her just-born, if she pottered around always doing something useful, it was because of her Humshira pack, soldered one by one to her breasts, when they didn't know better. If she were to drop dead, none of the sisters were capable of replacing her. The ingrates.

As the years flew faster than time, Mumtaz, the troublemaker, spoiled for a fight, for an upgrade. "Chudail, soowar, badmash, Munta believes she can be me," Iddanbi notified Allah, the force she wouldn't dare to visualise. That would have been blasphemous. Allah would compel Mumtaz to behave like a daughter should. "But tell me," Iddanbi would resort to deductive logic. "How can Allah watch over all of us? So many people to watch over, so many people! I don't know, but if I think this way, tauba, I will be punished. Desist, Iddan desist, carry on...some day, something will be done for you, only for you, the mother. Someday, something, Alhamdolillah, all praise and thanks be to Allah."

Distracted, spent, Iddanbi would catch fever spasmodically. When that tangled mind of hers stopped buzzing, the fever cooled. On placid evenings, she would sneak a look at the palm-sized mirror. "I am quite beautiful," Iddan would tilt the mirror in close-up and at distant angles. "Look at me! Pink as dawn...not really, but my skin is satin smooth, white as sugar during winter, my hair flows till my buttocks. I'm almost as tall as Saundha; I reach right up to his shoulders. No stoop, I can measure up to him. My nose is so right, a nice little slope, no dents. My lips are rose petals. Oh, why do I bring up roses all the time? Roses once bloomed in the gardens of my head. They were so fragrant and came in so many colours – pink, red, yellow, white. Roses are never blue. Why? Who knows? Let's see, my hands are callused, but they are not stone hard. After a wash, they are feather soft...again I am fooling myself...am I beautiful? I am, no I am not...desist!"

She couldn't, she would feel her tired breasts. Her obsession, she would rub them with rationed drops of almond oil, her fingers circling her inflamed nipples. Her breasts had served her well; she wouldn't let them sag. It wasn't her fault. Those wretched girls, the Humshira had done this to her, milking her dry. Dear Murad was feeding on trickles, the last drops. The infant never howled for more.

Iddanbi's eyes were her prized possessions, large, shaded between grey and yellow. "Who can deny this? I'm a lovely creature," she would chat with the mirror. "None of the girls has inherited them. They have Saundha's ember eyes. My heart aches - what can be done about Ameena's bad eye? Must be a mistake made by the midwife. Aah well...I've preserved my sight with surma...cooling surma. I use very little to make it last. Will Saundha ever replenish my dibiya? He will...he has to... The very first night, he had looked into my eyes, I had closed them for him, so shy I was. His first kisses were on my eyes. On the windows of my soul?" she'd chirp like a sparrow, "Those girls, if they hear me, they'll think I've gone mad. I tell you, give me madness over sanity."

Those convoluted conversations with her Allah were as essential as breathing. She couldn't live without her monologues, which were increasing at an alarming rate, making her as remote as her daughters believed she was:

"Ammi doesn't care. She considers us as liabilities. She has defecated us out of her system. She can't bear the stench. She keeps muttering on about roses, as if she wants to drown us in their fragrance." This theory was devised by Mumtaz and indoctrinated into her sisters. Ammi was mean. They couldn't weigh Ammi's burden of dreams, her concealed desire that the brood would be relocated in a salubrious place on earth. The permanence of Qalayat spelt despair.

Rain or shine, their father Saundha Bhai...bhai a brother! – so inadvertently incestuous – could have found a more compatible woman, Mumtaz would wager. If Abba was uncommunicative, it must have been Ammi's doing. He wasn't to blame. For the six sisters, he was a hero, their father, the provider, toiling whenever he could to bring home whatever sustenance he could.

Occasionally, Jameela and Fayazi would confide in Mumtaz, imagining Saundha Bhai casting fugitive smiles at them, dazzlers in the gloom. When he saw Ameena and Ferozi playing with the stray cats, fabricating a fantasy world for themselves, he did look on lovingly.

He never raised a hand or his voice on the girls. It was Ammi Iddanbi who would let them have it when rules were transgressed. Mumtaz agreed with Fayazi and Jameela, churlishly, "Abba loves us, he doesn't show it. You don't have to tell me what I know already."

No straying away from the house into the thickets of fields. Ammi could be obdurate: the wheat fields were especially dangerous, bristling with dagger thorns, infested with snakes, scorpions and worse. From there, a hideous stalker, the devil himself would whisk her girls away to a necropolis. "Out out, damn shaitaan, you despicable heretic," she'd add the plea to the verse she had learnt by rote: "Rabbi najjiner minal qawnidh dhaalimeen" – the Lord would have to save them from evil, from that devil who had refused to bow down before Aadam.

There would have to be a saviour. If not, the sisters would have to be tolerant of Iddanbi's whims and glorify Saundha Bhai's torpor. Once, when he was bathing, Mumtaz had heard him recite poetry, staccato lines which rhymed, "Karna hai pahad ka saamna / Zindagi ki niyamaton ko jaanna." (I have to face the mountain / To discover the divinity of life.)

Which mountain was he thinking of? Let that pass. The rhyme sounded soothing in Qalayat, a quarantine planned by nature.

The furnace summers followed by paralysing winters were in keeping with north India's mercury levels. The Aladia family thought otherwise – the extremes were a penalty reserved for them.

This much Rehaan Salamat Siddiqi, a mid-rung journalist, could reconstruct, refurbish from conversations amidst his maternal grandmother Fayazi, and her sisters Mumtaz and Jameela. He would eavesdrop on them, pretend to be asleep when they flapped like pigeons on a ledge before taking flight. His first waking memory was of his grandmother saying something to the effect that they hadn't been fair to their Ammi Iddanbi. Her words had stayed, "We should have loved her. A mother is always right. Alhamdolillah."

Brilliantly, they had devised a private Aladia language. Some of the words Rehaan could decode: loora (boy), loori (girl), kurchani (alcohol), jhola (be careful), nhupki re (keep your voice low) dhandoora (wealthy), baidaloo (poor), khaangi (low-life prostitute), itrahoon (haughty woman), Baraatoosh (British), ghartoosh (neighbours) – a comprehensive lexicon, most of which had been disappointingly auto-deleted from the grandson's mind. Fayazi, Mumtaz and Jameela could have taught linguists how to deconstruct and construct a vocabularly.

3

On a Jagged Beat

Formally Fayazi was Rehaan's nani, grandmother, and her sisters his grand-aunts. He felt as incomplete as a book with ripped pages; he had to know more about the sisterhood. The search for the missing pages could be iffy; it could be revelatory. Either way, he had nothing to lose but his tears. He wept readily, smiled with effort, maintained an impassive Buster Keaton face with a natural ease. His thin lips were arranged into a straight line. Tears were his inheritance. Like the Humshira, he could cry up a river at the quiver of an aching memory.

Rehaan was into his emotionally lacerated middle age, on the precarious side of his 30s. The image of the six sisters once huddled out there in Qalayat, conspiring a breakaway, would moisten his eyes. You're a ninny, a cry-baby, Rehaan would cringe. Not a worthy quality in a writer. To be sentimental is to be weak, shallow, immature. Can't be helped, he'd appease himself. He was sentimental, therefore he was devoid of any delusions of emotional neutrality.

He was an Aladia boy, and proud of the lineage. He had to know why. Perhaps the pride could diminish like a library of unreturned books or fast evaporate like ether. Rehaan, buckle up, confront the truth, the real.

Denial can stoke high anxiety verging on panic like a child about to be born kicking at the walls of its prison. For deliverance, the search for the story of Humshira, the six sisters had to begin. Or shelved.

Initially a crime reporter, he was now Media Editor with Mumbai's widely circulated newspaper *The Daily Chronicle*, half-a-century old and some. Located in Mumbai's business hub Fort, off Flora Fountain in two separate wings – one for the management executives who fixed rates for the revenue-generating ads, and the other for the editorial ranks – the workplace was within a heritage building, a carved brownstone edifice facing the Fountain. Editors, sub-editors, lay-out designers and reporters, were the doers, the executives, the fixers who kept the institution in the flush.

The 19th-century Fountain which depicts the Roman Goddess of Flowers and Spring, was mostly bone-dry before the inordinately delayed renovation by the city's civic authorities. At the square, five streets meet - the city's retort to London's Piccadilly Circus, Paris' Champs Elysees and New York's Times Square. A vintage poem by Niranjan Bhagat had waxed on Flora Fountain:

A glass and concrete jungle;
In its midst always
Quiet, comely,

With a hope-filled face,
She stands

A dream of spring in her matchless eyes,
Holding in both hands, stone flowers.
About her, in all corners,
Iron butterflies fly round and round
And lifeless insects play…

Names were rewritten even if history shouldn't be tampered with. In 1961, Fort, crowned by Flora Fountain, was renamed Hutatma Chowk, in the wake of a peaceful demonstration by the Samyukta Maharashtra Samiti for the creation of the state of Maharashtra. The police had opened fire, resulting in 105 deaths. The chowk housing the Fountain was dedicated to the memory of the martyrs. The metropolis was an archive of avertable tragedies.

Rehaan belonged to the metropolis, to Bombay rechristened Mumbai by the right-wing Shiv Sena on the heels of a traumatic spate of communal riots in 1992–1993. Memorials and the Sena's symbol, a tiger…martyrdom and communal hatred were like bookends.

Grandmother Fayazi, ever the worry wart, wouldn't approve of his brief out-of-town trips, assignments picked for him randomly by the paper's editor. Least of all, she wouldn't have ever endorsed his investigative trip to Qalayat. She wasn't a fan of yesterdays. She had drawn the curtain on nostalgia. There could be no life for her grandson in Qalayat, no iron butterflies there. Ma had set him in a groove. He was to a metro born. Stay there. Be grateful for the flora and the fountains.

He was schooled at Cathedral and John Connon followed by three years at St Xavier's College and two at the Bombay University campus, all top-of-the-line institutions, none of which proved to be a passage to instantaneous placements. After post-graduation, he couldn't find gainful employment. The gold medal for clearing the Master of Arts (Hons) examination from the university in Political Science was valueless. Tags of Cathedral and St Xavier's on his bio-data weren't an upper. A pedigree in Political Science was way beneath a Bachelor of Arts supplemented with a Business Management diploma. As an honorary tutor invigilating examinations and correcting the answer-sheets at the St Xavier's, he filled in a six-month term.

After a carousel of interviews, round-table discussions with other candidates and written tests, he was accepted as a trainee in a corporate ad agency, where he lasted a week, exiting without collecting his full-and-final payment. They could keep it. They'd made him feel substandard, rejecting his texts for the print advertisements. "Make the goddamn tagline crispy. You're too roundabout, too pompous," the head honcho among the copywriters would carp. "You're selling sliced bread. Get crispy, not wispy. Geddit?"

As a ground administration intern at Air-India, at the ticket sales counter, he was hopeless. Sales, not his scene. In a part-time job of editing the house journal of an inter-state truck transport company, the boss had gruffly ordered him to brew a cup of tea in the office-kitchen. "Not my expertise," the part-timer had gruffed back. In between the walk-ins and walk-outs, he'd read dog-eared copies of American authors – the musts…Mark Twain, Ernest Hemingway, John Steinbeck, William Faulkner, Tennessee Williams – at public libraries which didn't charge a yearly membership fee. Wilting copies of Maxim Gorky and Fyodor Dostoevsky were picked up for half a song from pavement book vendors. At the British Council, he revisited Jane Austen, Charles Dickens, Thomas Hardy and Shakespeare. At the cavernous hall of the Central Asiatic Society, he'd go through the pages of the day's newspapers, confounded by their flip-flop editorial stratagems.

Through a school friend's father – a venerable newspaper editor – Rehaan chanced upon his niche. He had to be recommended to the training officer, who took one look at him and said, "You don't look the sort who has news sense." The editor couldn't be bypassed though; the appointment letter reached his address within a week. Fayazi wasn't upbeat, "Let's say you are no longer one of the unemployed millions. What kalyug we're living in. Such a dark age where a first-class M.A. degree can't get you a job which pays you a better wage. Five hundred rupees a month to start with? With all that money invested in your education, you're worth at least a couple of thousands a month, and you know that."

"Ma, it'll all work out. I don't want to sell my soul for money," the grandson retaliated, bristling at the hollow ring in his voice.

Fortuitously, Rehaan was at home in the newsroom of *The Daily Chronicle* as a crime reporter, and the night shift warden who'd cover outbreaks of fire, road accidents, house collapses and miscellaneous tragedies which oddly left him unmoved. After a decade-long slog, he was entrusted with the portfolio of the newspaper's Media Editor – his daily beat encompassed Mumbai's glamour gulch, Bollywood movie stars, music wizards, business czars, master painters and upcoming artists.

On this beat, the Aladia sisters would show up in a dream haze. He had romanticised them into an Olympian warrior bunch. Ambiguity dogged him. Come to think of it, if he wasn't an Aladia grandson, at this very moment, would he have contemplated travelling the Bombay-Delhi-Qalayat route?

His patience was on a slow burn. Impetuousness would be self-defeating. He would rewind as if to a favourite retro-ballad on a playlist. Get real – investigative reporters can make Himalayas of molehills, the way he had as a rookie crime reporter, his debut designation on completing the one-year term of a trainee.

An adolescent Muslim boy, arrested on the charge of a petty theft, was subjected to rough treatment during police custody at the Arthur Road jail, built in 1926 to pack in 800 prisoners. The average number of inmates had mounted to over 2000. Space crunch, you see, the state police personnel had thown their hands up. The boy died after a day of being brutalised in prison. Grabbing that lead, Rehaan had dashed out a front-page news report, partly true, partly exaggerated. A month later, he was summoned as a witness by the violated boy's parents to Mumbai's Small Causes Esplanade Court. *Small causes?*

Rehaan hadn't reported the truth unvarnished; the story could have been unfounded. He had no evidence to substantiate the allegations: the boy was subjected to third-degree because he belonged to Mohammed Ali Road. He was a Muslim more vulnerable to cell torture than most. Stumped about what he could say from the witness box, Rehaan hadn't fetched up in court. The heat would abate; it did. The parents' plaint begot justice. Perhaps it didn't. He didn't want to know. To date, he's relieved that the unanswered summons didn't lead to a recall from court.

He'd seek a summons from his grand-aunt, by now monikered Mumtaz Chaudhran. She wouldn't respond. She had barricaded herself. She wasn't an inquiry counter. He'd drop by to see her at the slightest pretext to ask about her health. She'd see through his game and snarl, "As if it would make any difference to you if I drop dead today."

"Tell me, how have you been, Mumtaz Nani?" Rehaan would go on solicitously. He called her 'Nani' because he had no other form of address for her. His real nani, Fayazi would be addressed as 'Ma'; she was his mother in absentia. Her sisters were Nanis, for want of a convenient word.

Rehaan's biological mother, Zahira, had died at the age of 18 a fortnight after he was born. "Delivery complications," he had been told by Mumtaz Nani. "Even the surgeon who had attended on your mother, was reduced to tears." Ma Fayazi had corroborated that reluctantly, "Forget the past. I'm there for you. Isn't that enough?"

The son was Zahira's only nishani, a memento. He would maintain a straight face on being reminded by the irrevocably vitriolic Mumtaz Nani, "You are responsible for her death. If it weren't for you, Zahira would be among us today."

For the nth time today, she had repeated haughtily, "Why do you call all of us sisters Nani, boy? That you should only call your grandmother, your Fejji Nani. Fayazi is insanely possessive of you." Mumtaz had swivelled her face histrionically, "Call me Mumtaz Chaudhran, the chief! I've always been the eldest one, remember? Let me be now. Come back next Sunday if you must. And draw the curtains before you leave. Too many mosquitoes bigger than elephants, here."

Beige polyester curtains, imprinted with bleeding-red poppies erased the view of the high rises, myopically raised, planned and architected by real-estate profiteers. The concatenation of apartment complexes had sprouted right in the midst of Mumbai's Oshiwara, Andheri. The outback of the seven-island city housed countless families which had sold their cramped apartments in South and Central Bombay for relatively more spacious space, vended at deceptively low-cost prices. Freckled with mangroves which gave the impression of bountiful greenery, Oshiwara is a deceptive haven.

Mosquitoes and blue-bottle flies swarm into the apartments. The water supply is moody, but what the hell, Oshiwara was better than subsisting in those uptown crannies. Shops hawking jeans, T-shirts, household bric-à-brac, predominantly vases for paper flowers, and more textile yardage than could be worn by the entire city, aggravated the bustle around the neo-housing colonies.

The swishier, gated housing colonies close to the Arabian Sea-lined Seven and Four Bungalows, had been appropriated by the constellation of movie and TV professionals and, in many instances, rented by show business aspirants. No more than a marshland during the British Raj, the Seven Bungalows precinct was once punctuated by coconut palm trees and glass shards embedded on walls to prevent trespassing. One of the bungalows, city chroniclers testify, belonged to the founder of the Indian National Congress, Dadabhai Naoroji. The city father's bungalow, along with five others, had given way to high-rise towers. Nazneen, an ancient bakery, occupies in part, the sole surviving bungalow.

Mumtaz Chaudhran's apartment in one of the high-rise towers was a two bedrooms-hall-kitchen – 2BHK – acquired at a cut-rate price since it faced a mangrove infamous for mafia-controlled hooch distilleries. A piffling amount of surplus money after the sale of her Central Bombay home, was invested in mutual funds and fixed deposits at nationalised banks. These were safer than private banks which could go kaput any time, or that's what Mumtaz proclaimed. Never trust private enterprises. The government-sanctioned banks wouldn't dare to deprive anyone of hard-earned savings.

The Chaudhran had her theories.

She spoke telegraphically as the Oshiwara people do on being asked for directions, which would be, "Take a left, then a left, then a right." It would work. The lanes were chaotic, but landmark restaurants, Sasural, Jugheads, and Urban Tadka, were useful in the absence of signage.

It was at the bidding of the Chaudhran that Rehaan was about to travel to Qalayat, to scavenge information. Ha! Info was 'intel' now in the newsroom. At diverse phases in his life, Rehaan had talked to three of the six Aladia sisters: Fayazi Ma, Mumtaz and Jameela Nanis. It was imperative to know more, trace the three missing links – were Allarakhi, Ameena and Ferozi still alive? – extract intel to accessorise the fantasised chapters of a novel he had filed, deleted and recovered.

4

Train to Nowhere

There he was, then, on 10 December 2000. The thoroughly Mumbai-bred Rehaan Salamat Siddiqi procrastinated: to catch the snail train to Qalayat from Delhi or to turn back. The train was to leave at 6 a.m. from the Paharganj railway station between the Minto and Hardinge bridges which have been renamed Shivaji and Tilak bridges.

At that hour, towards the year-end, the railway station is a mist-covered spectacle. Stubbled, marble-eyed men in shawls and pugrees glare at those privileged to alight from autorickshaws, buses and yellow-and-black taxis aged to chrome-and-grey. Migrant workers from adjoining states gape at the blur of seemingly busy men, dazed women, jumpy children in Spider-Man imprinted factory-manufactured sweaters, aviator-collared shirts, windcheaters and jerseys tagged with faux designer labels.

Iodine-red uniformed porters heckle; they don't have sufficient workload. Neither are they paid enough. The coolies canter through the maze of overbridges, knee-length shirts bobbing through waves of fast-motion commuters. The train has been delayed by 40 minutes, which extends to 90 minutes. From a cold hardwood slatted seat, a somnolent rural scape wings past the iron-grill window minutes after the train chugs out of Paharganj.

In the snap of a finger, Lutyens' New Delhi – so called after Edwin Lutyens, the British architect responsible for much of the capital city's architectural splendour – transforms into satellite townships. TV antennae, satellite dishes and yesterday's laundry left on the rooftops to dry are a constant. The two-tier compartment of the train is overrun by hawkers of silver foil packs of potato chips, flavoured Mexican Chilli and Barbecue Americano. Rehaan doesn't buy one to get another pack free.

Come on, these are commonplace hazards, chill (how paradoxical does that sound in Delhi winter?), and smile. In any case, the stout, sanguine papaji with his family of miniature clones is offering to share breakfast paranthas and pepper-smeared potato wedges from a stainless-steel tiffin with Rehaan, now bonding with a community of travellers.

He should have travelled to Qalayat much earlier. He had dawdled because he was a hopeless traveller. He had wasted years to find shortcuts to the lowdown land. He was apprehensive. Out of spite, Zeus, the King of Gods, had presented a clay jar – containing sickness, death and disease – to Pandora's brother, Epimetheus. Instructed never to open the jar, curiosity had prevailed upon caution. From the jar, untold calamities had erupted. Only hope was left before it was closed. The reporter and his curiosity were in conflict.

Come on, what does Greek mythology have to do with the train-hop to Qalayat? At most, a shaft of optimism to reach a story.

As it turned out, Rehaan spent a futile day and night in Qalayat, which could have been one of those one-horse towns from the classic Hollywood cowboy Westerns auteured by John Ford. There was a shade of Bram Stoker's Dracula as well. "There is a reason why all things are the way they are", that pontificating line from Stoker's cauldron surfaced, but to no effect. The solitary tongawalla outside the railway station where he alighted alone from the train en route to the Golden Temple town of Amritsar, hectored him towards a magnificent, piceous horse. In the misty noon, the tongawalla whipped the Black Beauty.

The tongawalla didn't wish to know the passenger's destination point. Ensued a turbulent ride – the roads weren't tarred. The tongawalla salt-and-pepper bearded and earth complexioned, deposited Rehaan at Super Hotel. The lustreless, one-storey cracked cement structure must have witnessed more hospitable days.

Fixed rate for the ride: 250 rupees, give it or bargain in vain. Tossing a fold of an olive shawl to his mouth with a ramp model's flourish, the tongawalla at long last disclosed a shred of curiosity.

"What have you come for? All the ice factories are closed till Holi," he snapped, implying Rehaan was a businessman on a recce acquisition trip. Following the mixed blessing of industrial development, Qalayat was freckled with over a score of factories supplying ice to the cities: coffin-sized slabs of frozen water doomed to melt. Connecting bridges and railway tracks were being uprooted. An expressway under construction promised boom time. More factories, more modernisation, more trade.

Rehaan turned away before the tongawalla drawled, "Our ice is used in abattoirs to preserve meat…bade shaheron ke hotels and slaughterhouses need them…what-what business goes on? Look at me and my faithful horse, Chabook, who will also leave me some day, but I will never sell his meat. He will be put to rest with dignity. We are the load bearers," he groused, concluding with a non-sequitur, "You're not fat, you're a gentleman."

'Not fat' equals 'gentleman'? Possibly Rehaan had inherited the Aladia physique and carriage. None of the sisters, or at least the three he knew, had added ungainly amounts of lard as they had aged. Their bones were calcium firm, their backs ramrod, holding out against the onslaught of age and myriad stress factors. The sisters continued to consider themselves bread earners for the next in line. Rehaan, you're a progeny of matriarchy. Be thankful, he'd glow within.

A gender twist here. Uncannily, for the runaway sisters, a girl child was a joy forever. Boys, like their detested Murad, were an extra mouth to feed. Ne'er-do-wells, they were reflections of the wastrel wimps who crowded the TRP-rich TV serials, in which women did all the dialoguing, nurturing, while the men's jaws dropped to the studio's ersatz marble floors.

The louts in the extended families of the sisters wallowed in indolence; they had become cyborgs within four walls.

The younger lot hung out on the margins, again so much like the expressionless dudes in those TV series, dominated by angry young and old women dressed in crimson-and-gold bling.

Rehaan's stream of thoughts was getting muddier. There was so much more to cover, to discover. And many miles to go before he slept, he reminded himself, kicking himself for regurgitating a line from Robert Frost's poem, 'Stopping by Woods on a Snowy Evening', which he had used excessively as quick-fix headlines for newspaper reports.

To purely fictionalise the long and winding journey of the Aladia sisters would have been facile. It couldn't be done without grabbing at the errant straws in the wind. There had to be an essence of truth, the real over the chimerical. "Truth is stranger than fiction," Mark Twain had posited, "but that is because fiction is obliged to stick to possibilities."

The reporter in him was vigilant yet defeated. In Qalayat, he couldn't find straws in the wind. There was merely the vague update that the sisters' birth home had been converted into a factory producing ice slabs for hotels and slaughterhouses. The Aladia home was located in Dhairyapur, which had evolved into Qalayat's industrial belt; the wasteland had gained gold real-estate value.

The sale of the homestead had fetched a sizeable amount of cash, which Murad, it was alleged, had connived to pocket. He had stayed there till the deaths of Saundha Bhai and Iddanbi. The home was his by prescriptive right. The sisters didn't exist any more for Murad, but they could resurface to raise objections. The home was as much theirs, as it was of their parents' privileged one, the male heir. Between right and wrong, there was an in-between. The house which Saundha Bhai and Iddanbi had once built, was under a shadow of doubt. As parents, they could be considered unjust, scaly monsters turned to dust in a Qabrastan somewhere.

Rehaan had to re-try, penetrate the winter smog of Qalayat. Wasn't there a Lathwal here? Lathwal Laala, was the high-caste trader whom the sisters, Mumtaz and Jameela, had a crush on, etc. Rehaan added etc., to veil sexual insinuations. Lathwal Laala was said to be as enormous as a door, corpulent – a bison of a man. By contrast, the docile, dove-like Mander Bachu, his brother, younger by at least a decade, was scoffed at.

'Laala' meant a man of money, a benefactor, a de facto monarch. 'Bachu' meant a child, a natural-born slave at the beck and shout of the Laala.

Mumtaz would clap her hands to applaud, "Lathwal was a Laala among Laalas, a greedy king among paupers! He could still be alive. Swines like Laala don't die soon; only good people do. A palmist, and mind you, his words carried weight, had told the Laala he would live forever."

"Would you know of a Lathwal Laala?" Rehaan had inscribed in a notebook as the first question for anyone he could direct it at on reaching Qalayat. The tongawalla had cold-shouldered the question. Neither a yes nor a no.

Conduct your inquiries casually, Rehaan urged himself, dithering with an emaciated key to unlock a deluxe room of Super Hotel. Hopelessly inept at keying into locks, the square brass padlock opened at the nth attempt. Rather than urbane, the visitor looked clumsy before the Super Hotel's team, five or six of them maybe.

He had counted two inscrutable, middle-aged men behind the polished plywood counter; two younger men in the lobby – possibly valets-cum-waiters uniformed in baggy blue cotton trousers and dark blue striped shirts embroidered with a tilting red *S*; a 50-ish woman, her face covered by the ghunghat of a khaki nylon sari approximating the drapes of Mumbai's women constabulary. Presumably, it was her sullen adolescent daughter who carried a dented plastic pail. Housekeepers? None of them spared a glance at Rehaan. He was a wayfarer, who would probably leave the next morning, adding 1,000 rupees to the till, maybe 1,200 rupees with tips. They didn't have to ingratiate themselves with this guest. He hadn't arrived in a private taxi. The strap of his wristwatch was frayed. His white cotton shirt, navy blue jacket, a clashing maroon scarf and baggy black corduroy trousers made him resemble a downmarket showroom dummy. Whoever he was, made no difference. Nothing made a difference in Qalayat.

The deluxe room was extravagantly capacious, X'rayed just about by the winter sun. The room was fitted with a bed backed by a plank of polished plywood for headrest, a single pillow cased in white, spotty linen, a thick tassled blanket the colour of a sinking ship of a camel. By the window, a lean unstable desk played host to a lamp crowned by a polka dotted paper shade, a upturned glass of water, a metal jug, an ashtray shaped like a doughnut, ashen and scarred. Smoking encouraged.

A sienna door with phenyl stains led to the bathroom where a bucket bath would be possible under a tap marked red for hot, blue for cold – no power shower. Rehaan smirked, as a pardesi babu would, at the carton of fuchsia pink paper napkins and a blood red towel. A couple of hand-towels by the cracked water basin were emblazoned with the crooked embroidered emblem, *S*.

Super Hotel is a franchise of economy budget hotels, a hybrid between a hotel and a lodge, sprinkled across the northern states of Haryana, Punjab and Uttarakhand. The hotel's proprietors, the Chadhas, were a feuding clan of ageing brothers, sons and cousins, who had individually staked claims to the various properties. Extended hoteliering families usually do. Or so Rehaan was informed in Delhi before the train ride. "That shouldn't bother you," his news reporter friend, Anikendranath Sen nicknamed Badshah, committed to covering the rural beat for a newspaper, had decreed while guzzling Old Monk rums-and-water at the snug bar of Delhi's India International Centre, adding gratuitously, "You will find a roof over your head. You're not looking for a castle out there, are you?"

The acrylic mushroom-white paint on the walls was peeling. Overhead a fan rested covered with dirt flakes. There would be no need to switch it on. The windows let in a dire December breeze. These couldn't be closed either – the boxy windows were the only form of ventilation at the Super.

Lie down on that bed Rehaan. Gather your thoughts. Take a break from your surliness. You're on the soil of the sisters. Your roots are here. Images unspooled of the girls en route to their dream destination – womanhood.

The sisters couldn't wait forever. They had to jump aboard a train ticketless. Absurdly, he wondered if they had carried food and water for the dare of a journey, the absurdity stoked by the misgivings about his next meal. The Super couldn't have a dining room, a kitchen. No chance. Fitfully, he leapt towards the desk. Wonder of wonders, a cyclostyled typed sheet of wrinkled, pumpkin-sauce-stained paper announced crisply, "Room Service from 8 a.m. to 8 p.m. Veg-Non-Veg. Call extension 235." The extension crackled, puttered, died.

No TV, no alcohol, no guests allowed in the room – the restrictions had been stressed at the desk by one of the two middle-aged receptionists, indigo mufflered and sleeveless sweatered over the Super striped shirt. But for succinct smiles, the receptionists had been mysteriously nonchalant. So Transylvanian. If there were other guests at the Super, they were probably out for the day although a woman could be heard in the next deluxe room, shrieking about the murderous winter, the aches and pains targeting her knees and temples. "Dard, badan ka dard, dard," went her drone.

The drone wasn't obtrusive; rather, the woman's monotonous whines soothed Rehaan. He wasn't alone. There were signs of life after all. Yet Stoker's words gnawed, "Loneliness will sit on our roofs with brooding wings." What roof? What wings? Dump Dracula and vampires. No fangs. Quit punning, you dolt.

At a loss about negotations with room service, Rehaan made a meal of a chocolate bar stored in the overnight bag. Brittle, stale, sawdusty. Disoriented, he dropped on the cot, perchance to dream. No don't. He would see the sisters in flight again, their faces. The textures and silhouettes of their clothes would alter, they always did. There was no way of jigsaw puzzling their story together. Shut up and sleep. Perhaps they would leave him be tonight. Do the traveller that favour Humshira, you Aladia sisters, but there they were, his dream companions, those sisters tethered by their jehad to escape Qalayat.

Sleep came in installments. Wide awake at midnight and then at 5 a.m. or earlier, he scanned the mustard field from the boxy window – sows grazing at the parched grass by the roadway, grunting, dissatisfied with the bland vegetation. A knock at the door. Mercy be. He was sure he had been left for dead. A waiter with a fluorescent smile on a hairless, ivory-white face – could he be an albino? – handed him a ceramic mug of steaming tea.

"Good morning sir, chai for you," the waiter announced sunnily. "Breakfast? Toast omelette chalega? Aloo puri? Gobi parantha, achaar?"

"Toast is good," the Super guest smiled back. "Only toast."

"Sir what is your good self doing here?" Curiosity was raising its antenna.

"I'm a writer, a journalist...patrakaar."

"Then you must be a big man," his smile stayed. "Myself. Born, brought up in Qalayat only. Very fair and white I am.

Don't know why, my face, all white-white scares people." Voice lowered, he fluttered, "Can you give me job in big city? Not gone to school, not studied. Don't go by my face. Disease nahin hai, I am 100...200 percent fit. Kuchh bhi kar loonga. Aapki seva. I can cook, clean house. I want to leave this place."

Rehaan waited for more.

"No opportunities for people like me," the waiter continued. "No money for poor people. Myself Arjun Singhal, Arjun...taken from Mahabharata you know, name of the archer... Singhal, family name, but I'm not single. Married, two little-little children, boy and girl."

"Arjun...do you know of a Lathwal Laala? Can you take me to him? I will pay you if you can help me."

The waiter considered the deal, and said, "Laala Saab's address I can get...he is not here, but..." he held out a cupped palm.

Before Rehaan could fish for a hundred-rupee note from his wallet, a deep hectoring voice from the corridors intervened. Arjun's face slumped. He scampered away. The archer's parting words were a mix of a request and a command, "You will talk to me later. Address, will give you. Toast omelette will take time...chalega?"

The guest's "Let it be," was answered with the irritating, "As you wish."

Rehaan didn't wish, but.

The door had been left ajar. The tea was thick, bitter, ending with a swirl of sugar since it hadn't been stirred. The woman drone in the next room flew in, a bat who needed light, and cackled straight to his face, "You drank that tea. You're dead." She flung a tattered red sweater in Rehaan's hand, and bellowed, "Guard that. Everyone's a thief here."

Next, the Tweedle-dee Tweedle-dum receptionists from the counter, entered as if they had been waiting in the wings, choreographed in step, and chimed, "If you are staying for more time, pay in advance." They took turns to slap Rehaan hard across the face. This couldn't be happening. It wasn't, it was an ignis fatuus of his imagination. A symptom of panic. He could diagnose the symptom, no need to worry. He couldn't be going cuckoo. This must be the tea's side-effects. Hallucogenic? Get in line, Rehaan, he demanded of himself. He could be as methodical as a Mathematics professor. He could be strong-willed.

He was alone in the room, feeling the cold Kota limestone-tiled floor beneath his feet.

He pulled up his socks, conscious about the irony of the phrase, laced up his perforated leather shoes, checked out of Hotel Super, no questions asked. Credit card not accepted. 1000 rupees, inclusive of taxes, counted out in cash. The Tweedles checked every note, raising them up to a naked light bulb – alright the money wasn't counterfeit.

The hotel guest brought up Arjun Singhal, the waiter, the tea-boy. The Tweedles said there was no such employee at the Super.

"He's very gora, white as an egg," Rehaan persisted.

"Egg?" one Tweedle replied, the other one smiled, "This is veg place. No eggs."

"The room service menu said veg-non-veg."

"Which menu?"

Either crackpots or liars, they were like Mumbai's police inspectors who'd fob off his cross-examination about the missing Muslim youths after recurring incidents of gang warfare, with a "Missing? No one missing. All is quiet – sarva shaant aahe. Have a good day."

Used to being rebuffed, Rehaan walked towards the Qalayat railway station. Might as well hike, inhale-exhale the mist. An hour or two later, the station was forlorn, empty. The tongawalla was waiting right there though, with the stationary Chabook, outside the platform, but wouldn't approbate his passenger from yesterday.

The ticket counter was closed. "Anyone here?" Rehaan yelled at the top of his voice. "Koi hai, koi hai kya?" Hours later, a train pulled in. No passengers, no ticket required. He sat alone by the window, a knee-high boy as pale as the Super's vanishing waiter, held out a chit before him, and murmured, "My father said first take 500 rupees and then give." This had to be Lathwal Laala's address. Grabbing the demanded money, the boy fled. In a caterpillar scrawl, the chit said, "Lathwal Laala, Bajrang Niwas, Khudan, Jhajjar District, Haryana."

The train was already on a fast roll out of Qalayat. Rehaan neither had the stamina nor the bravado to jump off, and head for Jhajjar District. Too late, he would have to fortify himself to track down Lathwal. Qalayat had spooked him out. A detour to Bajrang Niwas could be one more ass-decision. Some other time. Maybe later, maybe later.

Such postponements wouldn't do. He waited, dithering, till the train's pace dropped at Narval Garh. Hopping off, he was taken aback. Outside the station, there were as many taxis, bicycle rickshaws and tongas, fighting for his custom, as they would in any metropolis. The most belligerent one, a taxi driver, ushered him into a bulky Ambassador, and quizzed, "Where to, Babu? You're lucky to be in Kamran's chariot. Others would have cheated you. I give you fixed rate."

"How far is Khudan, Jhajjar District?"

Kamran braked the taxi to a halt, and muttered, "Five hours. Not enough petrol. Fare will be to Khudan and back, you have to pay double bhaada. Theek hai na, Saab?"

Saab agreed. The driver fired off like a bullet, initially that is. Followed an hour's bumpy, back-breaking ride. The taxi was refuelled at a gas station, deserted except for a flashy, ear-ringed, baseball-capped attendant in a pair of acid-washed jeans and a Minnie Mouse tee-shirt. Moving to a distance beyond earshot, he spoke in Haryanvi with Kamran. Next, the attendant returned towards the taxi, his face resembling a frownie emoji. Rehaan saw himself being knifed in the heart. Should he fish out the cell phone in his overnight bag? Dial 100, call the cops? No, no, take-it-easy policy, you coward. He sat in the backseat inert.

The attendant asked, not without menace, "No one goes to Khudan, except to Bajrang Niwas. If you are headed there, don't waste your time. All dead there in fire two years ago. No survivors."

Apparently, Mander Bachu oppressed by his bison-like brother Laala Lathwal had, in a fit of rage, set fire to the joint family's mansion and then immolated himself. Their wives, children and Laala's granddaughter had perished.

No survivors. Gold and silver ornaments, valued at an inestimable amount of crores of rupees, were recovered from the charred basement. Bajrang Niwas was sealed by the state government to be auctioned, which could take forever. So much for the palmist's prediction – Laala Lathwal had succumbed to mortality.

"This can't be true," Rehaan said more to himself than to the attendant or to the taxi driver. Seeing him shaken, Kamran drawled, "Are you from Delhi, the government? Some minister's secretary?" Without knowing it, the taxi driver had done him a favour by granting him importance. Government equalled awe, not to be trifled with. Don't contradict him. Inadvertently, the the gas station's attendant had saved Rehaan a trip. He was tipped modestly, evoking a look which suggested oh-well-you-governmenty-miser-get-going. Kamran drove his passenger back to Narval Garh station, after being assured he would be paid the fixed rate, no refund for the aborted ride to Khudan.

The driver chortled, "What a day! You don't know your own destination. Sitting back there quietly, not even asking for radio or cassette tape. Truth be told I suspect you are not from the government, no attitude, no ghuroor shuroor… you're so ordinary, seedha saadha. Your name?"

On being told the name, Kamran softened, "Oh you're a Musalman. Apni qaum ke ho! May Allah always guard your health and wealth. Aameen."

At the Narval Garh station at the ticket counter, Rehaan was told that the next train to Delhi was full-up but he could go ticketless, standing, and pay a fine to the ticket checker on board. The Indian Railways' routine was complied with. Rehaan paid the checker the fine and a little extra for chai-paani – tea-and-water, an inventive euphemism for a bribe. So did a dozen other passengers. Ticketless travel was as much of a crime as plucking raw mangoes from a neighour's farmyard.

The ride back to Delhi was uneventful. The ticket checker abandoned his seat for some more chai-paani. Again, Rehaan slept in snatches, alighted at Paharganj listelessly, consoled by the thought that he wouldn't have to go through the process of extracting information from the Lathwaals.

It wasn't his imagination. No symptom of dread. He hadn't tripped out at the Super Hotel. The day and night in Qalayat were as real as the next-room woman's tattered sweater, now inside his overnight bag. He felt its coarse material. Those slaps were real. He should have retaliated. Why had the Tweedles slapped him? Eff, eff, zoned-out zombies they were. No, that didn't happen. Or did it?

Before office working hours, in an autorickshaw, he circled Lutyens' dozy business hub CP – Connaught Place named after Prince Arthur, first Duke of Connaught and Strathearn. Some places are immune to renaming. As the white columns blurred, Rehaan sent an SMS to himself from the cellphone: U wre ther u hv the rd swter. Yet he couldn't possibly play back the overnight trip to anyone. They would have advised psychiatry. If not, they would have made all the right empathetic noises. His journo friend in Delhi, Badshah would have guffawed, "Chum, you must have had too much to drink. You lush. Take it from Badshah, go back to Mumbai. Take the first flight out, home sweet home and all that. Cheerio!"

Cheerio? Badshah must have grown up, if he had at all, on P.G. Wodehouse. Never mind Rehaan, Sen is a nice egg. *Egg*? Could that be an echo of the half-offered toast-and-omelette at the Super Hotel? Of Arjun Singhal the tea-boy?

Watch it. The story of those sisters could be your undoing. It's pointless. It's killing you Rehaan. Not softly. Go away Roberta Flack. Her cassettes no longer played on his sound system anyway; they had come undone. A Flack compact disc...get one. You're quite a crackpot yourself.

5

On the Couch

"Chances are that you overreact," a professional psychoanalyst had once synopsised the condition of the Media Editor of *The Daily Chronicle*. There has to be a cause and an effect. It would have been far too queasy to enroll for formal, bi-weekly sessions on the couch. Go ahead, forget the stupid stigma associated with analysis. Rehaan *had* consulted Dr Abhay Mehta when he was stonewalled in his quest for the story, before the trip to Qalayat.

The analyst's couch was located in a spiffy spotless white-walled clinic, facing the Worli oceanfront, where pairs canoodled on the balustrade, oblivious of the lacerating lashes of the sun. Before climbing the stairs to the second storey of a high-rise, he was smacked by envy. He longed to hold someone's hand – a woman's, a man's – in his. Delete immediately. You're no longer a spring chicken. Romance at your age? Too late my friend. The hours of wait for the consultation were a help. A bunch of patients, men and women, seated solemnly on straight-backed chairs leafed through backdated magazines, snatching insolent glances at one another. No change of facial expressions and body language, no companionable nods, no sound except for the waves lashing the weathered rocks bulwarked by cement tripods. So therapeutic...a cursory visit had made Rehaan steadier.

He couldn't afford regular sessions at 5,000 rupees a pop. No way. Dr Mehta had said wanly, "I tell my patients to pay whatever they can whenever they like and only if they wish to." He was offering psychological charity. Rehaan was a borderline case for the couch. Hang on, he couldn't be labelled psychologically disadvantaged. Not yet. Psycho, unstable, insecure, complicated – he could be one or all of these. Could he be suffering from paranoia? No self-diagnosis, please. Take advantage of that pro bono offer, Rehaan smiled beatifically. At most, in his capacity as a patient – that's what analysts' regulars are called – he could have brought the doctor gifts, a lithograph or a personally painted water colour still life for the clinic's walls, which wouldn't be used, but accepted. The analyst would have praised the art dabble, fibbed that it was striking – "such bold strokes" – and in his practised professional tenor, would have exhorted, "You have talent, paint more. I like the water colour, the lilies in a bell jar."

The acquaintance with Dr Mehta had been facilitated by an investment banker who was in a live-in relationship with a high-society editor of a higher-brow arts magazine. The banker's relationship with her seemed smooth, silken. If there were any schisms, these were beyond perception. He had met Dr Abhay Mehta and his wife, Dr Nandini

Mehta, who specialised in Child Psychiatry, at a New Year's Eve soirée in the Feng Shui-energised apartment of the banker and magazine editor. The outlay of the pseudo-oriental furniture, the wall décor of Chinese scrolls and bell chimes, vouchsafed the pink of health and boundless wealth.

The difference between Psychoanalysis and Psychiatry is incalculable but tends to be treated synonymously. Analysis involves theoretical and therapeutic techniques to reach the subconscious for mental disorders. Psychiatry involves medication; it's a "medical treatment of the soul." Sounds simplistic, but it isn't. Just give me chicken soup for my soul, Rehaan had thought-bubbled facetiously to himself at the soirée.

Into his third vodka – his chosen poison if it was a Russian brand – he had asked Dr Mehta if they could meet up at his clinic some day soon. The doctor had said, "Why not?" No brows raised.

Months later, Rehaan called up the clinic to fix an appointment. The secretary transferred the line, after the mandatory, "Is this call personal or professional?" The caller chose personal. A tractable pause later, this time, the analyst said, "Sure let's meet, but not at the clinic. Come over and have dinner with us. Nandini will be happy to see you. We are vegans…suits you?"

"Fine, thank you," the potential patient said. "Would Saturday early evening suit you?"

"See you then," the analyst replied, attaching a caveat. "Just come as a friend…you know the place?"

Rehaan did.

The Mehtas, evidently had a yen for a sea view and pristine white walls. Their apartment on the fourth floor in a heritage structure on Breach Candy was pure vanilla albeit cluttered with books related to mind matters, and ribbed black files, perhaps of their patients. A silent Labrador ambled by as if on an evening constitutional. A maharaj, the epithet given to cooks of egalitarian households, gaped at Rehaan with gauzy eyes. The Mehtas' shy schoolgoing son retreated wordlessly to his allocated room. Nandini Mehta, without standing on ceremony, intoned, "What can I get you to drink? Whisky? We have a smoky single malt. Beer? Rum? Vodka?"

"If it's Stonichlaya...vodka."

A vodka-tonic, bereft of a slice of lemon which he would have liked, materialised from an inner-room's bar. Nandini said her husband was delayed at the clinic. He would be here any moment. Then she remarked casually, "Abhay never invites his patients home."

"Mrs Mehta, I am not a patient, I think. Not yet," Rehaan said tentatively.

"Just Nandini will do," she tilted her single malt towards his vodka, and smiled, "Cheers." On sensing Rehaan's awkwardness – he was propped on the edge of a furrowed black leather sofa – she pointed at an antique rocking chair.

"I'm fine here," Rehaan pleaded. He would have been far more klutzy while trying to calibrate the rocking chair into rhythm.

"To be comfortable on that chair, you have to be comfortable first," Nandini said seriously. This was getting to be much of an ado. The man who would be a patient, slipped into the rocking chair to rock.

"This is so relaxing," he asservated, balancing the crystal glass of vodka in his hand precariously. Ice cubes rattled.

"You don't look comfortable. Abhay is usually punctual, but the Mumbai traffic you know...getting worse day by day. The city still has such vitality; it's so vibrant and all, like New York."

"But where is Dr Mehta?" Rehaan asked, which wasn't a question to ask.

Nandini looked at him as if he was either demented or impertinent, and said haughtily, "I never ask, and he never tells me. Would you like some walnuts? Almonds? Healthy. We avoid fries, greasy stuff."

"That's so thoughtful of you," he flung his arms wide apart, regretting right away that his body language could be straight out of a school play. At the final year of school he had played the brooding Jacques of Shakespeare's *As You Like It*, pitching an untrained, paper-thin voice to reach the last row, "All the world's a stage, and all the men and women merely players; they have their exits and their entrances..." He was the prime choice for the part. When it came to mugging up lines, he had a photographic memory.

He had hammed outrageously then. The school play's audience had appreciated the over-the-top performance. How sweet, how talented! At the Mehtas, he was overacting all over again. Why? Don't get into that now, Rehaan. You'll make an ass of yourself if you haven't already.

Dr Abhay Mehta took the longest time to get home, apologised with the predictable, "Mumbai chi traffic, you know. Getting worse day by day. Are you being looked after?"

Raising his second vodka-tonic, Rehaan shone, "Absolutely."

The analyst poured himself that smoky single malt, neat, and said authoritatively, "Get off that chair. It's not good for the spine. Do you suffer from any back problems?"

"No, not really, but..." Rehaan leapt off the rocking chair to join him on the furrowed sofa. The analyst edited the conversation to the chase, "Something's bothering you, but I wouldn't advise you to become my client."

"Why not?"

"Perhaps you can tell me what's on your mind in a line or two, just as you'd update your Facebook status."

"Dr Mehta, it's not that simple."

The maharaj had to to be told when the dinner could be served. Nandini refilled her single malt from the invisible bar. The son bounced in to say he was facing problems with his New Mathematics homework, to which the analyst mock-scowled, "You have to solve your own problems, don't you? No cheating."

The boy returned to his room. Cleverly Dr Mehta cued in, "See that's what I meant. You have to solve your problems yourself. In your case, believe me, you can analyse yourself. You don't need a helping hand. I cannot do your homework for you."

"You do it for others."

"Only when I can sense they need analysis."

Dr Mehta was styming Rehaan whose spine ached though it had never acted up before. He winced, "Then why am I here?"

"For a drink and a vegan dinner. Cheers!"

"Cheers, Doctor. Okay, I'll tell you what I'm going through in one or two lines…I'm trying to write a novel, but there are too many loose ends. If I use dramatic licence, the story would be a false one."

"There, you've said it. It's up to you how you fill in the blanks."

"Doctor, let's not go around in circles. You still won't take me on as a patient?"

The analyst threw an admiring look at the white walls as if they had sprung up out of nowhere, and concluded, "No, not in your present condition. You're not ready. Maybe after you've done some more work on your novel."

The spine ache wouldn't subside. The patient who wasn't yet ready for the couch was sweating, itching to escape the dead-end conversation right away.

"Doctor, do you mind if I skip dinner?" Rehaan swallowed the remainder of the ice-cubed vodka, "I'd like to leave."

"I understand," the doctor reacted courteously. "Do you have transport?"

"I'll take a cab. And please do thank your wife for the hospitality."

"I will do that," Dr Mehta nodded curtly. "Update me on your story, maybe in a month or two, if you like. Do your homework."

"I am not your son, I'm not in school," Rehaan said rudely. "I came here for professional assistance; you don't want to help me. Thank you very much."

"Take some time, my friend. Then let me know what's on your mind."

"I'll inbox that to you on your Facebook page. Goodbye."

Cabbies refused to ply for a short haul. Rehaan's house was a five-minute drive away – from Breach Candy to Malabar Hill, minimum fare. He lurched homeward, extinguished his disappointment with Dr Mehta, a disappointment aggravated by anger.

That night, he slept the sleep of the dead. Anger worked as a narcotic. After years, he didn't dream of one of those sisters or the collection of them, embracing him, a stillborn adult, a child who in their eyes, had devoured his mother. The dreams would end with the Aladia sisters shooing him away as they would an urchin begging for coins with that plea, "I'm hungry and thirsty…haven't had a square meal in days." The Aladias wouldn't let him touch their hands either when he begged for information.

From now on, after sleeping soundly this night, would the man-boy have to down quantities of vodka and lather on anger every night? No, he wouldn't, he wouldn't think of Dr Abhay and Dr Nandini Mehta, the maharaj, the New Mathematics-challenged son again. He would forget the

Labrador who had been trained into ambling, without a syllable of a bark.

Shortly after the evening at the Mehtas, he could no longer stick to Maths, adding to and subtracting from the facts, secrets and lies extracted from whomsoever of the sisters he had probed without any let-up. They had been rigidly recalcitrant. And his speculations had carromed between the implausible and the contrived.

Dr Abhay Mehta had meant well. Value his words. Rehaan, do your homework. Perhaps, there's a cause and an effect behind every malaise.

Perhaps? Why perhaps?

No doubt the sisters had interred their past in a graveyard for the living dead, without so much as a tombstone.

6

Emotional Rescue

Around 1990, Mumtaz Aladia – the Chaudhran – had moved from central Bombay close to the Royal Opera House, to the Oshiwara apartment with her daughter Shuhaba and two grandsons Saagar and Sameer. She revelled in being surrounded, the queen bee that she was, calling Shuhaba 'Mother India' for giving birth to two children as if two were one too many.

Mumtaz's own sons, Abu Bakr and Abu Fazl were a curse. They didn't live with her any longer. Rehaan had lost track of how many children were born to the Abu brothers, and after how many nikaahs and relationships. Abu Bakr was self-taught, could read and write Urdu. Abu Fazl, wont to hurling abuses at teachers, was expelled for unruly behaviour after scraping through junior school.

Willy-nilly, Mumtaz had reared Shuhaba and her progeny, Sameer and Saagar, who looked as alike as a pair of eyebrows. On reaching adulthood, Shuhaba's two strapping sons were evicted, relocated, rent paid, the price that comes with grandmother-hood. Right from adolescence, Mumtaz's grandsons were hooked on opium. They had moved on to brown sugar and cocaine, funded surreptitiously by their mother, who assumed they would come out of their purple haze. When and how? Never mind, they would. They were losing weight. Their cowrie-shaped eyes had narrowed. They could barely speak. Their football-shaped arms were no more than deflated balloons; they resembled the discombobulated figure from Edvard Munch's *The Scream*. "Chutiye druggies," they'd be heckled when they ventured out for a heroin fix.

Mumtaz Chaudhran, the boss lady, had done her bit to drag her grandsons back to the straight and narrow. What a waste. She had given up. She had to survive, stick to her clockwork regimen. Draped in soiled white cotton saris, she wouldn't bathe or change her clothes except on Fridays after the jumu'ah prayer. Her teeth were coal black with stains of opium and paan coated in kattha, chuna sambhaal ke. Betel leaves were her narcotic, a common addiction peculiarly for Muslim women of her generation. Near about the age of 80, consolably she hadn't withered, was large-boned, wide shouldered, hair hennaed a hue of a rotting orange, a dangling-to the-waist braided tail fastened by a black rubber band. The scent of stale attar filled her chamber, to which Rehaan would be permitted entry refractorily.

"Salaam alaikum, Rehaan miyaan, sit sit," she signalled at the rim of her rumpled bed. "Chai peeyega ya sharbat? It's warm. Sharbat will be cooling."

As always, the rose sharbat, Rooh Afza, wouldn't materialise. Tea would, since a kettle was always on the boil, the brew acrid, undrinkable. Rehaan affected a polite gulp and left it to cool, a wrinkled film of cream floating on the brown swamp.

Mumtaz kept the narration of the escape of the Humshira from Qalayat wrapped under that shabby sari. She would have to be blackmailed.

"You owe my grandmother money. Tell me the story and I will ask her to give you an extension on the loan," Rehaan said jejunely.

"Wah, extension! For how long?" she bargained.

"A year," Rehaan said quickly, to which she laughed. "Make it three years. I'll be gone by then inshallah. I don't want to live longer than that."

"Three years! Ma will throw a fit."

"What makes you think she won't throw a fit even if it's for a year? She can be heartless you know. Fejji doesn't listen to anyone, not even you when it comes to money."

"Leave it to me," Fayazi's grandson said glibly, au courant with the fact that his ma had never pressed for the loan payback.

"Make it two years. Till then, I won't see her or your face."

"You just say that. You don't meet or call her because your ego won't let you."

Mumtaz Chaudhran looked away, drawing tears as if she had rebooted her ducts.

"Call her on the phone, you mean? Fejji can't hear a word unless she wants to. And you know something, boy? No one can turn back the clock. You don't have to blackmail me emotionally. I'm immune to emotions, whatever they mean.

Come back next week…you don't go to work on Sundays, do you?"

"Sometimes I do."

"Then don't go next Sunday. Have lunch with us. Chicken shorba, biryani, fresh buns from Nazneen bakery… shorba and seviyan we'll make at home. Don't tell Fejji about it. She'll think I am doing some jadoo-tona on you."

"Don't be absurd. Why would you cast a spell on me?"

"Ha! Frankly the thought has often crossed my mind. You're too self-righteous, bahut neq banta hai. You're as cunning as a fox, acting karta hai. You could have been an actor. Now go, we will wait for you on Sunday, 2 p.m. Not sooner or later."

Of the sisters he had met, Mumtaz Chaudhran maintained the sloppiest table: the meals overcooked, over-spiced, over-served, a pyramid of biryani slapped on ceramic plates. That lunch, sorcery or no sorcery, had to be avoided. The very prospect was as oppressive as the crows cawing themselves hoarse on the narrow ledge of her room's window divided into four squares of thick glass panes.

"When will we get the time to talk?" Rehaan hemmed.

"After lunch, if you're still alive after my witchcraft," she cackled. The Aladia sense of humour was patently taunting, wicked.

"Getting here from town takes two hours. If it's alright, I could come at 4 p.m. for tea."

"Don't throw your south Bombay-attitude. Doesn't impress me," she scowled. "You're tiring me with your *if it's alrights*. *No,* it's not alright. You want to meet me. I don't want to meet you. 2 p.m. or go fuck yourself."

"That's rude. Why are you like this?"

"It's a long story," she rolled her pink-veined eyes, and shifted gears. "I have nothing against you. So *alright,* come for tea...you won't drink it anyway."

Rehaan swallowed the ginger-devastated tea in a gulp, and began to take leave of her, to be chided, "Proper Muslims say something before taking leave of their elders. You are not a Muslim."

No point defending the credentials to his faith. "You're right as always," Rehaan conceded, "Khuda haafiz."

"Allah haafiz to you to, alrightwalla bache," was her parting shot, ratifying Rehaan as a child of the Aladia clan, a child she probably detested from the day he was born. She detested every grandchild born to her sisters, as if a male beauty-cum-talent pageant was on. Which sister would succeed in rearing a child who would grow up right? Which child would grow up to look presentable if not drop-dead handsome? At the hour of Rehaan's birth, May 10, 5 a.m., she was at the St Elizabeth's Nursing Home, manned by nuns, at a bifurcation of the steepest Malabar Hill slope. She had tipped the nurses a couple of tenners, "Tell the doctors to do something about his mother...she hasn't even regained consciousness. Till then, also pray for the child's health." After a grotesque wink, she had added, "and wealth."

Wealth, Mumtaz Chaudhran, could never amass. The middle class to which she belonged overtly, nevertheless had its upper – privacy. The Oshiwara neighbours weren't clued into her antecedents, nor would they dare to pry. Chez Mumtaz Aladia, it was barbed wire, no trespassers.

The Oshiwara apartment was a depressing meeting point. The walls, chlorophyll green, had caked in less than a month after a re-paint. In the living room, sofas and chairs of pistachio rexine and rusting steel armrests had been transported by a truck from their central Bombay home. The utilitarian couldn't be junked. Framed photographs of shrines and Urdu calligraphy were nailed on the walls. A baithak – a mattress covered in a white bedsheet topped by large sausage-shaped pillows also sheathed in white cotton – could not be complete without a paan-daan – a faux silver box topped by a handle, with receptacles for kattha-chuna and diced supari. An Urdu calligraphy-engraved tray held the washed paans, betel leaves.

Those leaves were chewed by Mumtaz and Shuhaba, as if a paan famine was about to strike within the next hour. And where there's a paan-daan, a less ornate brass ugaldaan, a spittoon, was like a signature on an amateur artwork. The mother and daughter would jet-spit the red fluid during and after every session of paan-chewing. The paan and thook smell was overpowering, best left associated with public toilet stenches.

"Why do I even come here?" Rehaan asked himself and answered. "Idiot because they are your relatives; they mean something to you. Why be so effete? If it's paan and spit, so be it. You used to eat paan too, occasionally, with extra cardamom and soft supari, didn't you? Stop being a snob. Mumtaz, I don't like. Maybe that's not fair. She wasn't born evil. She did so much for her sisters…for my beloved Fayazi Ma."

Such attempts at playing fair with Mumtaz and her family, he admitted, were partially put-on, fake. She was a witch. The bitch word he wouldn't use for her. Fayazi Ma had brought him up, mild-mannered, polite, Boy Scout-correct. Not the ideal qualities for an investigator of a past which could well meander towards the murky and the profane.

"Maadar chod, behen chod, falaan pitti" – the regularity with which the sisters used cuss words would startle him, but with time, they had become harmless volleys. Mumtaz and Fayazi cursed like boorish men because he presumed men had abused them with viler words. How come, he reasoned, the male gender wasn't part of the scatology? No father chod, brother chod, no you arse hole. The male equivalents didn't sound as vivid and colourful, not even close. Indeed, cuss words had become as familiar to Rehaan's ears as traffic sounds of the city. They were a part of the Aladias, the Humshira lexicon.

Their abuses would embarrass him, discouraging him from any resorting to any form of gaalis, except the occasional "Fuck you", an anti-reaction used in extreme, half-extreme situations and even as a term of endearment. Cyber intel will tell you that 'fuck' is a bad good word dating back to the 14th century. According to the British court records of 1310–1311, there lived a man – Roger Fuckbythenavele – an inexperienced copulator, a dimwit.

Not the sort to read a book in a moving vehicle, in the course of the two-hour cab ride home, Rehaan had scanned websites on the smartphone for the fuck word. Let the gaalis be.

Mumtaz Chaudhran would derive pleasure too from the prospect of mortality. "I don't have many more years to live. I could die today, tomorrow," she'd grin that black grin of hers. Seemingly, she was in great health. Her daughter treated her as a saint.

Her sons didn't. Abu Bakr who had moved to Delhi, to a barsaati in Darya Ganj – within the the walled city of Shahjahanabad – eked out a living by freelancing for Urdu magazines and newspapers. He had flunked his matric exams at the municipal school. Contemptuous of his teachers and the curriculum, he would play truant. He read Leftist pamphlets, ploughed through the Urdu translation of *Das Kapital*, strove to be a card-holding member of the Communist Party of India (Marxist), but was advised to retry when his precepts could be put to practice. It was decided perhaps that he would be a liability, not an asset.

The Internet boom had hit Abu Bakr hard. Editors no longer solicited his writings which were naïvely Left of centre and sanctimonious, carping at whichever political party was in power. He'd attack the state of the New Delhi governance and civic issues, blindfolded. Few readers, fewer takers. He'd been asking Mumtaz for a raise in his monthly allowance. She hadn't agreed, not yet.

After all, Abu Bakr was the certified prodigal. Besides his salvos of political rubber bullets, he had married a Hindu woman. One of his three daughters was named Shabnam, a non-communal name. Mumtaz had expressed her wish for any of her granddaughters to be named Fatimah – the daughter of Prophet Muhammad. Wish ignored.

The other son, Abu Fazl, an alcoholic, had settled in Karol Bagh, Delhi. He lived with his wife in an airless motor garage close to a maze of bargain-friendly textile shops. Mumtaz money-ordered him a monthly stipend. The rest, Abu Fazl's wife, Chanda, earned by cooking at neighbourhood homes, part-time. Chanda limped, the impairment, a testimony to her husband's schizophrenia. He could be violent at home.

Rehaan was advised to keep out of their range. "They're born liars," Mumtaz would thunder. Caution be damned, he had met them, and was treated like a benign stranger who possibly had money to spare. Abu Fazl and Chanda had hinted at loans. Sorry, Rehaan had said, he didn't have any savings to spare. 'Intel' about the Aladia sisters was denied.

Abu Fazl had huffed that any facts or corroborations were none of Rehaan's business. The sisters' story could not and should not be retraced. "Look at the way that Mumtaz Chaudhran has brought us up to be dependent on her. Why did that...that selfish woman bring us into the world if she couldn't take care of us?"

"How long do you expect her to take care of you?" Rehaan said politely.

"Khuda haafiz," the bombed-out-of-his-skull Abu Fazl had ended. Matriarchs, by his logic, had a lifelong responsibility to tend to their children. At 60 and a little plus, he looked like a haggard nonagenarian. Any story leads from him were as inconceivable as logging into a mind which didn't have so much as a password.

Shuhaba was the Chaudhran's sole sliver of solace. Whatever Mumtaz wanted, Shuhaba did. Willowy, unusually cocoa-complexioned, and pragmatic to the core, she was an exemplary daughter. No schooling for her during her childhood, but for Quran lessons from a maulvi five times a week. The Chaudhran abhorred education, be it in Urdu or English. Knowledge meant profane thoughts, borne out of ungodly upbringing.

Shuhaba couldn't have been muzzled if she had been permitted to go to school. She would have rebelled. The prestigious Queen Mary's School for Girls was right opposite their central Bombay home. She would look on enviously at the girls in uniform, who looked back at her as if she belonged to an exotic menagerie which they couldn't access.

Educated or not, Shuhaba did rebel during her early teens. She fell in love, or that's what she fantasised, with a much older man – Rajendra Bhalla of medium height, scanty hair and a broad forehead almost always beaded with perspiration. Married and a father, polygamy was a badge of manhood for him.

The 50-ish news photographer, Girish Karmarkar at Rehaan's office, would talk boastfully of his mistress, "She's got her act right; she satisfies me in bed when my wife acts up. My kept woman...I keep her in a room far away in Kandivli... Have to go by local fast train...just one hour... She also makes excellent omelettes for breakfast. Fluffy! What more can a working man ask for? You're single. Shall I find a woman, someone regular for you? At the very least, she can give you an awesome hand-job as often as you want." The offer was refused ad nauseam. The colleague would repeatedly conclude, "You're a mouse, not a man." So be it.

In all likelihood, Shuhaba had wished to break away from Mumtaz's stranglehold. She was pregnant with Bhalla's child at 18. Without throwing a fit or berating her, Mumtaz had gently steered Shuhaba and Bhalla into a secret nikaah at a mosque. "You can love any lousy man, but you cannot invoke Allah's wrath," she had cautioned. The clandestine meetings at rooms rented by the hour between Shuhaba and her man stopped. They were assigned a windowless backroom in the Chaudhran's house, with the proviso, "Tell that prick he must respect me. And I will need a monthly sum of money from that lund for your upkeep from now on."

Bhalla's family business in auto spare parts on the Royal Opera House traffic junction, was running full speed ahead. Shuhaba was his equal in bed. He hadn't ever met anyone like her, nor was he likely to. His first wife was a nag. He spent little time with her, turned deaf whenever she brought up the subject of Shuhaba. Bhalla's parents had acceded to the second woman in his life; their daughter-in-law hadn't given birth after five years of marriage.

Nikaah done, Shuhaba gave birth to a son at Dr Vidyadhar Sakholkar's hole-in-the-wall clinic. This ensured the continuation of the Bhalla family. Sameer and the next one, Saagar were quasi-illegitimate. With time, the Bhalla family would get around and induct their grandsons into the family trade. Wittingly, their names were common to the Hindu and Muslim faiths.

Around the time Mumtaz became a grandmother, a nani, she earned the title of 'Chaudhran' by a majority vote. She was acknowledged as the leader, the commander of the registered association of the naachnewallis, dancing girls – the British argot for them was nautch girls.

Kennedy Bridge bordered the ill-reputed association and the genteel St Mary's School for Girls. The bridge was built by the British railway engineer, John Pitt, around 1850, it is said, to prevent commuters from crossing the railway tracks to their deaths. Under its archway, abandoned syphilitic women would wait to crumple up and die. The British called it The Bridge of Sighs. Others called it Pawan Pul, The Bridge of Breeze, for reasons unknown. Could it be because a soothing breeze blew whenever a train thundered past?

Rehaan could recall the hierarchy there: the naachnewallis would dance at nights, flanked by a team of musicians on harmonium, dholaks and tablas, but wouldn't be game for sex with random clients. Below them, in subterranean rooms, migrant women from northern states had no pretentions. They were kamaanewallis, sex workers, and that was that. He knew so much more about the downbeat side of Bombay than the other boys at his elitist school.

At the kothas of the dancing nautch girls, there were handmaidens and male domestic workers who engaged in sex with one another and deluded themselves for a while that they had fallen in love. On being caught in the act, they were presented before the Chaudhran for a verdict. "How dare you mate like dogs in the heat!" she would declaim. "This is a respectable place." Without exception, the menial staffers who'd had the nerve to defy the code of the dancing association would be exiled forever from Pawan Pul.

The clientele for the obedient nautch girls came from the aristocracy. They gave the kothas a patina of class. Films stars would arrive too, to pick up the art of dance – Kathak – from the nautch girls. The young Congress party was to establish its city headquarters close to the circular compound of the kothas. The legendary Sadaat Hassan Manto found fodder for stories and joy at the Kennedy Bridge address, besides plot material at the kothas where crafty matriarchs drafted film star careers for their daughters.

The Chaudhran had her calculations – the Bhalla trade would be her grandchildren's, but she hadn't accounted for choppy weather ahead. The auto spare parts business crashed. Bhalla stopped visiting.

At the end of the cab ride, Rehaan mulled, "My family tree's roots are too gnarled, spread out. Sleazy, redolent of titillating dance performances and sexual trysts, but so what? Are you a sissy, are you scared? Scared of what? Search on."

The search was conducted from a fairly commodious apartment in Hill View (not that the six-storey building offered one). A view of overlapping trees and bougainvillea it did in the upscale real estate precinct of Bombay: Malabar Hill. The building wasn't swanky. The horseshoe-shaped colony divided into five blocks, contained at least six to seven homes on every floor. Tailors, grocers, hair salons, snack kiosks on the ground floor added to the clutter. The hill was an avidly desired address anyway, made for evening strolls past the going-to ruins South Court – the residence of Pakistan's founder Mohammed Ali Jinnah – cordoned off from the public because of property disputes.

His room on the sixth storey of Hill View, D-Block was stocked with books, music and artworks. Fayazi Ma's room was spartan. The stories of her sisters, his other nanis, were like the blank sketchbooks in his room. Some day he would sketch the Aladia sisters' faces in charcoal tints and abstract draftsmanship.

The generations before Rehaan had been way more adventurous. Born in the post-Independence age, getting slavishly committed to the Internet, for him other eras were distinctly more audacious. Romantic.

There was no didacticism, no feminist ideology to catalyse the women who had warred with their own shortcomings under the looming shadow of the British Raj. The Aladia sisters should have belonged to the footnotes of history pages but were neither chronicled nor investigated. How could they be? They were ordinary. None of them could boast of achievement, public recognition except Jameela, who, for a brief span, became a recording artiste of light ghazals. She was the sole celebrity among the Humshira. It was recapitulated that her legion of fans was star-struck enough to fall at her feet or catch a glimpse of her, a largesse she wouldn't grant. She would venture out only under the cloak of a burqa.

Jameela Begum was an accomplished singer of ghazals and geets. Mumtaz, ever concerned about her own superiority, claimed she had been formally trained in Kathak, the sensuous dance form accentuating beauty in motion, form, speed, range and pattern. Where could she have picked up the basics of Kathak. In Qalayat? No one demanded proof of the Chaudhran's Kathak credentials.

Rehaan had been made privy to the fundamentals of the Aladia story, primarily by his grandmother, Fayazi. However, he could never coax her into an authorised rewind. The truth, or something close to that, wasn't attainable, unless Mumtaz deigned to speak at length. Rehaan could pre-empt her hissing, "You will write out a story in words, publish a book which will wither away on the shelves. We weren't born to wither."

That next promised meeting on Sunday would be the same ol', he suspected unless the modus operandi was re-strategised. Politesse and curiosity hadn't worked. Mumtaz had to be seduced with what she craved most: flattery and money, in that order. Flattery could be laid on thicker than butter. Money would dent the ATM. Financially, the revised strategy was dicey.

No publisher was willing to give him an advance on this book – he had communicated on email with the most-wanted imprints working out of teakwood-panelled offices in Delhi. "We will go through the manuscript and revert with our decision," would be the bland response of the self-important publishers. They wouldn't take on any yarn, however valuable it may be to the writer. At the same time, the publishing trade's axiom is – outright rejection can boomerang. What if the nixed manuscript were to laugh back from the bestseller ratings on amazon.in?

International publishing houses, the solitary route to broader recognition, were too pernickety, conjuring up images of boardrooms in New York and London of editorial executives in suits, emperors downing thumbs as if the unpublished author were a scrawny gladiator. In the 1940s, J.D. Salinger's seminal *The Catcher in the Rye,* on youth angst, had to go through the baptism of publishing fire. So, who, pray, was the hack journo Rehaan Shafaque Sidiqui?

Alternatives were to self-publish, waltz into the cyber whirligig with an online edition, or knock on the web portals of self-anointed indie publishing houses which often inbox-messaged him on Facebook, exhorting a newspaper byline to try his hand at writing a non-fiction book of topical relevance. Or if not, humour. A movie star biography, fantastic.

Last resort: just take the story of one sister, time travel with her to the here and now, garnish the drama with love, sex, deceit and half a happy ending. Cram the sisterology into 250 pages, negotiate with the publisher to sell a copy for 99 rupees, and hello lightness my old friend, Rehaan would be reconnected to talk to you again, oh readers, probably figuring on the best-seller shelves of the airport bookstores. That's if the publisher cared to make the sales from a push to a shove.

Easier imagined than done. The investment, the toll to be paid for his emotional rescue was inescapable – no one pays for that. Don't bring up the loan payback rigarmarole ever again. Over to a new financial investment. ATM wouldn't do, limited withdrawal a day. A cheque – an incentive? – would have to be encashed for Mumtaz Chaudhran.

7

Fragments and Shards

She had cut her hand while shutting a window with needless force against the noon shine. The glass had shattered. A shard had pierced the Chaudhran's age-gnarled wrist. A home-made bandage was being tied around her right wrist. An antiseptic had been applied with gusto by Shuhaba, who stood at a distance, admiring her basic para-medic skills, "There, it's under control. No need to call the doctor."

"I will die of this injury, I tell you. That's what you want, don't you? To see me dead and gone," Mumtaz daubed insult over her injury. "Anyway, doctors charge too much. As usual, you don't want to spend a single rupiya on me. My wrist is paining but what do you care?" She looked at the bandaged wrist as it were a burnt-out candle.

In the sulphurous humidity of the room, Shuhaba cajoled her into reclining on the mattress and the mound of pillows, "Don't think about it. You'll be fine by the evening."

Rehaan reached the apartment half an hour late. Arching a thin white brow towards the wall-clock, she complained,

"You don't value time. See, I've hurt myself. There's been blood…go away."

Rehaan handed over a briefcase, a shiny new one of imitation crocodile skin. Her interest piqued, "What's in it? Is it for me?"

"It is for you, Chaudhran. There's money in there."

She'd been expecting the cash exchange: "How much?"

"One lakh rupees."

"That's all for your grandmother's sister? Take that cheap briefcase and the money away. Leave."

Negotations weren't Rehaan's forte. Summoning up as much servility as a speeding driver does with a traffic cop, he said, "This is all I have right now. Take the money, please."

"Organise a lakh more, next month."

"No really. This is all I could spare from my savings account. I had to break a fixed deposit," he was progressing somewhere with this woman. Like a traffic cop after grimacing and gabbing, she would accept the bribe.

"Get him tea, Shuhaba," she screwed up her face. "And you, you come sit beside me. I don't bite."

"You're a darling, Chaudhran," Rehaan tried to shake her left hand as a sign of agreement.

She ignored the offered handshake, grousing, "Miyaan, Musalman ho, that's what everyone says at least."

"Meaning?"

"Nothing, nothing at all. Boy, you don't shake hands with your elders. Have you forgotten your manners?"

Handshake no, salaam yes. The etiquette of cupping the right hand into a salaam alaikum approved, she advanced her bandaged wrist for a kiss. If she had wanted Rehaan to genuflect before her that afternoon, he would have.

Shuhaba left the room, saying, "Don't mind Ammi's ways. She's like this even with strangers."

"Hanh, yeh ladka stranger hi to hai," Mumtaz wasn't about to forsake her imperiousness. "Some years he doesn't bother to see us even on Eid days. And now he's sitting at my feet. Strangers behave with more courtesy."

Rehaan switched on a compact tape-recorder. "Put that silly thing away," Mumtaz pumped up her voice to an unpleasant level. You're not a duffer, I hope. Remember what I say. And don't interrupt."

"Whatever you say, Chaudhran," Rehaan assented obsequiously.

Intermittently tapping the briefcase, as if to check it was still there, the Chaudhran began her narration, fragmented, the sort a journalist was accustomed to, of reading between the lines. "Whatever prejudices you have against me, wash them down with a glass of water," she snarled. "Allah would turn me into a leper in this room if I were to lie. The truth is that we sisters adored our brother, Murad, and worshipped our parents. We abided by their every rule and command. They loved us, we loved them, but there was something unequal about that love. My heart, as the leader of the sisters, told me we would never be happy in Qalayat. I told you to go there. Did you?"

Rehaan nodded perfunctorily. She didn't have to know. The Chaudhran spun on, "We wouldn't have become the women we did if we had spent our adult lives as spinster kitchen maids or were married off to some elderly widowers. So many of those curs in that village were eyeing us and sending proposals for nikaah. Some of my sisters hadn't menstruated yet, but the men said they would *adjust.* I'd curse those impatient fuckers, behind their backs of course. Neither could I see myself being raped night after night by a wretched maadarchod. Qalayat's Maulana had lost one of his three wives. She had cholera; she croaked before she could be transported to a city hospital. I didn't want to die like that wife. A woman of virtue she was. She would get us bead necklaces and amulets from the dargahs. Maulana, that man may have been God-fearing. He was good-looking, with the eyes of a leopard cat. Wives were just a number for him. Two had survived; I would be the fourth one. I trembled at the prospect of spending the rest of my life with him. The kismat of my sisters would have been no better. We had to run far, far away as soon as we could – before I became the Maulana's haque ki chauthi biwi. Do you understand? Why are you looking at me that way accusingly? Lower your eyes, with respect."

"I'm not looking at you accusingly, Chaudhran. I'm listening."

"Then tell me I did right for myself and my sisters whom I regarded as my own daughters. They were not born from my womb; they were my property, my sweet burden. Speak up, did I do right or wrong?

"Right, absolutely right."

Dramatically, Mumtaz lifted her bandaged wrist as if it were a toll gate, "I wrote their destinies with this…this...and what do I have to show for it but blood and a cheap bandage? My own blood doesn't bother to get a clean one from the chemist's, and mind you, there's a day-to-night medical store just around the corner. Every one of us – you, also – is alone. All this garbage about family unity, love, care, should be fed to the vultures.

"Looking back, I should have left Qalayat on my own, but stupid girl that I was, I carried my little girls along. I had to steal the money for the train passage, so what? Allah will forgive me for the sin. So many sins committed for my sisters' well-being, not mine. Do you know what I stole? Did that Fejji ever tell you? I stole my father's savings which no one knew about. That miser Saundha Bhai would store half of the money he earned, I presume, to run away himself from Qalayat if he ever had the guts to abandon us to our fate. There were, believe it or not, 150 rupees and some coins in a tin box which he had hidden. He was foolish; he thought no one knew about that box buried under the bargad tree. He would look at the tree every morning he left home. I could read his eyes; I knew something was there. The village and my mother believed he was spotless. He wasn't. With prostitutes he couldn't get it up. But ha! No one could have told you this. I will. He was a 'kept' man of one of the Maulana's wives – the one who croaked. She would pay him I suppose whenever she needed him. Who knows? The child in her womb who died with her of cholera, could have been Abba's. And…and… the fucking nerve, he was plotting to get me married off to none other than the Maulana. Should any father do this to his child? There, I've given you full value for your money. Paisa vasool!" she stopped.

Rehaan wasn't about to give up. She was pandering to his curiosity, and to his relief, rattled on. "So with that tin box, we fled under cover of the night to Qalayat railway station. A train for Delhi was about to leave. We jumped into a compartment barely in the nick of time, ticketless. If we were caught during the night, I knew I could handle it. The ticket collector babu noticed us cowering in a corner of the crowded compartment. He was moustached, sword-sharp bristles over red lips, and had a fleshy waistline. I would have married him on the spot if he had asked me to. The babu had brains. He called me towards the exit gate, and said, 'I will have to report you girls to the chowki at the next railway station.' I began to cry, he pulled me towards him tightly, stroked my hair and lifted my chin up and asked how old I was. I didn't tell him. Sick paedophile he must have been. Plenty of those around those day, plenty today also. The train was due to halt in a few minutes. He said kindly, 'Get off at Narwana station. Don't say a thing. I'll see how I can help you.' He let me out of his grasp. I was sure he would help us.

"The fucker. It was a trick to get us off the train, with the least resistance possible. Either he wanted us to take us to the chowki and earn praise for doing his duty, or he may have had something else on his mind, like all men would have under the circumstances – to sell us into the flesh trade. We could have ended up as inmates of a brothel. So many girls from Haryana, I'd heard, had been sold by their parents to pimps. The only alternative was to let the homeless girls die a natural death. Between shame and death, I couldn't tell which fate was worse. The ticket babu was all smiles, brought us glasses of water and shelled peanuts...those mungfalis which you don't get anymore in the market, not easily anyway. I had to take charge."

Mumtaz stopped. Shuhaba bustled in to request, "Please let her be for now. You can come again some other day for tea."

"Kya tea tea laga rakha hai? This rude fellow doesn't touch the cup as if it was lavatory water. I'll be alright. Shuhaba, for the Lord's sake, get me a proper bandage. This rag you've used is itching; it could develop into gangrene."

"Ammi, gangrene doesn't happen with a simple cut," the dutiful daughter mumbled. "I'd get a fresh bandage, but it costs money."

"Take it from this boy, then."

Rehaan handed over a hundred-rupee note from his wallet. Mumtaz beamed triumphantly, Shuhaba lathered chuna-kattha on a paan leaf, applied khizaab, a mild intoxicant, and fed it to her. The Chaudhran vigorously chewed on the supari, reducing it to a rubble. Shuhaba said she would be back soon.

"Don't spend that money on yourself. Remember it's for the bandage," Mumtaz hectored. "Bring me back the bill and the change. Understand?" Shuhaba left the oppressive room, without a word.

"So where was I?" the Chaudhran pretended to lose the story's thread.

"You were telling me about the ticket collector and Narwana."

"You tell me what could have happened?"

"He must have taken you to the police chowki."

"Rubbish. We were offloaded at Narwana like cattle. He promised to return in a few minutes, said alright, alright the way you do, and he bought us tickets – half-tickets since we were underage – to take us to Delhi. We crossed the railway tracks to another platform; we changed trains. My sisters slept peacefully for the next four or five hours. I kept vigil. The other passengers were kind; they offered us food from their tiffins, paranthas and shalgam gravy. The ticket babu would return every now and then. He called me towards the passage, and said, 'You are brave. Just tell me what you're up to. Why have you left home?' I explained 'why' in the briefest way I could. 'All will be well,' he said again and again as if he had been created exclusively for our escape. He would think of something, kuchh na kuchh for us when we reached Delhi. I had the presence of mind to thank him for his generosity, nodded gratefully, knowing that only a miracle could save us from this man when we reached Delhi in the morning…you know at the Paharganj station. It was so vast and crowded. I prayed for a miracle. But Allah doesn't dispense miracles just like that. I managed to outwit that arsehole," she was chortling by now, a chortle limned by pride.

"How did you do that?"

"You don't need to ask me questions. You're breaking my chain of thoughts. Let me tell you what I remember. Next time, you interrupt, I'll stop."

"No more questions."

"Morning had set in. Paharganj was still as dark as night. It was freezing. I think it was the month of November. The Delhi weather you know. I had to trust the ticket fellow. Who knows he could have been our saviour who would take us to his family, deposit us under their care and we would live happily ever after. But your Mumtaz Chaudhran is no idiot. I had to do something, anything. I called him over, away from the girls, and said, 'What do you want to do with us?' He didn't say a word. I had to. Pulling down my dupatta, I warned him, 'I will scratch myself on my neck and breasts till they bleed and shout out so loud that the whole of Delhi right down to the Viceroy will hear. You will be arrested.' 'Rubbish, no one will believe you', the fool said.

"I screamed louder than a train's whistle. A huge crowd gathered, excited to watch the fun. It was as if they had formed a protective ring around me. That behenchod babu slipped away. Mind you, he took to his heels or else he would have been beaten up black and blue, all the colours of a rainbow. My dear sisters clung to me. I had to explain. I howled with tears that we were yateem, besahara orphans on way to an orphanage in Ballimaran... Ballimaran I wanted to be there. Abba had once told us of a poet who lived and died there... I can't remember his name."

"Mirza Ghalib?" Rehaan butted in.

"Jo bhi," the Chaudhran railed. "You want to know about the poet or about us? Poets can express themselves in sher-o-shairis of love and longing. That morning at Paharganj, it was as if I had gone mute after that scream on the railway platform. That was it. I was paralysed. I didn't care what Allah had in store for us. If you visit Paharganj right to this day, you will always find a mullah or two catching a train for a pilgrimage...to Ajmer Sharif dargah. That day, so long ago, was no different. Three mullahs, all old and beyond any bad thoughts, volunteered to help. They gave us a few coins which would get us to the Nizamuddin Aulia dargah, the mausoleum of Amir Khushrau – woh poet tha – is also there. I was told by the mullahs to meet the Sajjad-e-Nasheen, the chief administrator Abdullah Ameen there...to tell him 'Tauheed Bhai gave you his name...Ameen Saab will guide you. Any tongawalla will take you to the masjid.' Then those goat-beards hurried off; their train was about to leave. Next, we selected a tongawalla with the whitest hair in the group outside the station. He did look at us as if we were freaks. When one of the girls...probably Fayazi...told him to take us to the dargah, he said, 'Alhamdolillah.'

"The city was a blur. The girls and I were shuddering in the biting *cold*, but in our own way, we were jubilant. We were in Delhi, imagine Delhi, which had become the country's capital around then. Pehle capital Agra tha. Do you even know that? At the end of the horse ride, which didn't take too long, the old tongawalla refused to charge us the fare. He patted our heads; all of us had covered our heads with dupattas, of course. He said, 'You girls are all so small and innocent, like my own granddaughters, but I can't stop to talk to you. I'll lose passengers. This is the peak hour. May Allah be with you.

"Gullies as twisted as the veins in an old woman's hands, led to the dargah. We sat on the cold marble of the courtyard, exhausted, thirsty, hungry. Jameela, ever the spoilsport whimpered, 'Are we going to die, Aapa?' I ignored her, those hurrying to the masjid for the fazr prayers ignored us. They probably mistook us for beggars. We prayed to ourselves. Once the namaaz ended, we sprinted towards the water ghadas there. A mullah gave each one of us sugar tabarruq and rose petals. Not that he singled us out; he was distributing tabarruq to all who came towards him. Then he looked at us curiously. We were sitting still, silently on the cold floor. The girls were afraid. What next? That depended entirely on me. I went over to the mullah, taking care that my stride shouldn't look urgent or desperate. I told him quite plainly, 'Tauheed Saab has told us to meet Abdullah Ameen Saab.'

He looked shocked. What was he thinking of? Were we the chaste Sajjad-e-Nasheen's bastard children who had surfaced from nowhere? The very notion made me grin.

'Why are you smiling like that?' the mullah wasn't amused. He couldn't meet anyone who walked into the dargah. 'Namumkin,' he said. 'Ameen Saab is a very great man. He is leaving for a pilgrimage this afternoon. What do you want of him? You aren't his relatives, are you?'"

The Chaudhran dealt her trump card, "We have run away from home. We are here to convert to Islam."

"You are wearing clothes which indicate you are Mohammedans," he snapped, but since he wouldn't dare to miss the opportunity of converting six girls to Islam, he decided on the spot, 'I feel something is not right, but your jazbaa is admirable. I will take you to the Imam. Let him decide.'"

With the crispness of a news reader, the Chaudhran wrapped up, "That's all for today. The past one remembers for its wonderful, aflatoon moments, not for the painful, behuda ones." Rehaan was being dismissed. He looked at the briefcase, a look that didn't escape her, "I may tell you the money is not making me talk. I may tease you, but you are the Aladia blood…to an extent."

"Extent?"

"Extent ka matlab from your mother's side you are. Come back in a day or two. I shall tell you more about our escape, my escape. Never forget, I was the chief, the leader, the instigator, the heroine."

"I won't, never," Rehaan bargained. "Should I come tomorrow or day after?"

"Day after," and she raised her voice, "Shuhaba, show the boy to the lift."

It was like being released from a prison from which Rehaan didn't wish to escape. At the elevator, Shuhaba, said, "Ammi is difficult. We'll see you day after. Thursday, please call before you come. You know her moods. Khuda haafiz."

Outside the Oshiwara towers, business was desultory at the mid-rung boutiques, shady spas, massage parlours, wine lounges, veg and non-veg restaurants, many of them exclaiming that they offered the luxury of airconditioning, and global coffee franchises dotted with wannastars struggling to find a foothold in the Bollywood firmament.

Autorickshaws waited for fares. Buses lumbered past, bearing numbers which didn't quite indicate where they were headed to.

Mumtaz had adjusted to the round-the-clock beeps, the blasts of trucks pounding by. Rehaan couldn't think of her as a teenage girl of fortitude in the courtyard of Delhi's Nizamuddin Aulia dargah. She was neither lying nor ornamenting the escape drama, but she was underplaying the role of her sisters, ordering them to the chorus back-up line in which she was the lead item girl. The heroine?

Except for Fayazi and Jameela who raised pointed objections, the others appeared to have followed Badi Aapa's commands blindly. Abba Saundha Bhai and Ammi Iddanbi, it could be inferred, had been buried while they were alive. Fayazi would display a tinge of remorse at intervals. Mumtaz never. The Chaudhran had assumed the responsibility of the parents whose stray disclosures of love and care, were exhumed by that escape from Qalayat to Delhi via Narwana.

8

The Embroidered Brothel

Quite characterstically, the Humshira was cavalier about the repercussions of the escape from Qalayat. "They were our father and mother. They brought us into the world. We owe our lives to them," was the regret which Rehaan waited to hear, but never did. Surely when they became mothers themselves, they could have regretted the escape, the abandoment of their parents.

A droplet of apology would come from Fayazi Ma in a self-righteous cadence, "Why do you cause me pain? Parents are parents, but we didn't return to Qalayat when they passed away within a week of one another. Like their lives, their deaths were as ridiculous. Our abba, Saundha Bhai, had a rotten tooth. His wisdom tooth just fell off in his mouth and he swallowed it, by mistake, I should hope! Some infection or the other spread, and he died at home. Ammi Iddanbi developed a fever soon after. She cried her eyes out. Which woman wouldn't? Her tears had always scored over her laughter. I cannot remember the sound of her laughter.

We were told by our brother, Murad, that she was confined to bed. She ignored the roots, herbs and tonics prescribed by the hakim. Our procreators were buried close to each other. They must still have so many conflicts to sort out in the other world," she tailored her version of the burial. As an afterthought, to absolve herself of evil speak, she muttered, "Allah unko jannat mein mehfooz rakhen. (May Allah safeguard them in heaven.) Why must you remind me? Are you subjecting me to a police inquiry?"

He couldn't see himself in a police uniform; he didn't have the physique to carry off the khakis. At most, he could see himself in a lawyer's robes. In hindsight, the schoolday aspiration of fighting petty or paramount cases in the courtroom for those who couldn't afford lawyers struck him as naïvely idealistic, and as fatiguing as the three to four years required for an LLB degree.

Miscellaneous and unsuitable jobs attempted against his principles – what use were they? – his schoolfriend's father was on the board of interviewees for the post of trainee journalists at *The Daily Chronicle*, where he would be taught to climb the ropes either of a sub-editor or a reporter at the daily newspaper. No-brainer. Sub-editing would entail cleaning up reporters' copies. Let sub-editors spruce up his copy if he could learn to dash out those snappy news paras linked by connecting bridges. The brief for a cub reporter was to seek information, verify it and precis it into a report, which the training officer said should make sense to an extra-terrestrial. "Suppose ET lands on earth and picks up *The Chronicle*, it (sic) should understand what you've written.

We're taking it for granted that ET can read…English," he'd wait for our approving smiles.

Over a decade later, the twaddle during the training had transformed Rehaan into a reporter on a closer-to-the-bone 'human-interest' trudge, dedicated to detecting why his extended family was the way it was, why the Aladia women had charted the family manifesto which had seeped through four generations, why the men became puppets on their petticoat strings. The sisters' history, or whatever he could configure, testified that more than their sexuality, it was their native intelligence, in a broad generic sense, which they used as their ammunition. Also, the six were locked in a lifelong competition. Let's see who wins – rivalry must have festered within the Humshira.

In their own right, the six must have been achievers – or losers depending on your perspective – in variable degrees. In any case, achievement is overrated, accompanied as it is with unwieldy baggage. Deceit, manipulation and ambition, checked or unchecked, must have been their modus operandi.

At home, among his books, movie and rock music posters, Rehaan was knotted up. He couldn't be treated as a child, dammit. Go ahead, untie yourself, apply if you can the words of the Scottish psychiatrist R.D.Laing, "Creative people who can't help but explore other mental territories are at greater risk, just as someone who climbs a mountain is more at risk than someone who just walks along a village lane."

Come, come Rehaan, don't kid yourself. Creative people? Don't kid yourself; you're not in that club. Journalists report impassionately. They talk to those who're superior than themselves. They hack out inappropriate questions for appropriate answers. Interviews are stimulating, he could tell, only when the interviewee reducts himself, becomes a conduit of information and comments. The approach with Mumtaz Chaudhran wasn't working. The option was to go through a far more aggressive route by painting her into a corner. No, no that would lead to self-loathing. He would become like those hectoring-screaming TV news honchos, repulsive, their sound and fury signifiying self-aggrandisement. Maybe a truth-or-dare challenge could be the modus operandi. To dare wouldn't take any effort; the truth could be wounding. Endure it or back off.

There were no leads left. Memorabilia was scant, no photographs of the sisters clicked together. There were some letters, in Urdu, frequently beginning with the endearing 'Pyaari Aapa', followed by a quaint, 'digar haval yeh hai' (my present state of being goes like this). The letters shifted gears, harped on recriminations and verged on abuse between the sisters. The Qalayat home they had abandoned was the bone of contention. The hovel had been reconstructed by their brother, Murad, who had lived up to his name – a wish come true. The property in the village could fetch them a substantial sum, not sufficient to alter their lifestyles though. No matter. Here was a fold of land each one of them were entitled to. The brother couldn't usurp it. He had monopolised Abba and Ammi the moment he was born. Surely that was treacherous enough.

Mumtaz Chaudhran didn't care about the law and its niceties. She quibbled that since she was the eldest, the ancestral property belonged to her exclusively. In that spirit of bravado, she contemplated a courtroom showdown. Legal proceedings were inevitable. Murad who appealed that he was the only male heir, quoted the sharia. Threats of a court case would be as slow as the hands of a clock following their adamant orbit.

The other sisters, it had to be presumed, claimed a slice of the Aladia land as well. Unresolvable trouble had persisted over decades. Allarakhi, Amina and Ferozi couldn't be assertive; they were faceless by their absence. Rehaan couldn't recall seeing them in person. Their names would crop up and wilt.

Mumtaz's share was at long last bought off in a flourish of generosity by Jameela and Fayazi who had ganged up on the land rights. The Chaudhran was handed over a by-now-barely recallable sum in thousands, and given a loan as well, but had not yet imprinted her signature or fingerprint on the legal documents. "What money are you talking about, bitches?" she'd go amnesiac.

A morning conclave had been called at the Chaudhran's old central Bombay house, at the Kennedy Bridge kotha. Furious with the Chaudhran's wiles and memory loss on the thousands of rupees handed over to her, Jameela, so unlike her, had rained expletives and then flung a brass ugaaldaan at Badi Aapa, hitting her on the forehead. Blood had cascaded from the Chaudhran's forehead to her eyes and cheeks.

Rehaan rushed to his grandmother and held on to her waist tight, imploring, "Ma, let's leave." A slap resounded on his right cheek. Fayazi Ma wasn't to be fazed; a child's petulance wasn't to be tolerated. "Go and sit in the other room till we've finished," she said firmly. "This is a matter between us sisters. You're just a child." Child equals moron.

Rehaan was led out by Jameela, consoled with a flummery of endearments, and latched in a room at the far end of the Chaudhran's kotha. He wept noisily. When the door was unlocked, Jameela was applying a turmeric-paste bandage on Mumtaz's forehead. Fayazi was lathering a paan. This was getting farcical. Mumtaz and Jameela hugged each other. Business-like now, Fayazi Ma said to both, "Remember we love one another; quarrels are momentary."

"Why did you slap me, Ma? I'm hurting," Rehaan dared to wince.

She snorted, "Sisters are sisters. You will never know what that means… I rue the day your mother gave birth to you. It was disappointing to see my first and only grandchild…a son."

"You love these women more than you love me?" the boy asked precociously.

"Love between us sisters can't be measured," she said, as if she was drafting the opening line of an ode to sisterhood.

The cause and effect theory was alien to the sisters. Endlessly through his adolescent years, the grandson had wondered whether they were mercurial? Temperamental beyond repair? Wrong buttons were being pushed by him here. The closest guess he could hazard was that they were beyond comprehension, particularly Mumtaz, Jameela and Fayazi. The other sisters, Allarakhi, Ferozi and Ameena couldn't be like them. They must be made of the same clay in deceptively gentler colours, reminiscent of Amrita Sher-Gil's faces of rural women - stoic but aware that they were sitting for a portrait. In the imagined portrait, Allarakhi was dumped in a remote section of the canvas, and the demeanour of Ferozi and Ameena could have been that of concealed amusement.

If Ameena had participated in that meeting over the property dispute, he imagined her lost eye wouldn't have reduced her vision, but she would have backed off. Her sisters saw Ameena as impaired, a kaani, cross-eyed. She wouldn't change their perception. She wouldn't protest. It was only a matter of time. Her silence would have unnerved the sisters; she couldn't be cheated of her due status in the tangled grid of the Aladia sisters either. If she and Ferozi had been present on the scene, they would have been disappointed that Mumtaz hadn't been hurt more grievously by the hurled ugaldaan.

As soon as he visualised the conclave ending, he imagined the pious Allarakhi excusing herself – it was time for her afternoon namaaz. She would appeal to Allah for sanity, unity among the sisters and above all, her rightful share of the property. In a rare moment of candidspeak, Fayazi had told him about Allarakhi. She owned a miniscule shop in a Muslim-dominated mohalla, which sold sweets, biscuits, bidis, cigarettes and matchboxes.

The shop's monthly take was paltry. Often Allarakhi didn't know where her next meal was coming from. She had to live; she couldn't subsist any longer, moving from the dank corners allocated in the kotha by the Chaudhran. Rehaan could see Allarakhi, if she had been there, recoil on seeing a child slapped for no fault of his. She would have cupped her hands and breathed on his face to soothe it, and would have berated Fayazi, "Don't ever do that again. It is not correct to raise your hand on a child."

The slap, she would have fumed, was on her face. Fishing out a few rupee notes from within her blouse, Allarakhi would have said magnanimously, "Buy yourself some sweets from a big store. They have lemon drops and bull's-eyes imported from England also. This grandmother of yours is mean; she can't appreciate what she has."

And Fayazi Ma would have silenced her, "Mind your own business. I'm raising this boy the way he should be raised. Get that in your foolish head, you troublemaker."

Allarakhi would have laughed drily and prayed on a folded red-and-gold jaannamaaz which she must have carried with her wherever she went.

He was lapsing, hypothesising, breaking his word that he would stick to reportage. This Allarakhi was Rehaan's creation, endowed with a tender heart. He would have liked to learn Urdu at the feet of Allarakhi Nani. She was the sister he adored; she was illusory. His Allarakhi lived in a nowhere sky with diamonds, an unseen face he associated for no reason with the elegance of the Urdu language.

It was a lacuna. Rehaan was left uneducated in the adab of Urdu, overloaded with the school's curriculum of English, Hindi, Gujarati or Marathi, and for a year, Latin – from the textbook *Ora Maratima* – which he could never comprehend. Lessons in reading the Quran from a maulvi had proved cumbersome. Fayazi Ma stopped the lessons. She contended, school first, faith later. "At least learn the kalima by heart. That's the least you can do to be a good Muslim." Easier said, easier done. Still, ignorance of the tenets of the Islamic faith was a void. Whenever the sisters prayed, they struck him as women of God – they were being watched, they were under the Almighty's custody. The boy would recite the kalima to be in line.

9

Negotiations

Reciting the kalima inaudibly, at the next meet-up in Oshiwara with Mumtaz Chaudhran, Rehaan mustered up courage to talk tough. Supine on that mattress, littered with pillows, the Chaudhran who had covered herself in a polyester fabric chudder, would have to be receptive to his outburst.

Shuhaba, the near-comatose handmaiden, would place a glass of water, the cup of dark tea and sugared biscuits by Rehaan's side on the mattress. These would remain untouched, as always, but Shuhaba had to be hospitable – the most detested of enemies deserve a traditional welcome. She left the room, as was her habit.

The rehearsed outburst flew out of the window as soon as Rehaan could pronounce, "Chaudhran, I have something to say today..."

"You always have something to say," she griped, "but don't have the bloody guts to. I'll say exactly what you want to, chutiya. You want to tell me, 'My great ma hasn't brought up the loan...the lousy karza... Now I've given you more money, but you aren't keeping your end of the bargain.' That's written all over your monkey face."

Let her vex and wane, but hang on, don't react to her next ruse. Shuffling the briefcase from behind a bolster, she announced with the authority of a potentate. "Take your money, take it away. Maybe I've spent four or five thousand from it, consider that a tax levy. The Chaudhran is not for sale."

She was smouldering as if speaking from a stake, the fire burning. Rehaan accepted the briefcase, admittedly with relief, and walked out without saying a word. The wait for the elevator was interminable. The operator had goofed off – a tea break would be the excuse. Rehaan was about to take the stairs down. Shuhaba whimpered, "Don't take her seriously. She has lost her mind."

"That's your cross to bear, not mine," Rehaan said heartlessly, without turning back. The stairs rolled on in a blur. He was about to cross the exit gate and turn towards the taxi stand when Shuhaba's voice called out from the window, "Come back. She will apologise." The sequence was like a negotiation with a vegetable vendor who shooes you away, and then recalls you for re-negotiations.

Mumtaz grabbed the briefcase back, and was as ready as a diva would be for an opera. Swatting the mosquitoes around her, she consoled Rehaan, "You're playing a snake and mongoose game with me, smartypants. *Alright,* so sit comfortably. Whatever I know, I will tell you. My parvardigar will vouch for all the suffering I have gone through... I will start again with that black night, that qayamat ki raat, when we ran away from home. There was no moonlight, no stars to guide us in the dark. It was as if Allah showed us the path, and an oil lantern which I allowed your grandmother Fejji to carry. She kept complaining that the light was about to go off. There wasn't enough oil in the lamp, pardon me but she wasn't carrying it correctly; the tel was spilling. I took over the lamp, the light shone bright. The rough, stone paths, gullies and finally the pukka road leading to the station shone as if they were paved with gold."

The Chaudhran, astonishingly, did not place herself on an indestructible pedestal while narrating the train ride, or her triumph in outfoxing the ticket collector. The flight to the Nizamuddin Aulia dargah she synopsised, "Naturally, there's no place like home. We missed home as soon as we had left it. Who wouldn't? For nights and days, the passageway of the dargah became our home. Coins and niyaaz food kept us going. We weren't permitted to use the courtyard. It was huge but if the mullahs and the imam would have allowed us to do that, the floodgates would have opened up for boys and girls begging for alms at the open path before the dargah... that's where they have all those seekh kabab kitchens today. My Allah knows I want to go there once before I die, but I don't have the nerve to travel. I don't want my last breath on a train of all things. Anyway, let me tell you, we never begged. None of us held out our hands for coins and food; these were given to us as zakat, charity. If we, the receivers, gained by that, the givers gained full marks, 10 on 10 , from Allah. I believe in that, too. There may be no money in the house but zakat is a must. After all, on the day of reckoning, everyone has to be accountable to Allah. Remember this boy, any charity you give, God registers that in his ledger.

"Often I feel my corner in jannat has already been reserved. I won't have to stand in a queue for eternal peace. No fire, demons and a new death every day for me in dozakh after I have quit this wretched apartment. This is where my dead body will go from. If you care for me at all, if you're capable of a shred of respect, bury me at the Marine Lines ka Bada Kabrastaan. Don't know why, but I want my soul to rest in peace there. Local trains pass by, there's greenery, shade, wild flowers and it's not as congested as the other kabrastaans. Still I'm worried. I've heard that there's shortage of space there. The graveyard is house full. Multiple bodies are buried in every resting place, even the Bada Qabrastan. How cruel is that? Maybe, we would have all been happier in Qalayat. There must still be so much space there, cheaper than it is in this greedy city. I could have rested, alone at last."

The Chaudhran was rambling. Mortality was her guillotine chop. She was diverting from the story. She was derailing Rehaan from the single track of his investigation, a personal investigation. The Chaudhran wasn't conversant with Urdu poetry. No Mirza Ghalib or Firaq for her. Not even Hindi film songs which were Rehaan's weakness. Immediately, the lyric lip-synced on screen by Raj Kapoor played on the turntable of his mind, "Ek Din Bik Jaayega Maati Ke Mol" (One day, you'll be sold for the price of dust). The joker in Rehaan was drifting. The Chaudhran was talking her head off. He heard nothing till she huffed, "Where are you? I may as well be talking to a statue whose head is covered with bird-shit."

"I'm all here," he lied. "Every word of yours is being recorded on my cellphone."

"Swine, why didn't you tell me before?" she asked. "I would have spoken louder. Is the cell phone in your shirt pocket. Take it out and keep it before me."

"No need for that. If you speak loudly, there would be an echo effect. It's better this way."

Her face turned as soft a gazelle's. For the first time in her life, she came close to tossing him a compliment, "Kaafi intelligent ho...you're the most educated boy in the Aladia tabbar. Have to give you a medal for that." Then she changed lanes, "Actually, if you're that clever, why aren't you capturing me on one of those TV-type cameras? No one has ever taken even a decent photograph of mine."

She was buying time.

"I will bring a video camera next time."

"Make it next week. I will dress up well for you, will add a dash of lipstick and powder. Don't bring anyone else with you, no one but a camera and you. I can only talk to our flesh and blood if I may say so - someone I can call my own."

A handycam could be managed. A video technician demanding nothing but a Scotch-and-home-cooked-biryani dinner, would clue Rehaan into cam photography.

The part-time domestic help, Najma, who suffered from seasonal ailments, couldn't rustle up a palatable biryani. Moreover, Fayazi Ma would have asked a hundred questions.

So Rehaan offered to rustle up the biryani on a gas cooking range at the technician's studio. With the aid of a Google recipe, he prepared a saffroned rice pyramid, dotted with chunks of tender lamb, cashew nuts and raisins. The Scotch he bought at a discount price from a bootlegger. If it was spurious, too bad. "Fantastic!" the technician marvelled. "No one can make a biryani like Muslims do." The technician wore a jade Ganesha pendant around his neck, fiddled with the Elephant God under the haze of five Siberia-sized Scotch and sodas. Handling a camera, which weighed like a cherubic new-born, turned out to be child's play. "Don't forget to carry a tripod. I'll lend you mine in exchange for another dinner… and drinks," the technician boomed. Done. Rehaan felt like a lighthouse in the monsoon month darkness of the studio. No one had ever praised his cooking skills before.

10

On Camera

The technical nitty gritty of the video interview wasn't a speedbreaker. The Chaudhran's wiles to come to the point were. Rehaan had to hear it from her, verify hearsay that was as slippery as a basket of eels.

He'd go with the technique of True or False? Were the six sisters handed away individually, like gift parcels, to Muslim families for adoption by the mullahs with the go-ahead of the Sajjad-e-Nasheen of the dargah?

Rehaan wasn't convinced after years of eavesdropping and coaxing stories from the Aladia women. "If you don't tell me all," he had threatened Fayazi Ma during his late teens, "I will kill myself," though he had no such intention. Once looking at the Bombay sea-line, the grey waves lashing the greyer tetrapods at the Marine Drive boulevard, he had flirted with suicide on the eve of school examinations, and also when slurs were sent his way by friends on the St Xavier's college campus. Friends! A whisper had gone around, "He comes from a rotten family.

He's actually a bastard, you know? His mother was from a family of whores."

After a slugout with two of the friends, his shirt was torn, his nose bled. Fayazi Ma was horrified and threatened to visit the school and complain to the principal. She was persuaded not to, "I beg you not to. I started the fight, they didn't," he fibbed. He never spoke to the boys again. The whispers persisted.

"See who tops the graduation exams, you bastards," became his theme-challenge." That he'd skipped the fourth and seventh standards in school and jumped straight into Inter Arts (without expending the mandatory first year at college) rankled the bastards. Bastards, bastards, bastards. He'd tar them with flying colours. The vilification abated; the scars deepened.

If Rehaan was endowed with any quality, it was constancy. The video interview had to work. It had to with his key-witness – prime suspect? – Mumtaz Chaudhran. Ornamented in a thin gold chain, gold earrings, a silver ring, coy in an embroidered green taffeta dupatta draped around her head, she was a sight. The talcum and smudged lipstick jarred. The silhoueteless, pitch black velvet kurta was topped with a crumpled chlorophyll-green dupatta. The salwar ballooning below her waist had to be kept off camera. "You may only keep my face in frame," she said, as if she had been through hundreds of on-camera interviews before. Where did that come from? From the Aladia reservoir of native intelligence?

Clearing her throat, not that she had to, she began slowly, picking up speed, fobbing off Rehaan's whys, whens and what-fors.

"Teri yeh Mumtaz has sinned without any embarrassment. What is a sin, anyway? The sins of the pious mullahs? I forgive them. We sisters had to be separated by those mullahs. We couldn't stay together in some paradise, away from harm and abuse. I was entrusted to a woman; Neelambai she called herself. She instructed little girls in the art of dance...meaning how to dance before men who threw hundred-hundred-rupee notes at the bells, those two-kilo-heavy ghungroos on the ankles of our feet generously...the miserly threw ten-ten or five-five-rupee notes on our feet, but money is money. Mind you, that was in appreciation of dance only. No funny business.

"Don't look at me like that. I know what's going on in that bheja of yours. Get a haircut, your head resembles a crow's nest. Right now, you're putting on an act of being brain-dead. Still, jo bhi. Let it be, you don't listen to anyone but that Fejji of yours. Do what you want...the way I used to... refused to get my hair cut; my head was a shelter for lice and bugs. They would bite me, extract blood from me. My hair was none of Neelambai's business. Better lice than her. But what was to be done? She had her way. The barber must have been a butcher in his first life. He chopped off my hair. Tufts poked out of my skull.

"When I wept, the bai assured me the hair would grow back and it would look better, more silky, more seductive. That raand had a plan. She was a madam, all said and done, she would sell me for my nath, my nose-ring, you know, my virginity, my izzat for thousands of rupees. This situation isn't uncommon; it's been shown again and again in the pictures, hasn't it? Let me enlighten you – those scenes in the movies are half-truths.

"Virgins are sold after much pampering; rough tactics don't work. Madams can be sweet, try to be like elder sisters, gentle, persuasive. They aren't stupid, least of all Neelambai. What a style she had. In her heyday, she must have looked more desirable than any heroine, that too without make-up. So vivacious, her smile could light up a room. She had learnt every trick of the trade – how to bargain and whom to bargain with, immediately separating the landed gentry from the lower-class louts. She was a money-making machine. 'Trust me and I will trust you,' she told me. 'No harm shall ever befall your sisters. I will try to make arrangements for you to see them whenever you wish. I have never been a mother; I will be a mother to you.'"

"Motherhood for her meant fixing marriages of convenience. Not exactly a matchmaker, she knew which man needed a woman, why and when. Like nowadays, I've heard marriages are arranged on computer. To be fair, she gave me a choice. Between Giriraj Gulabchand Seth of Delhi and Abdul Ghani Seth of Bombay, both businessmen over 50 years of age, nothing to look at, they were in need of a concubine.

"Tired of their wives – Gulabchand had two, Ghani had three – they wanted a regular prostitute to service them in the way others couldn't. Neelambai is a Hindu name;

that was her professional name. She was a Muslim, Bilqis Begum, she would observe all the rozas. She was nicknamed Neelam – she wore so many sapphire rings on her fat fingers, you see. Those who solicited women merely as 'keeps', during the Ramzan days were told to get the hell out of her home. A spick-and-span house it was...two rooms at Delhi's G.B. Road, you know that place I'm sure...where so many randikhaanas still exist. That's where my story with Neelambai began...like the first reel of a film... We moved to Bombay only years later. But what's in a city? They're all the same; men and their sexual urges are the same everywhere."

She looked at Rehaan with contempt, "I don't know if you are a man. If you were, you should have been a father of two-three children by now. Look, look, how you are blushing like a bride...a Vestal Virgin. You will probably tell me you've never visited such places, too lowdown for you."

Rehaan laughed timorously, "Believe it or not, I have been there, but not for what you think."

In the still unrealised ambition of filming a documentary on the children of sex workers, he had asked a city guide to take him around the road – the Garstin Bastion Road as it was known in the British era. A line-up of a dozen brothels had multiplied into close to a hundred crammed cabins in decaying three-storey buildings, with a tumble of shops at ground level. In 1966, it was officially renamed Swami Shradhanand Marg. Not that the change made any difference.

The road, now packed with garish neon signs, pokey restaurants, pokier shops and wandering migrant workers from other states, housed over 1,000 sex workers. He had met one of them. The guide had sought his permission to have "some fun" with a woman who was washing tin plates at a tap. While he did, Rehaan had watched her son, Govind, about five or six, draw crayon sketches artfully on a slate. The sex worker saw the guide off, smirking, "Your friend is in such a hurry, didn't last beyond five minutes."

Embarrassed to tell the Chaudhran about the G.B. Road experience, Rehaan refocused on the Chaudhran who was unstoppable now, "Neelambai would insist on a nikaah between a selected lot of her girls and the useless, old men. Saala whatchamacallhim…Giriraj Gulabchand was half my height, face like a brown rabbit's and a body going to waste. The moment he was shown to me, I wept. No Gulabchand Seth for me.

"So we travelled to Bombay – it would take as many as 36 hours by train. Abdul Ghani Seth was a relief – as tall as Abba Saundha Bhai, dreamy eyes and courteous. The moment he saw me, he touched my chin, lifted my face towards his and said kindly, 'Don't be afraid. Only if you want, I will go through a nikaah and look after your every need, financial and physical.' No contest between those seths. An alliance with Ghani Seth meant a quick nikaah… qabool qabool...and I would become his fourth wife. Mind you, not his mistress, but a wife whom he could not take home. Suited me – no soutens, children and grandchildren to deal with. No sin was being committed.

"I was sold like those slaves of ancient days, but with dignity, by Neelambai. Meanwhile, the mullahs at the dargah had made other arrangments for my little girls. Those were different times. They did not do any zabardasti. My sisters were sent to different places only after my approval. 'You are the eldest, you are like a mother to your girls,' the old goats said as if I didn't know that already. I came to terms with their decisions. The mullahs were neither messiahs nor monsters. Even the pious have some advantage to seek – whether they ask for that advantage in the name of charity or good deeds. Who was I to quarrel with any one of them? And you're well aware where the lights of my life were sent, or have you forgotten? Memories, like the skirts which girls wear today, are becoming shorter and shorter."

Rehaan didn't need a memory recall. Jameela was adopted by a childless couple of Chandni Chowk. Her foster mother was a failed semi-classical singer, her foster father, a trader in gems and rough diamonds.

Fayazi was accompanied on a two-day train journey by a mullah to Bombay, where she was settled in an orphanage, the Sadqa-e-Hind Yateemkhana.

The orphanage funded by Sir Osman Baksh Mitha, a trader in salt and a troubleshooter for the British Raj, had a flawless reputation. Girl children were taught embroidery, cooking, and whichever natural-born talent they seemed to possess. It could also be swabbing the floors of the one-storey orphanage, in a clean alleyway of Byculla.

Allarakhi, more submissive than the others, was sent off to Lucknow, to be with the Sayyeds, a Sunni Muslim family in which the patriarch's teenaged son, was mentally a four-year-old. Daily prayers would go up in Lucknow in hope of the day when he would stop talking gibberish and hopping around like a monkey on their grand manor's tiled roofs. No one would marry him. Except for Allarakhi who would have to barter her gratitude to the Sayyeds by becoming the demented boy's humnasheen, the love and bride of his life. Bravely she resisted, she wouldn't let the monkey touch her. The Sayyeds waited. She would come around.

Ameena and her twin Ferozi found no takers, not immediately at least. A vacancy would have to be awaited at Bombay's Sadqa-e-Hind Yateemkhana. Till then, they could stay in a storeroom opposite the dargah, which had been mysteriously abandoned by its owner. No objections to the twins staying there, as long as they read the Quran diligently and daily. Their meals would be brought there. A maulvi taught them to memorise passages of the Quran by heart. Distraught on being isolated from their sisters, they moved like automatons.

After spraying the ugaldaan with paan spittle, like coloured water from a pichkari on Holi, Mumtaz Chaudhran resumed her video interface. "I'm enjoying this," she purred. "When will I be seen and where – will it come on TV? Which channel? – I'll be remembered. Mind you, don't show this to the public while I'm alive. Till I'm gone, my story, my sisters' stories, your story too, are to stay within the family. After I'm no more, who cares. Understand this, you selfish boy, saale ehsaan-faramosh, I'm giving you the story in my will. Not that I have anything else to give to anyone. Which is why that Shuhaba is always staring daggers at me. She stays away from me. I stay away from her as much as possible, I like to be alone in my room. At this age, I'm looking after her, not the other way around. My own first-born."

The Chaudhran's disappointment with her daughter was justified to a degree. In her teenage years, Shuhaba was a handsome woman, her complexion the colour of dawn – brown limned by a golden glow. She couldn't quite accomplish what her mother had wanted her to – become a movie actress in the early 1940s. Producers liked what they saw waist upwards. Her legs stretched on to the height of almost 5 feet 9 inches; she could rub equal shoulders with the heroes. A disadvantage – no hero liked to be paired with a towering woman.

Shuhaba found employment as an 'extra', a junior artiste in a couple of films, relegated to the backdrop in party scenes with nearly 50 others. She would be asked to sit on a table looking as expressionless as she could; she was part of the furniture, that's all. Ashok Kumar, then a neophyte, was the lead actor in one of her two films. Shuhaba caught his eye. He had ambled over to her, saying, "You could be a heroine, you know..." and sauntered away to chat with the formal leading lady of the picture, a tear-jerker in which he portrayed an upper-class man with faintly socialistic leanings, a part which was aimed at sniping at the British colonialists.

That brief encounter with Ashok Kumar had been clicked by an on-the-set photographer. Shuhaba had framed the print which hung in her room at the Oshiwara apartment. One of the peak thrills of her life was the fact that Ashok Kumar, years later, had recognised her at the premiere of one of his films. She'd beg or borrow passes from her neighbour, a B-grade film producer's wife. The matinee idol of yore had become a father figure on screen. When Shuhaba gaped at him at the premiere, he had called out to her, "Oh, it's you. Forgotten your name. Why did you give up? Good to see you," and he had hugged her paternally, before saying goodbye with his pearly-white smile. Shuhaba was over the moon but wouldn't recount her dream encounter even when she was prodded about the photograph. The Chaudhran didn't appreciate dreams retold.

Shuhaba's nikaah and separation from Bhalla were an open secret among the Aladia sisters. It would have been pointless to bring these up in the video-interview with Mumtaz Chaudhran, who, right then, raised her little finger for a piss-break. She returned to sit primly on the chair, prepared to dole out answers; no qs necessary. This interview would be her last hurrah on the subject of her family, in which she was the lead player, her sisters the supporting ensemble, with cameos by the men who criss-crossed their lives. The men had invited themselves over for dinner and overstayed their welcome.

The video camera's red light flared malevolently, which pleased her. She was being accorded attention. Expertly, she asked if she should turn her eyes towards the lens or at Rehaan on a settee, placed at a diagonal angle. Both are good, he told her shortly, drawing a look as if he was an amateur at a one-person filming venture, which he was.

"Jee janaab," she preened. "I told you where my sisters were settled. I kept track of them but didn't poke my nose into their destinies. I had enough on my plate to handle.

I had to organise my life too, didn't I? Neelambai's house, which she set up in a kotha of Bombay opposite Kennedy Bridge, was not a home. Ghani, my husband, legal husband, mind you, would visit once or twice a week, do what he had to, leave money for me with that Neelambai, the witch. He was loaded, quite a sethiya I swear. I'd call him Sethji. Quite a kind, caring man, at last he shifted me to a place of my own, closer to his home facing Girgaum Chowpatty beach. He wouldn't have to travel much; his visits became more frequent. Our lovemaking – if it may be called that – became a habit.

"Neelambai did raise a stink; she wanted more than the monthly stipend organised for her. She warned me, 'We have to demand more money; it's our right to. Remember, when you have no one else to turn to, my doors will always open for you, night and day.' As if her home…the kotha was a hospital to mend damaged souls.

"I was smart. Ghani Sethji was an easy target. He was besotted with me. I would dance with fury to the radio music in the bedroom. I tantalised him like no other woman could, demanded the price which comes with conjugal rights. Frankly, I extracted as much money, jewellery and passion, if you know what I mean, from the Sethji till one fine day, he suffered a stroke in the middle of the night. His family was informed. He was taken away to a rest house somewhere in Panchgani, a 10 or 11-hour' drive from Bombay.

"Months later, throwing caution to the wind – and with proof of nikaah – I went to see him in a hired Buick taxi. His wives and their children were there. They gave me respect.

I sat before Sethji, who was paralysed. He couldn't even nod to acknowledge my presence. Yet there was a hint of tears in his eyes. Don't know if I acted or I was moved. I broke down till his wife, the eldest one, had to calm me down with a glass of water. And I must tell you, the wife did the unexpected. She took off the four pure gold bangles on her right hand and gave them to me. My heart exploded; I howled some more. I shouldn't have. The bangles were crumbs, as if I was being given charity. I had been manipulated by that bloody wife of his. After that, I didn't have the audacity to demand my haq, my share of Ghani Sethji's vast property – farms, complete buildings rented to tenants in the heart of the city, the wads of cash in his tijoris, diamonds, pearls…the works. Don't want to remember what I was cheated of that day in Panchgani. I've been jinxed, you know. Never got my rightful share of wealth or gratitude.

"Those four bangles tied in a knot in my dupatta, I returned to Bombay in the waiting Buick. The fucking driver had the nerve to ask me how much maal…booty…I had got away with. I told him to mind his business; he kept talking. I had carried a small Rampuri knife for the journey. I flicked it open, moved it on his neck. He bled a little maybe; he kept his trap shut.

"It was the longest journey of my life. I was driven to Neelambai's kotha. It must have been 4 in the morning when everyone is wide awake like owls at such places. Real ullus, I tell you. Neelambai took me in her arms as if she would crush me to death, and said, 'I have kept your room as it was. I knew you would come back. This 'I knew it, I knew it' smugness was a knife stab, but you know me. Mazboot, solid like a truck. I had been away for two years at that Chowpatty love nest of ours; the months, weeks and days seemed like yesterday. That's what happens when women get sentimental and think of lousy things like love.

"I swore that night never to think of love again. Passion, lust, yes, because I am human like everyone else. I had my physical needs. Neelambai would find me another man, but I would make it clear that he would have to be a husband who could take care of me, a tiger who would treat me like his cub. By the way, before I returned to my room in the kotha, I also insisted that my sisters shouldn't ever know about my sudden exit from Ghani Sethji's Chowpatty flat. They would have to be told I left him because I couldn't stand him anymore. If my sisters refuse to believe this, it would their problem, not mine."

As brusquely as her departure from that Panchgani resthouse, she ended the interview, "Enough, go now," the pet phrase coined for Rehaan. When he didn't react, she crowed, "I've given you so much spice. Would any woman talk to you about how she was shamed?"

"You're a great woman, Chaudhran. Infinitely more honest than your sisters. Way more..."

"Don't use fancy words on me. *Infinitely* indeed. You're lying and you know that. Take that tinpot camera of yours and go now."

"Just a few questions," he protested.

"I hate questions," she hit back.

"I have to ask them."

She mellowed, "When you were a baby and your Fayazi Ma brought you over, you would want to jump into my arms. Then you'd shit on me. I'd say, 'Never mind.' and clean your bottom. You're one of us; you're an Aladia though you've taken your so-called father's name."

"So-called?"

"Yes, yes…forget all that. I say what comes to my head. Siddiqi…such a grand name...it means the truthful one, ha! You look soft on the outside. Almost like a girl you are, but you don't give up. Alright, shit all over me again now, but ten questions are all I will allow you to ask. Make it quick."

"Why ten?"

"For me, that's an auspicious number. We had escaped from Qalayat on the 10th of a month. That's also your date of birth, isn't it? I like the number. Take it or leave it. I feel as if I'm in court again, where Fayazi and Jameela had dragged me…do you remember? For our Qalayat property? I should have known you would also harrow me some day. Fayazi ke ho, you've gone on her."

He started gently, "Chaudhran, among the sisters, who would you say has been the most successful?"

"You want me to praise Fayazi. Like grain hoarders, she is flush with money. She is respected and above all, she has you. She has rutba…status. You're the only male in the family who has looked after his ma…his grandma. You have a job; she wouldn't have got the power she does without you. All the other males born to us sisters have been nikamma, parasites. They won't rest till they've sucked every drop of blood out of us. Second question."

"At Neelambai's kotha...establishment, were you ever forced to meet men...apart from Abdul Ghani Sethji?"

"You mean did I ever sell my body for money? Was I a glorified prostitute? The answer's 'No'. I am ashamed you ask me this. I don't want to continue...go away."

He rephrased the second question. "Did you ever fall in love, if that means anything?"

"Twice, if that means anything. Abdul Ghani Sethji because he was the first man in my life. Sadiq was my second man; he ran chores for Neelambai. A servant. He was beautiful. No one could help falling in love with him. He had the eyelashes of a woman. He pretended to be submissive gentle, making love to me as if I was an empress. Whenever I was alone, I would leave a soap dish on the windowsill. That was the signal for him to come over and make love for hours in the afternoon.

"After a while, I didn't care if our secret was out. It was my mistake that I didn't marry him. After that alliance with Sethji, I had learnt my lesson – nikaahs don't last. In any case, Sadiq wasn't faithful to me. He had a mistress, a hijra. Heera, that eunuch was called. I suppose they made love in a different way. At the very start, Sadiq had made it clear he would not be able to give up Heera...I gave in. He needed both of us to be complete... What this "complete" means, I will never know."

"There is still something I'm not sure about. Have you ever regretted for a minute leaving your parents and your brother to fend for themselves in Qalayat?"

"For your kind information, whenever I saved some money, I would money-order it to Qalayat. As for Murad

Bhai, like all Aladia men, he was good for nothing, a wrestler who could never become a champion, the best. We Aladias have to be the best. He was addicted to opium. He had our house to his name, he must have been 40 or 50 – who cares! – when he passed away. An overdose of afeem, I was told. We never saw him which is just as well. Our hearts would have melted. The property, then, rightfully belonged to us sisters. His wife and son believed otherwise. They wanted money.

"Once, in a fit of generosity, Fayazi and I money-ordered them 10,000 rupees at one go – a princely amount those days. The house was transferred to Fayazi, Jameela and myself. Murad's son – if I'm not mistaken, his name's Nauman Ali – did visit me in Bombay, at Kennedy Bridge. I fed him with my own hands – murgh musallam, tandoori rotis and kheer… I gave him some more money. He was a grateful boy, undemanding. But that was our first and last meeting. Often, I do think of Nauman – where did the boy go? Is he alive and *alright*? Such thoughts pain me. Your fourth question?"

"Why haven't you been kinder to your sons and grandsons?"

"Like my brother Murad, all they want is more, more and more. They want to devour my flesh to the last morsel. I did all I could to them, distributed big amounts of money to them. My sons are drunks, and my grandsons, fucking dukkars, druggies. Shuhaba is the only one I can tolerate, except on the days when she gets on my nerves. Of late, the days have been increasing."

"Question five. Do you think your sisters have been resentful because you made them leave Qalayat?"

"Yes. And only they can tell you why. Sixth?"

"Would you say you were the most daring of the sisters, the one who went on to become the madam of a brothel?"

"Silly question. Yes of course, this Mumtaz has been the most daring. Chaudhran ko English mein madam bolte hain...pata hai? Look...is Chaudhran called Madam in English? Say, say whatever comes to your fucking tongue. Fayazi didn't want me to be known as her sister. She would never let me visit her bungalow. She would visit me, if it was necessary, wearing a burqa and arriving in a tonga, instead of her cars. She'd even bring you along when you were as small as a shrimp. Kids are duffers; they are not supposed to know anything."

"Seventh question. Jameela rose to become a ghazal singer, cut records and had fans swooning over her. Were you envious?"

"Yes, very much. Jameela was also said to be a cheap gaanewaali – rumours which were false and soon died down. If you ask me, she should have been a classical thumri singer. The classical can never be tainted."

"Eighth question. How honest have you been with me... in your answers?"

"Fairly honest. No man or woman can be 100...200 per cent honest. There are some things which all of us carry to the grave. We have to."

"Chaudhran. Without elaborating on these 'things' to be carried to the grave, can you give me an indication of what these could be about?"

"These things are connected to the desire to be the winner. If you cannot understand what I mean, too bad. Enough?"

"Last question. Haven't you been unfair to Shuhaba Baaji?"

"Never. I don't need to answer that. Now, go."

Rehaan hadn't used a lapel mike. Her voice was hoarse, yet clear. The camera's in-built mike was sufficient for the video footage which would never be edited or posted on a website. The interview itself left a lot to be desired. Mumtaz wasn't provoked enough to break into tears; her eyes had indicated remorse, at most. The Chaudhran wasn't capable of 'speaking from the heart', a catchphrase in journalese. At which point she had become immune to heartspeak, was beyond plumbing.

Rehaan had conducted hundreds if not thousands of interviews – with police officers, constables, social workers, politicians, mafia dons, artists, movie celebrities – who could never jolt him out of his thick skin. Yeah, yeah, he'd be a put-on Noddy in Wonderland, sure, tell me another. The Chaudhran's tongue was as forked as theirs. Rehaan watched the Chaudhran's video footage a couple of times – an hour and some minutes.

For an overall perspective, it was imperative to talk with Shuhaba and her two sons, Sameer and Saagar. Shuhaba owed Rehaan; she would have to talk. Through an acquaintance, he had pleaded for the admission of Shuhaba's sons to a rehab centre. The Centre's counsellor had remarked, after a week, "They're too far gone. Still, we're talking to them and helping them with medicines at a subsidised cost, but we're not miracle workers. Sameer won't be able to last beyond a year. Saagar's case is terminal as well, but let's see. We haven't caught him lately with brown sugar and heroin, he's watched on CCTV."

"Who smuggles drugs in, anyway," asked Rehaan. Could it be one of the watchdogs?

"Are you casting aspersions, Mr Rehaan?"

"No, no, just making sure."

Three years had elapsed since the counsellor's dire prediction. Shuhaba deluded herself that her sons would be cured. She was vulnerable as ever. Rehaan could draw her out without being exploitative. The sons were beyond exploitation. After the Chaudhran's video interview, back in the unlit passageway to the elevator, he had asked Shuhaba, "Baaji, when can I meet your sons?"

The unflinching answer was, "Any time you want. I cannot say 'no' to you. Right now, you know they are recovering at the same Lonavla sanatorium - Happy Home. It runs on charity. Where else could I place them? My request is, be kind to them."

Rehaan hadn't dared to ask Shuhaba for a conversation. Not yet. He would have to wait – only when and if she was ready. As if she had read his thoughts, she said, "Be kind to me also when you're ready to hear my side of the story. I will not refuse." Rehaan let that pass. This was neither the time nor place to commit Shuhaba to talk ill of or defend the Chaudhran. The timing had to be spot-on.

"Do let me know if I can be of any help," Rehaan said insincerely, hoping she wouldn't ask him for a favour – more money for house repairs, more money for clothes for Sameer and Saagar, who were always in the same pair of jeans and checked shirts whenever he'd seen them.

"When we need help, I will phone you, Bhai." she said. "Allah haafiz."

'Nani' and 'Baaji' had become generic terms, convenient to address the grand-aunts and their daughters. For his sanatorium cousins, he couldn't find an apt word.

Fayazi Ma, though, was the apt word. She had raised and reared him, claiming that she had weaned him at her own breasts. He had refused to be fed till she had clasped him to her breasts. "Miraculously, I lactated," she'd claim. He wouldn't dare to counter that with a "Really?"

He couldn't tell her about the investigation into the Aladia story. She was nearing 77. She could shuffle around, and on some days, recoup her strength enough to wash the kitchen with damp rags and chuck cannisters of water into the toilet basins and commode. A neatnik, contradictorily she didn't care about what she wore. A white petticoat and blouse were her uniform at home. If and when she went out, she would fix a cotton sari on her emaciated frame. In summer, she would sweat profusely, breathe asthmatically, and banned airconditioning in their two-room apartment. "Those AC luxuries can be bought after I'm dead. AC is bad for asthma, so don't argue. I want to save every rupee I can, so you're comfortable after me. Beta, your job doesn't pay you enough."

When Rehaan returned home after the Chaudhran interview, Fayazi Ma said, "First you'd write with pen on paper, then typewriter, and now these costly computers. And what are you doing with that camera, bache? Don't ever wander off towards filmmaking. I am afraid of that. That Shuhaba became an 'extra.' Your mother wanted to join the movies...as a heroine...and see what happened. Nothing, zero. Mark my words, there is something evil about films."

Nevertheless, Fayazi Ma was a film addict. She'd watch every Sunday afternoon film on television. Her logic was, "Films are okay for time-pass. They are not to be taken seriously. No film is real."

With age, she had turned near-deaf. Any suggestion of a hearing aid would be rejected with a, "I can hear a little bit now at least. With those things plugged in my ears, I'll become a deewar, a wall." And after alluding to the title of the Amitabh Bachchan-Shashi Kapoor film, there would be the patented wisecrack, 'Tere paas Ma hai' (You have Ma). What else do you want?"

Paradoxically, Fayazi Ma had exposed Rehaan to films with a vengeance, bundling him up in her arms as an infant. She was a bundle of contradictions. Likewise, he adored and detested her for being a helicopter guardian. Whenever he wanted to go out to a film, the theatre or play gully cricket, her firman was to return before sunset, and to take care while crossing the streets. She dreaded dying under a speeding taxi – not a car, but a taxi.

She'd chat up taxi drivers, curious about their place of birth, marital status and families. At the end of the ride, she'd leave a small tip, not a custom to be followed in Bombay, and complain, "You were driving too fast. And you kept turning your head back to speak to me. Watch the road next time." More often than not, a cabbie would awww, "You remind me so much of my mother back in the village." She'd prefer not to hear the word 'village'; she felt she was armed with the arsenal of urban intelligence.

11

Just Don't Mean A Thing

The Mumtaz Chaudhran interview had to be kept off the record from Fayazi Ma. Shuhaba didn't bring it up either when she dropped by during an unannounced visit. She would wait till Rehaan returned from office. Fayazi was restless. Shuhaba wouldn't tell her the reason for the visit, except for stuttering, "I was in the area. Just thought I would drop by. It's been a long time…and also consult Rehaan about something important."

"Hasn't he done enough? Your sons are in a sanatorium, aren't they? Where else could they be? What more do you expect of Rehaan?"

"Nothing, nothing at all," Shuhabha said apologetically. "Just wanted to thank Rehaan."

"You could have conveyed your great big thanks over the phone. Don't fool me. No one comes to us without without demanding a favour. Tell me, has Mumtaz Aapa ever asked about me? Whether I'm living or dead?"

As Rehaan entered the room, Fayazi Ma persisted with her recriminations, as if he was invisible. Shuhaba kept a straight face, ending with, "You're right, Maasi. I cannot understand my mother. I don't know which clay she's made of. That's why I need to talk to Rehaan."

Rehaan dared to interrupt, "Ma, do permit me to speak to Shuhaba Baaji. Her sons are in bad shape. You cannot be so heartless."

Stung as she always would be by the mildest criticism, Fayazi Ma moaned, "I can't hear much anyway. My ears are becoming thicker than a wall by the day. That's why that Chaudhran mother of yours calls me 'saali behri', deaf, doesn't she?"

This just wasn't working. Shuhaba wouldn't be able to talk in the presence of Fayazi Ma. It was Rehaan's turn to lie, "I just remembered I have some writing to complete within an hour. Shuhaba Baaji, can we talk some other time?"

Fayazi Ma gloated, "See, he never does what I don't want him to. Drop her till the taxi-stand and return immediately. You have your writing to do. Work is worship."

Given a five-minute deadline, Rehaan sought to escort Shuhaba to the taxi-stand just around the corner. She said she would take a bus instead. He couldn't wait with her at the stop; the Fayazi firman could not be disregarded. He solicited a conversation with Shuhaba mid-town next Sunday. The traffic wouldn't be a bother. Perhaps they could lunch at the Delhi Durbar on Grant Road.

"As long as your ma doesn't mind."

"I won't tell her about it," Rehaan said, surprised at himself. He was Fayazi's grandson. No story could gain precedence over her demands, one of them being, "Don't you ever have anything to do with my sisters and their children."

Ineluctably, such moments made him ponder: Why didn't he have a will of his own, a mind of his own, a life of his own? Grow up, dimwit. The disturbing visual of a ghostly head on the album jacket of Emerson Lake and Palmer's *Brain Salad Surgery* would waft by. A campus favourite by the rock band went, "Do you wanna be the player? Do you wanna be the string? Let me tell you something...It just don't mean a thing." Not that those lyrics were relevant. Yet the 'just don't mean a thing' refrain would resonate from nowhere at the oddest of time and places – as right now at his desk, with him pretending he had something urgent to write. He didn't.

A slice of solid teakwood with three drawers frequently difficult to open during the monsoon season's abrasive moisture, had been dispensed with. The replacement, a certified antique from an American expatriate's garage sale was sturdier, the drawers unchangeably stubborn. They would have to pried open. The papers from the top drawer spilled over the ones below. Rehaan, like his ma, was a neatnik, but had delayed discarding years-old electricity and phone bills. What if he had to furnish them as proof of payments done some day? Power supply and phone connections are known to be cut off arbitrarily. Excuse: a bygone bill unpaid. A new table-lamp he had acquired, was retro-ugly, a moon cut out of sticky papyrus imprinted with a transparent dragon, made in China and bought from Chor

Bazaar, where there was no distinguishing mark between the priceless and the worthless. The bulb behind the moon shed a mottled light. So what? He would junk it only if the paper went up in flames. Such promises, vows made to himself – not to others – couldn't be broken.

Checking out the condition of Sameer and Saagar at Happy Home, the Lonavla rehabiltation centre, was one such promise. The early morning ride to the hilltown closest to the city would be calming he hoped. It was. The Deccan Queen, introduced in 1930, has assumed a legendary reputation, but it wasn't A-grade any longer, particularly the breakfast service and the manic jostling to clamber aboard the train. Still, it was deathly punctual. At a brisk walk of half-an-hour from the station, the sanatorium was stark and as dilapidated as a storybook haunted house. No greenery, no redeeming flashes of flower beds, no serenity.

Brothers Sameer and Saagar were rushing closer to hell. Their room was windowless, the ceiling marked by deepening cracks, the beds were bug-infested mattresses, the single pillows sweat-stained. They could have been in a forgotten jail. No supervisors, no warden. The centre was founded on donations from philanthropists, most of them dead or dying like the centre itself. If the brothers, size-zero and lantern-jawed, recognised him, they didn't show it. Sameer cracked his knuckles, breaking the silence. Saagar laughed, a weak cackle. Both looked away at the walls as if reading a secret text there. How and when they were initiated into drug abuse didn't matter. They were now in their 30s, addled beyond cure.

Rehaan headed to the Centre's office which was, wonder of wonders, manned at noon by a true-to-prototype portly matron. "No one here. All staff in kitchen getting lunch ready," she said, pushing forward a fat ledger. "You can write your complaint there. We will see what we can do."

"No complaints," said Rehaan. He walked aimlessly for an hour around the hilltown which was flocked with tourists from adjoining towns. Close to the peanut chikki and chocolate fudge shops, a share-a-taxi awaited the fourth passenger. The other three comprised a family of parents and their knee-high son, who were all morose, as if dealing with a tragedy of their own. They ignored Rehaan the way the brothers had at Happy Home. Dropped off in Bombay's mid-town, Dadar, Rehaan jumped into another taxi, solo, and returned home. The first thought, a cruel one, suffused him, "What a waste of time. I shouldn't have gone. Those guys have some complex about me. Their problem, not mine."

He had tried. Not enough. Selfishly, he was hungry about the story. The brothers were hungry for death. Shuhaba had wanted them to be like Rehaan - schooled, colleged, employed, successful. Her sons had been expelled from school; they had been caught with brown sugar. Scenting the unsubtle Brut on Rehaan, their mother had bought them the cologne. Neither of the boys had worn it, bartering Brut off for a heroin fix. "It's your fault," Shuhaba had wept. "They can't be you. I want them to be you. They wouldn't have become druggies if not for you. Whenever your grandmother showed off your school report card with high grades, they felt inferior. Allah knows there must have been evils inside them."

Yet those remonstrations didn't infect Rehaan with guilt. Rather, he felt superior and chortled within himself, "I'm good; those stupid cousins are pathetic." Belatedly, the feeling of being insensitive was seeping in. If he was ever offered a drag at a marijuana joint, after college hours on the campus, he would be disdainful. "No, thank you." Unknowingly, the brothers had made him clean-cut, virtuous, a can-do-no-wrong paragon – a prick.

Being judgmental came naturally. Redeemingly, Rehaan judged himself too, more severely than he did others. A childhood without a father and mother, with a grandmother Fayazi Ma who slipped into the surrogate roles of both – there was something unnatural about that. He could have grown up, warped, disturbed, if he hadn't used the liferaft of self-pity. Boy, accept the tragedies, the deaths, or else you can't live normally, or demand normalcy from others. Compared to him, Shuhaba was tragic, her mouth downcurved like a theatre mask.

12

Over the Parcelled Lunch

At the Delhi Durbar lunch, Rehaan was aware Shuhaba would not be normal. She would be melodramatic, distort reality, feeding him either generalisations or canards. Still, the lunch had to be done. At a veneer-laminated table pocked with gravy stains and water rings, he waited. She would be late, but she would be there. At other tables, Muslim families, taxi drivers and college students, were into the specialties of the house: tandoori chicken, naans, dabba ghosht, daal fry and phirni served in copper katoris. The restaurant, patronised by a regular clientele, was blusterous, facing the main traffic-strangled artery of that Playhouse, or Peela House. Such a quirky misnomer. Peela, yellow, an unintended camouflage for the red-light district Playhouse, a near-clone to Delhi's G.B. Road.

Shuhaba showed up an hour late. He had already downed two–three cups of tea, overburnt and extra-sweet. The fumes from the tandoor in the durbar's grotty kitchen were near toxic, but no one seemed to care, least of all

Rehaan. In a burqa, her face outlined by the black polyester fabric, Shuhaba didn't want to be noticed there. She looked around for familiar faces. Didn't see any but spoke as if she was being hunted by a posse of cops or gangsters. "Salaam alaikum, Rehaan. I am not comfortable here," she said nervously. "Can we go to the AC section?"

"Walaikum salaam," Rehaan leapt up. "Sorry, I didn't notice the air-conditioned section. Yes, of course."

"It costs a little more. Don't worry about it. I will pay the bill."

"You will not," he followed her into a dimly lit cavernous hall with foamed seats and cleaner tables.

A waiter ambushed them right away; the lunch traffic was about to thicken. "What'll you have?" he demanded instantly.

Shuhaba had planned the meal, "Parcel me a tandoori chicken, full plate, four wheat rotis, and a plate of shammi kababs. How many kababs in a plate?"

"Two in half-plate, four in full," glowered the waiter, snow-haired and bearded, wearing a long loose black shirt over a pair of blue striped pyjamas.

"Full," Shuhaba looked away from him. "Please parcel. Don't forget the onions and the lime."

Rehaan couldn't possibly eat while she talked. He asked the waiter for another cup of tea and like her, for tandoori chicken packed. Full.

After looking at Rehaan and Shuhaba as if they were thick in the head, the waiter left with the cryptic line, "As you wish."

Shuhaba leaned forward, her voice barely audible above the clatter of plates which were being thumped on the adjoining empty tables. Rehaan asked her, "Could you please talk a bit more loudly? Can't hear."

"I don't want to speak much, Rehaan. The food here doesn't suit me. It'll be a treat for the Chaudhran. She doesn't like whatever I cook at home. She eats, she says, only to stay alive."

"I'm sure she's only joking. A mother can be rough. She doesn't mean a word of what she says."

"But why?" she hit back. "Look at your mother, your grandmother. She would give her life up for you and you know that."

"Yes, I agree."

Shuhaba had calculated what she wanted to say, and that was to say nothing. Instead, she fished out a cassette from her fawn raw silk clutch embedded with artificial pearls – an heirloom probably. She mumbled. "It took me himmat… courage to record this cassette. Everything you want to know, should be there. Hear it when you get home. And if you can, please never ask me for another word after this. This is to be our last meeting. I have had enough."

The snowy waiter returned, "Will you have tap or mineralwala water?"

"Tapwala, will do," she said. "Get the order fast and bring the bill as soon as you can."

"Can't we talk? I won't ask you questions."

"All the questions you could possibly ask, and I could answer are there on the tape."

She began reciting the kalima silently to herself. She couldn't be interrupted.

She insisted on paying the bill for the packed lunch, resumed chanting the silent prayer, blew her breath onto her fingers and said she needed to catch a taxi and get home within the hour.

"Has anything happened? Why are you in such a tearing hurry? I will drop you to Grant Road station. A train will be faster."

Hurrying into a cab before closing the door, she said, "Forgive me for behaving like this. Sameer and Saagar passed away two days ago, within hours of one another. They were cremated by the Happy Home people. I did not call anyone there. Why trouble anyone?"

She announced the news as a death notice would, banged the taxi door shut. Before words of condolence could be offered, she said, "Allah haafiz," covered her face with a veil. She had lost her sons, but she wanted to 'treat' their grandmother Chaudhran to a meal – tandoori. The Chaudhran had to be kept happy by her daughter who had lost the capacity to grieve.

It wasn't possible to listen to the tape at home. Fayazi Ma would surely catch some snatches even with her walled ears. She could hear clearly when she wished to. The tape would have to be transcribed in the relative quiet of the office after the night shift. The paper had been put to bed at 1.30 a.m. A peon and another reporter who stayed in the far-flung suburbs spread themselves atop the buffet-large tables, using a stack of yesterday's newspapers as pillows. The last train home had already left. The next would only be at 5 a.m. or thereabouts. Rehaan would be left undisturbed in his cabin, a mid-sized room fronted by a sound-proof glass door.

He switched on the 60-minute tape on the now unfashionabale radio-cum-tape-recorder. Shuhaba had recorded her statement on one-side of the tape – 20 minutes. The rest was blank. The transcript:

Rehaan, my ammi – Mumtazbai, Chaudhran - you may call her what you will. I have noticed you fumbling whenever you want to address her. I am also intelligent enough, though it may not seem so to most, to know the answer you have been in search of. The answer would have been best left untold, but I have always looked upon you as a child, a spoilt child who must have his way.

The answer is yes, Ammi had to do what any woman would have had to under the circumstances. She has told this to you, making herself a victim. Let's grant her that. There was no exit for her. She sold her body, she took on lovers, she had to live. Neelambhai's trade was at an ebb at G.B. Road. Bombay promised more clients, more prosperity. Money was being being minted in the country's business hub; it was dwindling at the national capital.

At Neelambai's kotha at Kennedy Bridge, pakeezahs – pure virgins, what a farce – have no place. Pakeezahs don't just sing and dance… Ammi never ever danced... All that stuff about learning Kathak is drivel. Kothewallis don't await a knight in shining armour to take them away in marriage. They don't go through the luxury of a nikaah. They are high-priced prostitutes and let's accept that. A kotha is not a marriage bureau. Wahan dhandha hota hai, women are traded like cattle. Women there sleep during the day alone; they sleep with their seths at night. Ammi's Abdul Ghani Seth kept her for five years at Kennedy Bridge. At times, I've heard, it was for longer. It doesn't matter. The fact is that Abdul Ghani Sethji paid for her nath, her virginity – 10,000 rupees. The usual rate then was 5,000 rupees. Either Neelambai drove a hard bargain, or the sethji was so enamoured of Ammi that money didn't matter.

Why did my mother have to sell her body? I don't see any shame in that. She had to because she was alone. Her sisters were no longer with her. She was fighting for herself. She was paying the price of leaving home, of leaving her parents who saw their daughters as burdens. It's not like today when girl children have found acceptance. Or have they? Once, at a hospital where I was admitted for a minor surgery, a nurse told me that she has monitored the faces of the parents and the so-called respectable families of the new-borns. When a girl is born, the faces fall with disappointment. Then there are put-on smiles and consoling words like 'A girl is an avatar of Lakshmi, the Goddess of Wealth. We are very fortunate.' That's the way it has been. Disappointment masked with smiles.

At the kothas, a girl child is welcomed; she won't be another mouth to feed. She is like a fixed deposit in a bank account.

Ammi was Neelambai's fixed deposit, to encash as soon as she had her first period. She had begun menstruating already but lied that she hadn't. The bai was no fool. She humoured Ammi for five, maybe six months, before auctioning her virginity in the mandi.

Ammi didn't put up a fight. She was curious about love... sex. I suppose Ghani Sethji was an experienced and artful lover. He would arrive at the kotha over the weekends, return home under the light of dawn, dropped and picked up by his chauffeur whose salary and tips were commensurate with his discretion. Ammi had more lovers, men she took a fancy to. There was Latif Chacha, also old and wizened, whom she had sex with on the quiet, a British constable, sailors spending some days in Bombay, munshis...clerks, even Neelambai's brother... Many, many men, what can I say? She made love to them all. I don't know who fathered me. Does it matter? When Ghani Sethji learnt of her promiscuity, he was furious. He felt cheated; Ammi wasn't exclusive to him. All this he learnt through his chauffeur. After all, there were no secrets at the kotha. He didn't return, ending the weekend sex. That talk about living with Ghani Sethji in a separate aparment, that drive to Panchgani, the gold bangles are blatant lies. He moved on to another woman in a kotha in another mohalla. I can't say this for sure, but Neelambai would crow that men who left her dehleez either ended up bankrupt or succumbed to venereal disease. Ghani Sethji's condition belonged to the disease category...and then a stroke. He was paralysed. The Chaudhran was right about that.

Ammi, as she did say, found comfort in the arms of the kotha's servant Sadiq despite his love for a hijra. It could have been love. She was crazy about Sadiq. That he wouldn't give up on Heera, made him more exciting...who knows? Mysterious are the ways of the heart, they say. To that, I'd add the laws of sexual attraction are more mysterious. I am saying too much; I shouldn't be. If you do write our story, please do take care not to portray Ammi as a slut, a fallen woman. She wasn't. My brothers, Abu Bakr and Abu Fazl, were Ghani Sethji's sons. That much I know. Ammi wouldn't breast-feed them; the task was assigned to a professional woman, someone who fed her own child and my brothers, turn by turn, as if they were on dole.

I said I don't know who fathered me. My guess is I'm Latif Chacha's daughter. I have seen a photograph of his. I have his height and complexion. I've never cared to trace him. Where is he? Does he even know of my existence? Believe it or not, Ammi breast-fed me. She doted on me, and would sing lullabies to me about the moon, the stars and all things wonderful.

My brothers were brought up in the kotha…useless, oversexed, drunk till Ammi couldn't tolerate their presence. She encouraged them to move to Delhi, the city where she was brought up, without being sold, in the adas of the kotha at G.B Road. She sent them to her past, away from her present at Kennedy Bridge. Ammi could be cruel and she could be caring...always moody. She would send money for them. That's it. They grew up warped, good-for-nothings. Abu Bakr can read and write; that's not sufficient. His writings I have been told are against the government, always. As if he can run the government himself.

As adults, Abu Fazl and Abu Bakr Bhais joined in partnership to start a small restaurant at Ajmeri Gate, selling khamiri rotis, daal and lamb curry at throwaway rates to the labour class. I would meet them on and off down the years. Their restaurant was revolting. They weren't always in their senses, neither were they forgiving. They hate Ammi. Their wives and children have little knowledge about us, which is just as well. They only have mean words for Ammi, for me, for the Aladia tabbar.

Neelambai passed away howling and screaming; she suffered from so many ailments affecting every part of her body. She wouldn't agree to be admitted to a hospital. She wished to die in the Kennedy Bridge kotha; she would get a honourable send-off from there at least. All the kothewallis were there when she breathed her last. I felt a sense of relief. She had become so infirm, cranky.

Ammi pretended to mourn, howled like a banshee as she always does – a great performance for a woman who was straining at the leash to become the next Chaudhran of Kennedy Bridge, the official leader of the Dancing Girls' Association of Kennedy Bridge. You can double-check this. The association is a registered body with the trade unions of the city. It was formed following the freedom of India from the Raj. The association's signboard is still there at the entrance of the compound. No one can claim ownership right to the kothas there. The mafia has taken over…don't ask me which mafia. I don't want to get into trouble.

These are no kothas anymore, no dancing girls or mujras anymore. Beer bars were a rage and then closed down by official orders. The lovely kothas…really there was a charm about them…have given way to brothels, some licensed, some not. After 10 p.m., the area stinks of quick sex, costing anything from 1,000 rupees to 25,000 rupees, and more for 'extras'.

Rehaan, your Baaji is embarrassed...and tired. I cannot lie blatantly, which is my saving grace. Whenever I have had to lie, I have kept silent as if someone had cut off my tongue. I have not spoken to anyone till now, and I hope I never have to. Don't ask me more. About my own role in this story...if it's worth hearing out, it's just this. I went through the drill which Ammi had. In her case, Neelambai was the leader. In my case, it was my own mother. My nath was sold to a Hindu man, Bhalla Saab. His family, as you might know, had a chain of auto spare parts shops. Ammi would not dream of nurturing a Hindu man's offspring. She would make me go through abortions. I begged her not to; I would go to the police if I had to. Sameer and Saagar were spared. Bhalla Saab moved on, as all men do.

Then what? Another seth was arranged for me – Shakur Rawji, who manufactured firecrackers, of all things. During Diwali, when the sales of his firecrackers would soar, he would be generous with the excess cash in his wallet. He would buy gold jewellery for me, identical to the ones he bought for his wife. Men lose interest in their wives after a couple of years; their interest in 'kept' women also decreases with time.

Rehaan, you are an intelligent person. I don't have to tell you the demand for untried positions, anal sex and threesomes becomes natural. Shakur Saab was bisexual. One night he brought a boy, who seemed to know the tricks of the trade. The boy was manly, hairy. He had been picked up from the streets. Shakur Saab took off the boy's clothes, then his own, and took some pleasure in making me watch while they kissed and played with each other's bodies. I was expected to join them. He wanted to enter me; the boy would enter him...I don't want to say more. May God forgive me.

I felt cheap. I had to tell Ammi this. She was furious. Shakur Saab was banned from the kotha. Just as well,

I wouldn't have to hide the fact that I was a mother of two from that...that...pervert.

Now that Sameer and Saagar are gone, I have no idea how Ammi feels about the loss. Like my brothers, my sons grew up within the kotha, aware that their mother, I, sold her body night after night. They became dependent on country liquor, marijuana, brown sugar, cocaine, heroin. I can't help feeling that both had a death wish. What else could they wish for? A normal life within abnormal surroundings?

I should be weeping. Ammi shed some of her artificial tears for my sons; tears mean nothing to her. Just a way of telling herself that she is still human, capable of shedding tears, like hot water from a geyser.

Ammi is old. Officially, she is still the Chaudhran of the Kennedy Bridge compound. Maybe they just didn't feel the need of a Chaudhran there anymore; they make their own rules for the dhanda. We sold our rooms there and moved to the suburbs where no one recognises us. Like Neelambai, Ammi is in her 80s now and infirm. She sickens me with her abuses. She doesn't approve of anything I do for her. She calls the doctors 'greedy cocksuckers' when I somehow manage to pay them their house visit fees.

I am beyond caring now. For good or bad, Ammi is the only one I have, someone whom I can call my own.

Cannot say more, Rehaan. Nothing more that makes any difference to my story, the Chaudhran's story. I beg you to keep this tape to yourself. Use it for your book only if you have to, with some amount of dignity and respect for our khandaan. Could you wait till our story won't hurt anyone? Can you change the names of the real-life people involved? Is that possible? Above all, don't say anything about this tape to your Fayazi Ma. That would not be fair to Ammi.

Mumtaz Chaudhran, my sons and I were born cursed. Ammi's life would have been so different, so chaste, if she had not escaped with her sisters from Qalayat. Before I end, I do want to express one more wish to you.

Let the Chaudhran be. She believes she did right by everyone. Let her live with that conviction for the rest of her days. Don't visit us again.

Allah haafiz.

Shuhaba had shut the door on him. She had spoken with pauses but there were no stretches of silence which would have indicated that she has spoken unrehearsed.

The tape was a confirmation of what Rehaan had suspected all these years. Mumtaz Chaudhran was feared, but not respected by her sisters. If they hadn't cut off ties with her irrevocably, it's because she would have become spiteful.

For the world at large, she was the Chaudhran, the gutsy leader of an association. Fayazi Ma would retort sharply whenever asked about her eldest Aapa, "Let her live in her world" or "Stay far away from her. If she needs anything, I will look after that, not you," exacerbating her grandson's curiosity to know more about the leader who was now an outcaste.

Fayazi Ma would claim that all the sisters had conducted themselves respectfully but for the Chaudhran.

And she knew which bullet to fire at Rehaan. It was always, "I have done so much to bring you up, you parentless boy. Be grateful. If it weren't for me, you would have been dead, homeless or wasting away in a kotha," topping that with, "Am I not your mother?"

"Yes Ma, you are." His search for the Aladia story was an act of ingratitude, bordering on the mutinous, but without the story, in his eyes, there could be no redemption for the six sisters.

Shuhaba's tape was reassuring. He was getting to the core of the story. Jameela Begum of Chandni Chowk would have to be the next stop, the next chapter.

The Shuhaba tape he kept in the office desk, locked. On returning home, Fayazi Ma launched into her practised inquisition.

"Why so late? Have you eaten? Is that whisky on your breath? Have you started drinking behind my back? You do smoke, don't you? You wouldn't dare to smoke in front of me, would you? I suppose you're grown up...are you?"

She wouldn't wait for the grandson's answers, carrying on regardless, "Don't expect me to believe that you're a saint. Have you 'kept' a woman?"

And then her last salvo, "Tell me, are you a laundebaaz, you know...have sex with boys?"

"No, Ma, I'm your son. Would I ever dare to 'keep' a woman or a boy?"

"Who knows?" she'd badger him as always. "Have some fruit from the fridge, go to sleep. What are you waiting for? You want to tell me something?"

"Nothing, only next week I have to go for office work to Delhi?"

"Again? Go, if you have to. But remember, I'll be alone here. Phone me every day even if I can't hear you properly."

"Of course, Ma. You don't have to tell me."

"For how many days will you be away?"

"A couple of days at most."

"For me every day will be eternity. It's late now, go eat, sleep."

13

Songs of Love and Longing

In the December of Delhi, Jameela Begum would sun herself, a long-limbed, stick doll of a woman with conspicuous breasts, a pocket transistor snuggled in her cleavage, heaving up and down with her breath. Addicted to the broadcasts of vintage songs by Noor Jehan, Mallika Pukhraj and Farida Khannum on Pakistan radio, she would declaim, "This Mallika…my voice, my ghazals were as mellifluous as hers."

The reception was bleary, the transistor wasn't equipped with the crystal clarity of F.M. The songs were about unrequited love, endless nights spent in longing. Emblems of flowers, the moon, the stars, eyes and tears were used for imagery. Take the traditional "Ishq ek raat si hai jiski saher hote hi phool khilte hain, chand ki badmast nigaahon se, phir bhi aankhon mein shikayat kyun hai": a sonnet about flowers blooming at dawn, the moon casting a lecherous eye, and the eyes a-complaining.

Jameela Begum was a spent force, now combating her anonymity. She had retreated into a shell; she would listen, rarely talk. Begum connoted a woman of high rank. Added on indiscrimininately, once suffixed to a name the honorific wouldn't brook argument. Most women, once married, would wear it as an ornament. Those who hadn't yet gone through a nikaah, used it to sound superior, lady-like. Once she had cut her first record, Begum was attached to Jameela. The variables Jaan and Bai were rejected.

This Pakistani Radiowalli (neighbours had given her that sobriquet), at her peak of form, had been idolised by many, deceived it seems by the recording company's bossman who had drafted a contract, rescinding her share of royalties in the 78 rpm record sales. She had signed on three or four sheets of thick rubber-stamped paper, elated by the very prospect of a shot at fame. Not that she could imprint a signature; a thumb impression was enough.

The story of the chanteuse was linear enough. Adopted by a couple, the Qureshis, who lived in Kucha Lattu Shah, a Chandni Chowk backlane, named after a saint who was fond of spinning tops, she was ushered into a modest one-storey structure. Grandiloquently it could be called a mansion, a haveli. Jameela was to perform the role of a multi-purpose daughter. She was to help her foster mother, Zainab, in the household. She would be a maid-cum-daughter who wouldn't talk back, play truant or demand a hike in her needs and wants.

The Qureshis had seen scores of servant girls come and go. It made more sense to bring home a child whom they owned. Not that they were cruel slave-drivers; the Qureshis thrived on common sense. This was it. With a calf-like newcomer in the haveli, Nizam-ul-haque Qureshi, a jeweller by profession, would quit bothering Zainab. He would not have an excuse to humiliate his wife, "Go back to where you came from…that rat hole in a glorified jhuggi at Ajmeri Gate." He wouldn't threaten a nikaah with another woman who could procreate. "No shortage of girls in Chandni Chowk, you know," he'd rile her frequently.

"Marry that orphan, then," Zainab had retorted. "Wait till she menstruates and do your worst. I will not call that yateemkhana girl my daughter. Understand?"

Joining his middle and index finger, Qureshi said, "Remember the words of the Prophet," Qureshi said. "The one who takes care of an orphan, is with me in Paradise like this," pressing two fingers tightly, to illustrate his point. "The mohalla will no longer point fingers at you. They may not accept the girl as one of us, but time is a healer. They will get used to her."

"First of all, who knows if she is an orphan or not. We cannot accept whatever we're told as the written truth." Zainab had ended. "Second, I don't like the way she looks at me. The brazen chit of a girl."

Although Zainab Qureshi spewed anger, she was secretly delighted. She could play a mother, shower affection if not love on a child. Also, she saw in Jameela another Zainab, possessed of talent, which could be tapped, nurtured and encashed.

Born to a family of gawaiyas, Nizam-ul-haque's Zainab had repressed her aspirations to become a songstress, a thumri artiste. Thumri is associated with intricate illustrative dance movements bordering on eroticism. The form is an exaltation of romantic verses blended with folk songs of the state of Uttar Pradesh in the Awadhi and Brij Bhasha dialects, revolving around a girl's love for Lord Krishna. The intrusion of Hinduism in a Muslim household? Unthinkable, Zainab had to stop dreaming.

Ghazals revolved around loneliness, on love's labour lost, leaned towards romantic themes, verses composed in the same metre. Ghazals were flexible enough to apply to all faiths. At the Ajmeri Gate home, Zainab had furtively studied the form at the neighbourhood's tabla maestro. Her voice could scale heights, her mentor a singer with a high alto voice, had predicted a tremendous future for Zainab, which was never to be.

Perhaps Zainab would be able to transfer that future to Jameela, if the girl permitted herself to be moulded whenever Nizam-ul-haque was away. He would leave for Heera Mandi soon after breakfast and returned, way after sunset, often with the overpowering stink of hooch on his breath. "What kind of Muslim are you?" the ever-offended wife would trill. "You keep quoting the Quran. Let me remind you that it is clearly decreed that drinking is a sin."

Zainab, like most Muslim women, had struck a compromise, "As long as you don't drink in the house, I won't create a ruckus." If he was guilty of the sin of adultery, Zainab didn't want to know about his affairs. She wasn't cut out to be confrontational. Best to be in denial or else she would be isolated. Talaaqs initiated by men were common. Men, the beasts, always had the upper hand.

Zainab would have to make Jameela a pawn if she were to attain a semblance of authority in the Kucha Lattoo Shah haveli. It had to be her home for life; nowhere else to go. Her parents wouldn't have exactly welcomed her back. She had made attempts to leave only to be told by her mother, "Accept him as he is with his faults, like I did your father. At least you have a roof over your head. A haveli no less, and a man to call your own."

Vicariously, the mother had probed, "Does he perform his duties as a husband should?"

"No, Ammi," Zainab had clucked. "We have tried so hard to have a child that those duties have become a punishment for us. For months, must be a year now, he has not touched me. Tell me, is it always a woman's fault that she cannot bear a child? I should not be saying this, but I feel he is incapable."

"Are you saying he's not a man?" the mother asked, not quite sure whether that mattered.

"Nine times out of ten, he has...he has taken me from the back."

"That's normal," the mother said. "All men do that, for extra pleasure."

"I can't help feeling that he prefers...men...boys."

"Stop! You cannot jump to such depraved conclusions. Do you have any proof of that? Don't let your suspicions ruin you. You are about to adopt a child...you will be performing a good deed... you will earn sawaab. Don't lose heart, you could still be a mother some day. Now, will you wear your burqa right away and take a rickshaw home?"

The mother was always right. The adopted Jameela would have to be handled with tact. Whenever Nizam-ul-haque Qureshi was at home, the child was assigned menial chores and then taught cooking, which she was a natural at. Praise be, the child could deal with singing lessons, too – in light ghazals, not thumris.

The child would plead, "I will do every little thing you want. Ammi, can't you bring my sister, Fayazi, here? I can't live without her."

Zainab's clockwork reply would be, "Maybe some day, not now. We don't have the resources to feed another mouth."

"Can't she at least visit?"

The foster mother would fold her in her arms, "Aren't you happy with us?"

"I want to be with Fejji."

Under the cover of night, Jameela had sought to return to the yateemkhana. She had bolted out of the haveli, only to be caught by the mohalla guards who knocked the pavements with rattan wood sticks past midnight, shouting at the top of their voices, "Jaagte raho." The "Stay Alert" cry was redundant. The mohalla was as used to it as swatting the swarm of mosquitoes which stung only at night.

By the time, Jameela had reached the mouth of the lane leading to Kucha Lattu Shah, she was caught by the nape of her neck by the human alert alarm. Neither Nizam-ul-haque nor Zainab Qureshi were taken aback by her bid to escape. Without ado, Jameela was returned to her charpoy, a patchwork quilt was pulled over her, Nizam-ul-haque patted her cheeks, and promised, "I will find out whatever

I can about Fayazi tomorrow. By now she must have found a home."

The dargah's mullahs weren't forthcoming with details, but for the scant information that Fayazi had been adopted by a prosperous Muslim family in Bombay. Nizam-ul-haque hoped they were Sunnis. "They are Memon Sunnis," he was assured. After Prophet Muhammad's death, there was a fall-out over the choice of the successor. Sunnis and Shias follow different prophets and have never quite reconciled to the schism.

For years there was no news about Fayazi being transported by train to Bombay, rated as it is to this day – a promised land bustling with the mega- rich, compassless wayfarers and the damned. Fayazi would fit in, Jameela thought; her sister had to. Nizam-ul-haque would concoct updates, "All your sisters have found a good place. Don't worry about them. Worry about yourself, Munni."

That term of endearment, Munni, wasn't apt for Jameela at all. Munni suggested a petite girl of playful disposition. Jameela was lanky and sullen. Nizam-u-haque was not good with names. Zainab would argue, "Just call her Jameela. It makes her sound beautiful."

"Is she a beauty? Not that it matters. The Quran associates the name Jameela with someone of graceful manners."

"Manners indeed! It was your decision to adopt. Manners will have to be taught. I will call her Jameela. You can call her what you want. It will make no difference. It's only muddling up her already muddled head…"

"I can see what you're doing with her head, mohatarma."

"Save the mohatarma nonsense for other women. I don't need any honorifics. I am content with the way I am and always will be...at your beck and call."

"I know what you've been up to. Every child in the mohalla does. Instead of sending her to madrassa after she's finished cooking for the day," Nizamul-haque interjected. "I am informed you are taking her to Ajmeri Gate."

"Yes, so?"

"You want her to become a singer. Bring shame upon our family?"

"Two doesn't make a family. Besides, there's no shame in singing ghazals and geets, but what would you know?"

"Our daughter will not sing; it's a stricture in our sharia. Music is for heathens."

Their arguments would be inconclusive. To the new entrant in the skeletal haveli, they were no different from Iddanbi and Saundha Bhai in Qalayat.

Mumtaz had transferred the sisters to another land of want, of obeisance. Or had she? Jameela liked to cook and sing, in that order, and she did. At her new home, she could eat regularly, and possessed a corner of her very own, shared with a clay doll she had rescued from a garbage heap outside the khameeri roti tandoor down the lane. She had named the doll Fejji.

14

Still Voices, Distant Lives

All aspects considered, Jameela wouldn't have recoiled at the mention of Fayazi's transfer to a Bombay orphanage, funded by the philantrophist Sir Osman Baksh Mitha, who owned vast tracts of land and salt pans on the periphery of the city. His father had made a fortune in the salt trade and had adopted the surname of Mitha, which meant salt for some, sweet for others.

A trader in fabrics, too, Sir Osman was the man-to-go-to. Wives of the British officers would invite him for high-tea soirées, which he would attend to boost his high-society equity. He couldn't pronounce a word of English, but his feral eyes, crowned by caterpillar eyebrows, communicated with the lords and their significant others. The ladies swooned over the fabrics – the silks from China perfect for ball-gowns and the mulmul from Dhaka so cool for garden parties in the torrid summers.

A multi-tasker, he dabbled in other businesses, sanitaryware, upholstery, and had set up a workshop in the orphanage with a set of handpicked seamstresses who worked day and night shifts to dress up the alabaster-skinned ladies. Sir Osman's establishment was constantly on the lookout for interns. Fayazi learnt the skills of a seamstress, along with pre-pubescent girls housed in a dormitory, under the bridge leading to the Grant Road railway station, named after Sir Robert Grant, the mid-19th century Governor of Bombay.

Retail textile marts, tea stalls, theatres, cinemas and inchoately, that partly licensed red-light district Playhouse / Peela House, surrounded the orphanage, its looming windowless stone walls, guarded by a posse of strapping Pathan guards. The orphanage girls weren't permitted outside the gates; the dank hall of hand-cranked sewing machines, were Dickensian. Sir Osman wasn't primeval enough to deny the orphanage denizens three square meals and clothing. Fayazi never had to ask, "Please sir, may I have some more gruel?"

Back at Lattu Shah Kucha, Nizam-ul-haque had instructed Zainab, "Let her be happy with the doll and those wicked singing lessons." Jameela was progressing excellently. Her voice had a certain husky edge, a maturity, which wasn't in sync with her frail physique. The ghazal coach, Ustad Shaandar Khan, had advised her foster mother to feed her well so she could gain weight which would enrich her voice. She could barely touch the high octaves. With more riyaaz, she would get there. A daily, uninterrupted diet of dry fruit, apples, chicken and milk were the bare essentials – beyond budget, but the calf had to be fattened. Still, Jameela wouldn't gain weight.

As much as her talent for singing, Jameela was a natural-born chef, rustling up lamb shorbas, raisin-flecked pillaufs and pistachio kheer. Nizam-ul-haque, wiping his ceramic platter clean, would end a meal with a volley of burps, to express approval. Zainab and he were putting on more fat than their glorified house-help. As she grew, the least striking of the Aladia sisters in Qalayat, Jameela came to be identified as Chandni Chowk's reed-slim, curvaceous star of the gullies and kuchas.

The hours of practice at gawaiya Ustad Shaandar Khan's chamber at Ajmeri Gate extended from an hour to three hours every alternate day of the week. Jameela's voice at riyaaz ricocheted through the gullies. Connoisseurs were called in to check if she was ready to perform, but not at mehfils – Nizam-ul-haque had shot down all such proposals. No, he wouln't let her sing in public.

Zainab had to concur. A public display of talent would be akin to prostituting a child in a bazaar. Although it was not yet permissible for a girl from a respectable family to record a song at a studio, a settlement could be reached if her voice somehow caught the fancy of the decision-maker at Columbia Records, Rana Nihal Singh – a Rajput of royal descent – who operated out of an office-cum-recording-studio in Connaught Place.

Accompanied by Nizam-ul-haque, Jameela by then in her mid-teens, sashayed confidently into the compact, unfussy studio. Dressed to the hilt, in a coordinated leaf-green salwar kameez, white dupatta, and Zainab's heirloom emerald earrings, she had to catch the Rana's ears. She was crestfallen on being turned away. The music lord wasn't available for anyone who dropped by at the office randomly. Yet, as they descended the stairs, she said casually, "Abba, we will come again and again to this place if we have to. Yes?"

The rejection was a sign, Nizam-ul-haque concluded. Girls from a chaste Sayyed family would not and should not become singers. They didn't return to Connaught Place for months, till Ustad Shaandar Khan announced brightly, "I have personally spoken to Rana Nihal Singh. Be prepared to meet him on Monday afternoon, soon after lunch. Jameela don't eat anything in the morning. Just have sips of hot lime water...your voice will be clearer."

From the vignettes Rehaan could gather that Jameela was an instant hit at the afternoon session. Forget catching Rana Nihal Singh's ears, his eyes shed copious tears during her rendition of a ghazal by the 17th-century classicist Wali Mohammed Wali: "Kiya mujhse ishq ne zaalim kaun aab ahista ahista? Le aatish gul ko karti hai gulab ahista ahista" (My love has melted that despot, bit by bit /As fire distills the essence of rose, bit by bit). A contract was clinched. Its terms were Greek and Latin to Nizam-ul-haque who signed the batch of papers in fractured Urdu impatiently on receiving a hefty advance sum, half of which had to be paid as nazrana, a token of gratitude to the Ustad.

None of her record pressings is accessible, but the ageing Jameela Begum would brag that there were scores of them; they had brought her overnight stardom. Her fans – qadardaans, she called them – would wait outside the Lattu Shah Kucha haveli to catch a glimpse of her, which would be denied. Singers of stature had to retain a certain mystique. Moreover, Nihal Singh wasn't the classic benefactor. The contract was unsparingly draconian. Nizam-ul-haque received piffling amounts after the advance. They had been conned. The music baron was a cheat, claiming that her records weren't bestsellers. Within a span of 18 months, Jameela Begum's stardom dangled in the balance.

Nizam-ul-haque, without any evidence, contended that Nihal Singh Saab was hinting at a liaison with Jameela. She had conducted herself coquettishly and sung like a wanton woman. "You shameless girl, it's all because of your indecent behaviour! Instead of appreciation, I can see lust in that man's eyes. I'm putting an end to this claptrap."

It was assumed that Jameela was aware of the male libido. She was. The mohalla's girls would chatter on about their repressed sexuality, waiting to be awakened strictly after their nikaah to a man of their parents' choice.

"Abba, the Rana is older than you," Jameela fluttered with counterfeit innocence. "He cannot have bad intentions."

She liked to be lusted after. She liked Rana Nihal Singh, a broad-chested, silver-haired man of unlined neck, broad shoulders, sword-sharp moustached, laser eyes, immaculately dressed in tweed smoking jackets or blazers, his pierced ears sported diamond studs. He would place his heavy hand over her shoulder during late-night recordings, while waiting for the musicians to turn up. Nizam-ul-haque was not with her that night. Watchdog Zainab Ammi was, but had dozed off in the stuffy waiting room.

"We're alone," Rana Nihal Singh had said.

"I know," Jameela had whispered and come closer to him. She wanted to embrace him but moved away. If she surrendered easily, the Rana would have her eating out of hands.

"Ranaji, this is not right," she had said coyly, and pre-empted his retort, "There are so many Jameelas in the bazaar. Don't think you are the only one."

"I am not a child, I know that. Tear up that contract and I am yours."

Her career was at a do-or-perish stage. Nizam-ul-haque was summoned to the office, alone. The contract would be redrafted, the royalties and advances would be doubled. Doubled was not enough. A wildly improbable figure was quoted. Rana Nihal Singh laughed fiendishly. Jameela Begum had gained popularity, her records sold. Yes, but so what? His was a monopolistic music recording business, and he said, "With that amount of money, I can create ten Jameela Begums…and let me tell you, she would kiss my feet, if need be."

A Sardari Khatoon, also of Chandni Chowk, was being talked of as an incipient threat. She belonged to the mohalla of Farash Khana and was believed to be equally adept at ghazals and thumris. With the dissolution of the silent era of cinema, film music composers from Bombay had been asking about her. Nizam-ul-haque wouldn't pay heed to the upcoming competition.

"You want Jameela to become your mistress? You should be ashamed of yourself. I will expose you. I will let everyone know," he sneered at the music baron.

"Everyone knows. Go and expose me. That will only bring shame to your daughter, if she's is your daughter that is," the baron sniggered.

Nizam-ul-haque stormed out of the office, shamed.

Jameela Begum would have to quit singing, even to herself. She couldn't become a whore for all the money in the world. A husband would have to be found for her, a boy from a family which wouldn't take her past into account. Not likely, not in Chandni Chowk at least, where rumours would be relayed faster than morse code.

Ammi Zainab sulked. Abba Nizam-ul-haque was fretful. His jewellery business was in shambles. Consignments of fake gems from China routed through Bombay had flooded the market. He would have to switch from diamonds and pearls to costume jewellery. Adopting Jameela, in sum, had brought the Qureshis more grief than money, which was a must to maintain their lifestyle. No more dry fruit and dairy desserts.

Jameela Begum struggled with her composure. Stardom had meant wearing a burqa. She longed to run free in the gullies, walk past the dilapidated home of Mirza Ghalib in Ballimaran, comfort herself that the master poet had died unrecognised. Alcoholism, they regretted hypocritically, had devoured him. But she was still alive, wasn't she?

She had stored the letters from those who were smitten by her ghazals, of men who professed undying love for her. One of the letters, which Zainab Ammi had read out to her, was from Hamid Abdullah. In all likelihood, he was one among the many who would wait to catch sight of her. He would have to be searched out, another reason for ambling every early morning through Ballimaran, under the pretext of fetching a breakfast of nihari, slow-cooked lamb and marrow, from a vendor. The moment she saw Hamid, she would recognise him through the gauze of her burqa.

She couldn't. Ballimaran swarmed with sculpted young men, raw peach complexioned, blue morning shadows on their cheeks, which they would shave clean presumably only if they had to. One of them seemed to be always shaven, even perfumed, and seemed as if he was waiting for a vision of divine beauty to materialise. Poof, out of thin air! Perhaps he was an aspiring poet. No, no, admirers of poetry don't shave and perfume, unless they were emperors or princes. This specimen couldn't be her Hamid Abdullah. He couldn't be traced.

The walks down Ballimaran were wasteful till the year was about to wind up. On the anvil of winter, a hunched rug seller paid his customary annual visit, accompanied by his son, who had barely sprouted whiskers. Zainab pleaded off, "Mustafa Chacha, no new rugs this year. The ones you sold to me are still in shape." The old man nodded, but still rolled out a Kashmiri rug, "This I will give you for nothing. Just pay me whatever you can." The boy looked on stone faced.

"Is that your son?" Zainab Ammi's curiosity was piqued. "He resembles you. You must have looked like him in your better days...khubsurat hai mashallah...may the Lord protect him, what a looker he is."

"Khubsurati doesn't fill our stomachs," Mustafa Chacha shook his head penitently. "He's a good for nothing. Can you imagine, he has drowned himself in music? It would be better if he drowned himself in the Yamuna River."

Jameela Begum joined them, pretending to be interested in the rugs. So as not to sound too forward, she asked, "Chacha, what is your son's name?"

Startled by her cheek – girls would never display themselves before strangers – her ammi said, "Go inside. What will you do with his name? Make halwa puri with it?"

"I am Hamid Abdullah," the boy blurted out boldly.

Jameela Begum and Zainab Ammi recognised him as the letter writer. Ammi was prodded to buy a rug, "You do have some savings from my earnings, don't you?"

A plan was on the boil. Jameela could be given away in a nikaah to the boy. The foster mother hoped the chacha would ask neither for a dowry nor about her short-lived fame. Fame tantamounted to vulgarity.

Hamid was smiling beatifically at Jameela, who was wracked by mixed feelings. The boy wasn't the man of her dreams. She had longed for a man way older who would be protective about her as much as she was about her doll Fejji. "Come on, Jameela, forget about this Kashmiri boy. I would rather run away to the end of earth with that swine Nihal Singh," she told herself.

Too late. The ghazal artiste had outlived her purpose in Lattu Shah Kucha. The Qureshis were mildly fond of her, but still saw her as an 'outsider'. A girl couldn't remain a spinster. The sooner the nikaah was performed, the more expedient. Mustafa Chacha sensed the urgency. The smooth bargainer didn't ask for a dowry and circumvented any demand for a meher, the lump sum to be paid to the bride if the marriage collapsed.

Instead, the rug-seller hawked logic. Hamid Abdullah would find gainful employment soon enough. The vital clause in the nikaah hinged on the fact that the boy didn't have a home to call his own. "You are great people," Mustafa Chacha began. "We are your humble servants. Whatever you say, we will obey. I must return to Srinagar to be with my wife. She's getting on in years. Our daughter is married to a rug weaver there. They get by. How do you expect me to leave Hamid alone in Delhi? He's an innocent boy. Would you consider giving him and his bride the lower floor of your haveli. It is unoccupied anyway."

"No," Zainab Ammi exclaimed. "As soon as we have done our duty by Jameela, we are giving the lower floor on rent. Times are bad."

"When have they ever been good for anyone, Zainab Sahiba? Think about it. Your precious daughter will be with you, and also her groom. Two are better than one. Moreover, we are accepting Jameela without any questions. We haven't paid heed to the rumours. She's seen the world, she is a singer, and you know what that means. She is impure. May Allah forgive her for her sins..."

"Leave my house right now, you old fool," Zainab Ammi raged.

"Your wish is my command...sar aankhon par," Chacha had rolled the dice.

The nikaah was performed by a kaazi of the neighbourhood. No one was invited. Hamid Abdullah and

Jameela Begum, both in their mid-teens, were man and wife. The bride, decked up in a layered silk sari and gold-thread embroidered stole, didn't resist the marriage. The night before, she had wept to her doll, "Fejji, I wish you were here. We could have run away somewhere. Hamid is an idiot. I don't like him. He doesn't say a word, as if he's in awe of me. That could be a boon. Maybe I can use that, I'll make him my slave. For the first time in my life, I won't be at anyone's mercy. Hamid will be the woman; I'll be the man. Just you watch."

As if in a trance, Jameela Begum discarded the doll into the stove fire, watched Fejji burn, and cried to herself, "My sister, I pray for you every day. I will pray for the real you from now on. The doll's dead. For me you've just been reborn. Where are you Fayazi? Where are you?"

Fayazi was at a sewing machine, fixing the hem of a lilac velvet gown to be worn by Lady Hardinge to a summer ball. She had no time or leisure to remember any of her sisters. They should have kept in touch, through letters, a post-card. They hadn't. For Fayazi, it was each to her own. She'd show Mumtaz that she would be the winner in their undeclared contest, not for survival, but for an independent life of her own. Some day, she would wear a gown too, of lilac velvet.

The passage of Jameela Begum from ephemeral fame to ordinariness was devoid of shocks and surprises, according to the stories told to Rehaan by Fayazi Ma. Hamid was content to be a fanboy to the songstress he had adored. He took over the duties of the kitchen, and hawked Kashmiri rugs and carpets brought over by his father during the Srinagar winters.

In addition, Nizam-ul-haque employed him as a part-time courier for the fake gems ordered by the rising business class of Delhi. Zainab's knees had given way, and she was confined to bed. Jameela would administer her round of medicines, apply almond oil to Ammi's arthritic knees and listen to her remonstrations without hearing them. "It was all going so well...and then?" Ammi would moan. "Jameela beti, you should have given in to the demands of Rana Nihal Singh. We could have moved out of Kucha Lattu Shah, somewhere quiet, a small kothi with a garden. I wouldn't have had to see your shauhar Hamid behaves like a namby-pamby...joroo ka ghulam."

Zainab Ammi repeated the curiosity of her mother, "Tell me, does he fulfill his duties as your husband? Why haven't you given birth to a child yet. I would like to be a grandmother before I am carried to my grave."

"Ammi, I am carrying," Jameela Begum announced blandly. "I am three months pregnant."

"What? I must have been blind not to see that. May all go right with the birth of my first grandson...sum-e-aamin."

"It could be your first granddaughter, Ammi."

"Don't say that. You have a black tongue."

"I pray it's a daughter," Jameela said. Zainab rolled over to the other side of the bed and moaned. "There's a devil inside you. Which woman would pray for a daughter? You tire me."

"Ammi, rest."

End of another afternoon, with little to look forward to after sunset.

The girl child of Jameela Begum and Hamid Abdullah was named Noor by Nizam-ul-haque. Delivered at a clinic by a doctor who also part-timed as a dentist, the child couldn't have been God's own light. For the grandparents, she was a liability, another dark cloud like the ghazal songstress had become in the household.

The child gurgled at her grandfather. He couldn't be indifferent for long. Zainab Ammi ignored the child, but by then, she was as chronically unhappy as the piercing pain in her knees. "We were to misery born," she'd whimper.

Were they? Far from it, Kucha Lattu Shah was still one of the more prosperous addresses in the chowk. Their meals were cooked at home, the rotis ordered from the tandoor. They dressed neatly. Noor was a happy child, never shouting the roof down for her daily feeds.

"This girl is so much like my brother Murad. He was such a doll. Maybe we shouldn't have been so tough on him," Jameela Begum would muse, and return to Radio Pakistan.

15

The Weight of Postcards

Jameela Begum was glowing. She had received a postcard from Bombay. Fayazi would be visiting them next winter. The card said nothing more, nothing less. Days were counted for the dry season to abate. Fejji would arrive in December, if not in January.

Either way, Fejji was alive and had apparently done well for herself. She was married to Sir Osman, his third wife. The first one had died, the second was consumptive, Fayazi would probably be the last in the row. Osman Baksh Mitha, knighted by the British empire, was in his mid-60s and ready to croak, inshallah. Whether Fayazi had raced ahead of the other sisters, only the winter would tell. No news from Mumtaz and the other sisters, Allah preserve them. If He hadn't, too bad. Jameela Begum persuaded herself that she wasn't to blame.

Two winters elapsed, the next was one about to surrender to the lacerating summer. Fejji didn't show up. Again she had to be discarded like the doll, forgotten. The postcard – without a return address – was the only sign that the sister still cared. Jameela could have travelled to Bombay, Fayazi could have requested her to. But wait, perhaps Sir Osman could have stopped her, given her an ultimatum - it's either him or her sisters. Likely, very likely, Jameela Begum consoled herself. Adapting to the extended Memon family could have taken a toll on dear Fejji, and who knows how his family had treated her. Yet, nothing could end the jabs in Jameela's heart: how could Fejji announce her arrival, and not turn up for years? Where had she found the Kucha Lattu Shah address? The influential Sir Osman must have obtained it for her.

Rehaan could guess the reason for Fayazi Ma's delay. Sir Osman was insanely possessive of his wife. He worried about his advancing age. A stroke had paralysed the right half of his body. He was confined to a wheelchair, he was paranoid. If she left him, it would be forever.

Jameela Begum's daughter, Noor, was four by now. She had been enrolled in the Muslim charity school in Ballimaran. She would be educated in Urdu like all Muslims girls of the time. The retired songstress had felt it would have been more in order to send her to an English-medium school, a proposition rejected by Abba Nizam-ul-haque, "Who will pay the fees? That leech Hamid who isn't even ashamed of being a freeloader?"

"You have been unfair to him, Abba. Hamid respects me and he loves our daughter. That's more than all the blessings in the world. He has been contributing whatever he earns, which is more than you do nowadays," Jameela Begum countered. She had never used the word 'love' before. What did it mean anyway? Stolen embraces, stolen moments of happiness. More importantly, Hamid was a model father, rocking Noor in his arms, singing stanzas from Jameela's recorded ghazals to her, off-key.

Fayazi did arrive in winter, years after the post-card, in a horse-drawn rickshaw which had to halt outside the unnegotiable Kucha Lattu Shah gully. Laden with gifts – gold anklets, a pendant and earrings for Jameela, objets d'art and a Persian carpet, which she hoped they would use in the house right away. "It's precious," Fayazi announced grandly. "If you ever sell it, I will get to hear of it."

Jameela Begum pooh-poohed the gifts, "Fejji your presence means all the riches of the world." They wept in synchronised harmony. When they stopped, tea, kachoris and kalaakand were served. They sat on a bed together, and talked their hearts out.

"Where are the others?" wondered Fayazi. "Ask me if I care. They haven't bothered to find out what happened to us. Why should we?"

"They are our sisters, Fejji."

"That they are. But we aren't the police to launch a search for them. We have found each other. Isn't that enough?

"Your rich old man must have ferreted my address."

"Naturally, Sir Osman can do anything."

Fayazi's winter breaks in Delhi became an annual feature. Sir Osman would thaw and agree for Jameela Begum and Noor to return the visits, as long as they didn't stay for long in Bombay. They had to be endured, not endorsed.

Fayazi corresponded with Jameela though post-cards ghost-written by lettered munshis. The two sisters were unbreakably tethered, simply because they weren't beholden in any way to their party leader, Mumtaz. They wouldn't bring her up in conversation when Jameela Begum's family was around.

Without informing Rehaan, left to the care of the household helps, Fayazi Ma rushed to Delhi when Zainab, first, and then Nizam-ul-haque passed away – death by natural causes. The boy was told that his ma had gone on a pilgrimage, without specifying the location.

The Kucha Lattu Shah haveli was now Jameela Begum's, no questions asked. She continued to rent out the ground floor to Kashmiri families, replacing them every winter, so none of them could claim rights for permanent tenancy.

Noor was transferred from the municipal school to an English medium high school at an hour's distance. Its headmistress was a British woman, no less. Fayazi gifted the milady a zari stole with bell-shaped tassles; it would keep the headmistress warm and empathetic towards Noor, whose studying skills were thankfully, above average.

It seemed a perfect world – the alliance between Jameela and Fayazi. Meanwhile, the other four sisters must have flourished in their different homes, owners of different destinies.

Destinies – a gratuitous word in a journalist's dictionary. By the time Rehaan had begun scavenging the Humshira story, there were far too many simplistic suppositions and conclusions. They were all alive perhaps, fielding fluctuating health, but they were there, weren't they? Some of his Christmas school breaks had been spent in Kucha Lattu Shah. He knew Chandni Chowk, the Moonlight Square with its stenches and aromas.

For decades Jameela Begum's haveli had been denied sanitation facilities. Rehaan couldn't abide by the toilet which had no flush. A sweeper would clean the muck once every morning and evening. The place stank. The turmeric factory nearby stank. The nullahs were clogged. Yet there was something about the house with an atrium, surrounded on four sides by compact rooms of chalky white walls and a courtyard around the exterior. At the kuchas, specific professions proliferated, as in Maliwara, the gardeners' neighbourhood. The katras were home to artisans specialising in calligraphy and copies of Mughal miniature paintings.

Rehaan had learnt that a decade before he was born, amidst the pell-mell shops and the old-worldly havelis, the co-existence between the Muslim and Marwari communities had turned turtle, violent during the partition of the sub-continent in 1947. There were riots, face-offs, bloodshed. Jameela Begum's haveli was not part of the target area, quirkily because of her respected status as a ghazal singer. To some, she was an artiste who had brought the mohalla a modicum of dignity. Attitudes toward a woman who had stepped out of the house, were altering inchoately.

Chandni Chowk piquantly enough was designed by a woman - the Mughal Emperor's daughter, Jahanara Begum. The bazaar was once invested with elegance by a pool right in the centre of the main square, which shimmered on full-moon nights. Thousands of shops, originally built in a half-moon shaped pattern, were now grossly disfigured.

The communal unrest had stabilised. Over time, as Fayazi Ma and Jameela Begum continued to meet in Delhi winter, Rehaan hung out at the Paranthewalli Gali, at the Art Deco Moti cinema, travelled by the eight-seater scooters starting at the dry pool called Phunwara, a fountain with no flora. He had bought kilos of those jawbreaking sohan halwa and the hafshi halwa (racist that, the goo was black and some wise guy had named it 'Negro') to carry back to Mumbai. Sanitation had been fitted into the havelis, but Kucha Lattu Shah was no longer comfortable for the Mumbaikar journalist. On assignments or on holidays, he preferred to stay with his schoolfriend, Deepak Gupta and his family in a red-brick designer bungalow in South Delhi's Gulmohar Park.

"You've become too big for us," Jameela Begum's daughter Noor would huff. Older than Rehaan by 10 years and some, she doted on her grand cousin. Without any notice, Noor had eloped with Mannu Sharma, who studied at the same institute, the Delhi College, shocking all. Noor was excessively moralistic, would scoff about affairs and sex, was a devout Muslim, and then she had upped and married Mannu, the son of a Grade II government clerical officer. The civil marriage was annulled. Jameela Begum had seen to that, with the unspoken approval of Hamid. His silence meant consent.

Mannu Sharma had sworn that he would convert to Islam, would move in with his bride even if that meant evicting the haveli's seasonal Kashmiri tenants. He backed out without apology. The child Noor was carrying was aborted. To her credit, Noor did complete her post-graduation in English Literature from Delhi University. She wasn't the extroverted, chatty sort anymore. She would talk to herself, shoo off scorpions infiltrating her mind, hastening Rehaan's alienation from the haveli he once believed was his second home.

He would return for quick visits, carrying gifts – no longer expensive, but reasonably priced dupattas, shawls and trinkets – from Fayazi which Jameela Begum would accept nonchalantly. "Keep them on any shelf you can find, and give our shukriyas to Fejji," the Begum would purse her lips, switching back to that transistor radio propped between her cleavage. Noor would walk to the tandoor, return with naans to be served with the lamb shorba cooked on logfire. Its recipe would not be revealed. "You have to cook with love in your hands; the ingredients don't matter," was Jameela Begum's alibi, while she heaved herself up from her charpoy to add the coup de grâce, the tadka of burnt onions and a pinch of saffron.

Hamid Abba had become more withdrawn that before, roasting and then lighting up beedis on a hot coal. Rehaan couldn't extract any story for him. He didn't want to encroach upon the man's silent zone. In a way, he was once again up against recalcitrant sources, as he had been with Mumtaz and her daughter Shuhaba. Their stories were painfully similar.

Noor would have to be prodded whenever she was collected and calm. Whenever those scorpions within her were resting, she would have to be asked, "Could I speak to your ammi, about my mother...grandmother Fayazi Ma and about their sisters, about Qalayat?"

When he did ask, he could hazard Noor's response, "Ammi doesn't talk as you know. Why rake up old wounds, anyway?"

"Precisely. I'd like to know if those wounds have healed."

"Have you spoken to your grandmother...sorry I mean your mother?"

"Not yet. I've spoken to Mumtaz Chaudhran, her sons and daughter. I intend to meet up with Allarakhi Nani next...find her..."

"She could be in Pakistan. You know it's not easy to get a visa."

"Nothing is impossible Noor Baaji. But may I speak with your mother?"

"Let her be, Rehaan. She is not well. If you must, you can speak to me." Here was another Shuhaba Baaji.

"When?"

"Tomorrow if you like, but on one condition...you stay with us this time. I've always felt humiliated that you should stay with friends...with parayas...outsiders, when you have your family...connections...here. You used to love being with us. You used to love our walks to the municipal garden. You cut your right thumb on a kite string, remember? I rushed you to the hakim so the thumb would stop bleeding. I'm sorry to say, but you have been ungrateful."

"I'm sorry too, Baaji."

"What time will you come with your bag and baggage then, tomorrow?" she asked pointedly, then said quixotically. "Forget the condition. You are used to luxury, no need to come here... May I ask for something else instead?"

She looked away, circled around the verandah, babbling, and then returned, "Can you get Mannu Sharma to meet me...without letting anyone know?"

"I could try. Do you have his phone number, address?"

"Last I know he had shifted to Dehra Dun. He's married, two children. Happy family, I suppose. That's all I know."

"That won't be possible. I have just two more days in Delhi, I've to report back to office... Noor, I promise I'll track him down. Just give me some time. Meanwhile may I speak to you tomorrow?"

Rehaan attempted another ruse, "We could go for a walk in the municipal garden."

Noor didn't answer. She encircled the verandah again. Rehaan bid his salaams to Jameela Begum and the immoveable Hamid Saab, and went over to Noor, "I will wait at the Town Hall park around lunchtime...one-ish? Close to where you get the hand-made ice-cream."

"You no longer get ice-cream there, Rehaan. Even the benches aren't of the same colour."

This wasn't getting anywhere. Rehaan said, "I'm sure the playswing, the slide must be there. I'll be waiting."

Noor was there before he was. In a burqa, she was feeding pigeons. They walked over to the surviving Ved Prakash Lemonwale shop serving the spicy banta soda. Noor smiled, "You're still a kid." Then they jostled through the early afternoon crowd towards the Red Fort, thronged with policemen on duty to prevent any untoward incident. On a stone parapet of the fort, their backs turned towards the chowk, Noor tilted her neck towards the charitable hospital for wounded birds. "Some things never change," she smiled. "I would like to think you haven't – still so inquisitive, wanting to know more than you should."

"You're right. My profession has only increased my curiosity."

"Newspapers seldom write the truth. Do you?"

"I try to. Since politics isn't my beat, it's not difficult. I write on cinema, the arts…and occasionally human-interest stories."

"Human interest? So my ammi's story falls in that category?"

In more than an hour spent on the parapet, Noor at most corroborated what he knew, except for her take on the sisters' battle with Murad for the rights of the Qalayat property.

According to Noor, Murad had served his parents well. He had cared for Iddanbi and Saundha Bhai during their recurring illnesses, and their last years. A failed wrestler, his wife however had brought sufficient money in the form of dowry, to see them, their son Nauman Ali, and his parents Iddanbi and Saudha Bhai, through hard times. The Qalayat hovel-turned-lucrative-property by every moral stricture belonged to him. The sisters could have been more benevolent. Jameela Begum and Fayazi Ma had formed one phalanx, and Mumtaz Chaudhran, the other. It had to be assumed, the rest of the sisters had played along, always the marionettes.

Murad and his wife Waheedan had accepted one-eighth of the share, which amounted to precious little. Their son Nauman Ali had migrated to Dubai to work initially on the labour force of a power plant under construction, and then as a manager of a supermarket. Nauman Ali and family had prospered – he drove a car (a second-hand Benz), their sons were being schooled. One of them had revealed a talent for sculpting, a talent which his mother encouraged. Nauman Ali had kept in touch with Noor, never forgetting to mail her cards on Ramazan and Bakr Eid. The wishes were for Noor and for her father Hamid exclusively. Jameela Begum was never mentioned.

"I was so fond of Murad Mama," Noor said. "He would tell me I should find a man and get remarried – as if men are sold in supermarkets! You know about Mannu, I have never forgotten him. They say I'm mad. They've forced me to meet analysts and quacks. I was taken to an exorcism centre in Hyderabad. Frankly, that has only made me worse. I cannot forget Mannu. I cannot get our unborn child out of my system."

She took Rehaan's hands forcefully, as if she was about to handcuff him, "Tell me, you will find Mannu. I need to meet him once. That's all I want. Swear on me that you will do this much for your Noor Baaji...for the love I gave you when you were a child."

There were scores of Mannu Sharmas on Facebook and Twitter, but none with a double 'n' and none who fit the description of Noor's Mannu. Rehaan cancelled his flight back to Mumbai, reached Dehra Dun by the early morning train. The plan was to put the police through a wringer about a Mannu Sharma there. Or ask around with the locals. He drew a blank. He hurried back to Delhi to make it for the red-eye to Mumbai. The office needed him, he felt with misplaced pride, erasing the crushing reminder from the management honchos that a newspaper worked on the singular corporate principle – no one's indispensable.

Dehra Dun had left him disoriented, what with its rash of shops and pharmacy stores at the Paltan Bazaar. The mountain range which ringed the town stood there magisterially, but then every mountain range has that effect. If there was tranquility, it was to be found at the hillside cottage of a syndicated columnist, an astrologer. The clouds would enter his living room, hazing the face of the astrologer who wore make-up to camouflage his age.

The astrologer had heard Rehaan out, declared regretfully he knew of no Mannu Sharma, wondered if he could do a weekly column for a monthly stipend at *The Daily Chronicle*. "Doubtful," Rehaan had said truthfully, and right away gave up the idea of the astrologer consulting Vedic charts to search out the possible address of Mannu Sharma.

On his return, the beat at the newspaper office was cripplingly slow. The advertising revenue was falling, the pages had been decreased from 32 to 28, the entertainment section was reduced to four pages from eight. At home, Fayazi Ma wanted to know what Jameela Begum, Noor and her Hamid Abba had said. Had they asked after her? Did they want her to visit? Did they want to come over to Bombay for a few days? If not Jameela Begum, at least Noor could visit for a while and give her company. Rehaan said he would ask her to visit but wasn't sure if she could. "Why? Has she gone completely mad?" Fayazi Ma said cruelly, hoping for an affirmation.

"She's fine. I'll phone to tell her you were remembering her. She'll be pleased."

"Why is she behaving like a maharani? She probably thinks she'll be doing us a favour by coming here, Rehaan. Let her be. And listen, distribute the sohan halwa among the neighbours. It'll rot in the fridge."

With most of her teeth gone, Fayazi Ma couldn't taste the Chandni Chowk confection any more. Neither could Rehaan aggravate his cavities. The neigbours – the Kapoors and the Aghas – accepted the sohan halwa, since they had to. Perhaps they would distribute it to others. Dental hygiene was a priority.

Rehaan did at long last trace a couple of tracks of Jameela Begum in the archives of the National Centre of the Performing Arts. Listening to them over headphones was trying. The scratchy mono recordings had decimated their value. All he could figure out was, there was an anguish in her then young, modulated voice, but it was barely comparable to the renditions by the Pakistani divas she would hear on the transistor nestling in her cleavage.

Jameela Begum's story had reached a dead-end. Rehaan had to put it in the freezer, like he would have to keep Noor's solicited favour on hold. There were other immediate tasks: move from the newspaper to one of the fast-burgeoning websites? Impossible, he was a print man, the ink on a newspaper every morning had to kick-start his day. Print journalism was his calling. Banish the thought of a change, Rehaan would stick to the newspaper. At least there were no signs that the management wanted to sack him. He could detect that the divide-and-rule policy had intensified. He edited the entertainment section of the paper; a junior reporter was promoted to edit its website. The smarmy reporter would drop by in his cabin to chat, and repeat, "I'm a huge fan of yours, sir. I could never step in your shoes." Some nerve.

Rehaan would look at his perforated leather shoes. He'd have to buy a new pair soon, fast.

Back home, Rehaan thumbed through Doris Lessing's *The Golden Notebook,* which he would turn to whenever he was low, wallowing that he was alone. Lessing told him, "Because I was permanently confused, dissatisfied, unhappy, tormented by inadequacy, driven by wanting towards every kind of impossible future, the attitude of mind described by 'tolerantly amused eyes' was years away from me. I don't think I really saw people then, except as appendages to my needs. It's only now, looking back, that I understood, but at the time I lived in a brilliantly lit haze, shifting and flickering according to my changing desires. Of course, that is only a description of being young."

Lessing was his security blanket; he was no longer young. He was getting on at a workplace he could neither forsake nor escape from. He would follow, if he could, the Lessing route, "Whatever you're meant to do, do it now. The conditions are always impossible."

Impossible, impossible. But don't *let it be*; play Lennon-McCartney on the turntable of your mind. Rehaan played the vinyl L.P.:

"And when the night is cloudy,
There is still a light that shines on me,
Shine until tomorrow,
Let it be..."

No point, Lessing or Lennon-McCartney, no placebos. Get a life. Apply malice, if need be, which surfaced naturally on a Sunday afternoon when Fayazi Ma was dozing off to the television news. He shook her frame roughly. Not quite registering his anger, she dripped saracasm, "Do you want to kill me? Be my guest."

16

The Blue Cat, The Laughing Buddha

"Ma, I want that porcelain blue cat back, the one with the eyes tightly closed. Why did you ever give it to that Jameela of yours?"

"Don't you dare call her Jameela. Speak with respect. She is your grand-aunt. Call her Nani, and if you can't do that, Jameela Begum. Have you lost your manners? And no, you can't have it back. It was your grandfather's. If he was okay about gifting the cat to my sister, who are you?"

"It's a priceless piece, an antique. I saw it at the Kucha Lattu Shah haveli, gathering dust in a corner."

"You want to sell it?

"No, I'd like it back... It's ours, my grandfather's. It was not for you to gift it to anyone without my permission."

"Nonsense," she ended the exchange. Retreating to her room, she shut the door hard, switched on the fan, and foetused up for a nap. She wouldn't entertain confrontations with her grandson. She would not be questioned.

Rehaan entered the room. Changing his tone, he sat down at the edge of the bed and pressed her feet – an everyday duty.

"Ma, as always, you win."

"That I do," she gloated, her half-shut eyes signalling to her toes. "Massage them. You're a good boy, you love your Ma."

"Sometimes, I'm not sure that you love me, Ma."

What she didn't wish to hear, she ignored.

"Ma, it's just the cat I want, not the diamond pendant you gave Jameela Nani. Why did you ever give her a diamond? We could have used it. Our rooms need air conditioners."

"You know very well the diamond was gifted for Noor. Would you have wanted me to go empty-handed to her house? Whatever else I have, is yours. And I will not let you buy air conditioners. They are harmful for my bones."

"Point noted, Ma," Rehaan nodded. "Can I get one for my room?"

"Your salary won't be enough the pay the electricity bill," she said groggily. "As long as I'm alive, I will not permit living beyond our means. What's with you today?"

"I'm fed up Ma, tired of living with half-truths. You keep secrets from me. Why are you partial to Jameela Nani? You care a damn about your other sisters."

"The others are witches. Stay away from them. They're all jealous of me. Jameela isn't, never was. Do you understand?"

"I don't."

"Let what you call secrets remain secrets. Now, leave me alone. Switch off the television in the hall. It's such a criminal waste of electricity."

From the top of the TV set, a porcelain Laughing Buddha grinned back at him. Who knows, Fayazi Ma would have also given it away to Jameela Begum or Noor. When it came to them, Nani suffered from fits of generosity. When the Buddha was under imminent danger of being gifted, like the cat and the diamond pendant, Rehaan, all of five or six then, had cried, "Ma, neither Nana nor you ever laugh in the house. The Buddha's my friend, he's the only one who laughs here..." Fayazi Ma's heart had melted. She had hugged him and apologised, "Your Buddha will always be with you."

Rehaan adored the Buddha. He was mortified that he could fall from his perch from the TV set some day. The Buddha had survived. If he was shifted to another perch besides the one chosen by Fayazi Ma, the laughing one would crash to pieces.

A year whizzed by, maybe a bit more. Jameela Begum's health was on the skids. The doctors had given up hope. She had a brain tumour. Hamid Saab was befuddled. Rehaan would phone Noor on the landline. She wouldn't ever pick up her cell phone. Her phone manners wouldn't permit her to say anything besides, "All's the same. What do you care?"

The phone calls to Noor were made with an ulterior motive. Fayazi Ma craved her company. She would not go in for a cataract surgery without her. Rehaan, with more demands at the desk for exclusive stories, needed Noor to be by Fayazi Ma's side or else she could become blind as a bat. She continued to watch TV news unfocused.

He was alone, Noor wasn't. Hamid Abba, staunchly faithful, never left Jameela Begum's side. In addition, the

Chandni Chowk neighbours were willing to spend their vacant time with an ailing old woman. At the end of the day, Hamid Abba would repay their kindness with tea, fruit biscuits and home-cooked shammi kababs.

In a Bombay housing complex, the neighbours would drop by for rationed minutes to check on Fayazi's impending eye surgeries. No more, no less. If the cataracts had to be removed, it couldn't be done without Noor by Fayazi Ma's bedside. Without a pay-off for Noor, forget it. The search for Mannu Sharma would have to be resumed.

Although it was years since he had been on the crime beat, he had maintained a few contacts at the Press Room at the Police Commissioner's headquarters bang opposite Crawford Market. Perhaps there could be a lead. The Public Relations officer, appointed to spoon-feed journalists with news about cases solved (the unsolved ones were never mentioned) had retained his thankless job, post-retirement. Mr Congeniality himself, Jal Taraporevala, with a (retd) on his business card, was more than likely to remember Rehaan from his days as a rookie reporter. Taraporevala didn't.

A grizzled crime reporter, Anand Desai, did. He freelanced for a Gujarati language newspaper published from Mumbai and Ahmedabad. Desai was an evening fixture at the Press Club, known to be the cheapest bar in town; the alcohol came at subsidised rates. Resembling a glass-windowed ship at dock, the club faces the triangular-shaped Azad Maidan, often the site of hunger strikes, protests and police lathi-charges. A TV set blared on day and night. Computers in the club's anteroom would be used when reporters had to file stories. Sections of the club were sponsored by industrial groups. Vintage film posters carried the logo of a video company.

Desai, in his 60s now, recognised Rehaan right off, booming in a cocktail of English, Hindi and Gujarati, "Rehaan, you've become rarer than the Eid moon! Any problem-shroblem, dear? Saala, you've put on kilos, such a toothpick you were. What's the matter, yaar? What's bugging you? Main hoon na. Will sort it out. Medicine for every illness." On hearing Rehaan out, Desai beamed, "Your problem? My shroblem. Tomorrow Sunday chhe. I'll take you to the cyber cell on Monday fatafat, the jagah is chikkar with data. Drinks on you today, dear." Journalists, Rehaan included, had a thing about free drinks.

Anand Desai was on his nth rum and water. He was the one who had ballooned over time. Rehaan had lost weight, but why go into fitness fundas now? Rehaan, buoyed now by a certainty of sorts of tracing Mannu Sharma, ordered vodka-tonic and drank Desai under the table. He was flying. His breath was a sewer. Fayazi Ma would be waiting up for him, never mind the hour. He chewed on elaichis, soaped his mouth clean. Not enough.

As he tiptoed towards his room, Fayazi Ma raised her voice, "Don't think I can't see. I haven't gone blind. Come here, you've forgotten my foot massage... I've been waiting."

Dutifully, Rehaan sat on the edge of her narrow bed. The massage was a form of pressing the feet – mutthi; it had to be executed with a cupped palm. He held his breath to the extent he could. Ma's eyes may have dulled, but her acute sense of smell hadn't. Without shifting from her supine position, she announced, "You have been drinking yourself silly."

"No Ma, not at all."

"You're no saint," she reiterated. "I will ignore your weaknesses, but don't you ever drink at home. That's all I ask."

"Yes, how many times will you go on with that? Believe me, you've got me wrong, Ma," he lied, and was prepared for the next ritual admonishment which she would frame as a question. It was her favourite, "Have you come from a brothel? A randi? Do you expect me to believe you don't screw around?"

"I don't, Ma."

He anticipated the next pronouncement, also a question. When she didn't throw it at him, he waited. The pause was calculated to hurt him deeper. The curiosity about his sexuality was offensive.

"For the last time, I will ask you...and give me an honest answer," she restarted. "Are you a homosexual? Have you kept a boy? Or has someone kept you. Be careful...aajkal AIDS is spreading. Even I know that."

Rehaan didn't retaliate with his customary peal of laughter. He said, "You have a one-track mind. Stop."

"I will not stop. You stop the mutthi! Enough. I must have brought you up wrong...tu namard hai, incapable of being with a girl. At least I hope you have had some experience with girls."

Furious with the either-or supposition – a man who either whored around at the brothels or fucked around with men – Rehaan's eyes smarted. He was guilty – guilty?

– of short-term relationships with women. He wasn't the marrying kind. How could a grandson dedicated to his ma ever think of that? And he was guilty – guilty! – of being bi-curious. He had allowed himself to be seduced by two older men – once, during an overnight train journey and another, on a date fixed on a gay website. Neither of those encounters had given him 'pleasure' if pleasure could be derived at all from sex without anal penetration.

She can be mean. This ma of his could be hurtful, but so what? He didn't expect her to be perfect. He didn't expect her to realise that he could enjoy and needed sex. Yet, his basic instincts were secondary. He loved her to death; he had to be the perfect son as long as she lived, and still saw him as a child who could never grow up.

"May you see my dead face soon," she would curse. "Let's see how you can live without me. You'll be visiting my grave every morning to repent."

Repent for what?

Assistant Commissioner of Police, Sajid Yaar Jung, would report around noon at the cyber cell set up in one of the few surviving heritage British-era buildings at Kala Ghoda – the black horse referred to a black stone statue of King Edward VII, Prince of Wales, mounted on a horse commissioned by the Jewish philanthropist Sir Albert Abdulla David Sassoon. The Sassoon Reading Library was another contribution by the Jewish settlers to the city. The statue was removed from the precinct in 1965 and stored at the Byculla zoo. Lately, a simulacrum of the horse had returned to the area, but without the rider.

Jung was drop-dead regal. He could have been the missing rider from the horse. Rehaan shuffled from a computer-buzzing hall into the ACP's musty cabin, and couldn't resist asking, "Sir, do you belong to the Jung family of Hyderabad?"

The ACP waved him to a rickety chair, "We can talk about that later. I'm told you are looking for someone. I don't trust journalists, bloody muckrakers. Present company excluded, I should hope. I don't have to give you any information, but you seem to have top contacts."

Jung wouldn't raise his eyes from a diary. He was writing away furiously, his handwriting resembling hieroglyphics – perhaps his self-created short-hand.

"What're you looking at?" Jung frowned. "Ask me and I will tell you. I write every word which is spoken here in a diary. I finish an entire diary in a day, even two diaries when things are chaotic."

"You could record me on your cell phone, sir."

"I don't need your advice, Mr Rehman."

"Rehaan Shafaque Siddiqi."

"Rehaan, Rehaan, fine. You see I have a fading memory. I can't remember names or events easily. I'm retired, age 65. Yet the police commissioner has put me in charge here. I suppose I can handle computerised memories, but not my own."

The ACP was also stone deaf. Rehaan's voice pumped up, as if on an amplifier, when he explained the whys and whats of his hunt for Mannu Sharma. A peon was summoned by an electronic bell. Acrid coffee and biscuits were placed on the worn-out desk topped by a grimy glass sheet. Rings left by the teacup hadn't been wiped clean in days. "Drink that coffee," Jung commanded. This hospitality was the sort which marked every meeting everywhere in Mumbai. To please him, Rehaan finished the coffee. The biscuits were extra-sweet, flecked with grains of sugar.

"Eat the biscuits. Millions of people in our country go hungry. Consider yourself lucky."

This man was approaching senility. Rehaan toyed with the idea of leaving the cabin. In a twist of efficiency, the ACP buzzed the electronic bell, wrote down the name, Mannu Sharma, Delhi, on a chit, sneezed hard twice, and handed it over to the peon, saying, "Give it to the criminal records department."

"Criminal?" Rehaan was daunted. "What makes you think Mannu Sharma is a criminal?"

"My dear man, everyone commits a crime in some form or the other. Leave it to me, will you?" he continued his hieroglyphic notations in the diary, and explained. "The cell is in its infancy. We have Census records and all that. But if this Mandu has done something wrong, he'll be faster to trace."

"Mannu, not Mandu."

"Yes, yes, I have written Mannu with a double 'n'. I suggest you return in an hour, maybe two."

Rehaan exited from the stuffy cabin. The windows were tightly shuttered. Jung had a sinus problem, going by the crumpled paper tissues in a straw wastepaper basket. The hour spent at the Jehangir Art Gallery opposite the cyber cell, was oppressive. An extensive show was on, exhibiting the works of fresh graduates of the J.J. School of Art. Abstracts – layers and layers of vibrant colours on large canvases – were on display, punctuated by pictures of the city's street children, the grand CST railway station, and a fairly evocative one of commuters swarming their way out of Churchgate railway station at peak hour. If he had the money, he would have bought that painting. At 2 lakhs rupees, it didn't fall into the category of buyable art. Mannu Sharma could have been a part of the commuter crowd at a Delhi metro station. Maybe. Stop it Rehaan, this Mannu could have vanished from the face of the earth.

After a burger-and-fries lunch, two hours had ticked by at tortoise pace. On returning to the cell, he was told that ACP Saab would be back in five minutes, at the most ten. He had been called over to the police commissioner's office for an urgent meeting. Five or ten minutes in Mumbai argot can mean forever. To reach Jameela Begum's story, Rehaan had switched to another lane. Get me out of here, he wished. Dump this nonsense of a search for Mannu Sharma.

Incredibly, ten minutes it was exactly. Jung Saab returned to his desk and diary, forwarded a sheet of paper to Rehaan, and said in sotto voce, "Two Mannu Sharmas have been traced. Two ns. Both are middle-aged, 40 and 42. One is in Noida and the other in Purani Dilli. Both have committed crimes. The Noida chap has broken traffic rules, his name is registered at the toll booth there. The Purani Dilli fellow, I'm afraid, is dead. My sincere condolences. He was mixed up in the drug trade; he was let off with a warning due to lack of evidence. A year later, he was murdered in cold blood, case still unsolved. So which Mannu is your brother?"

"Sir, he's not my brother. And it's *the* Mannu I hope."

"Good luck. The names and addresses of both these Mannus are written on the paper. May the dead Mandu's soul rest in peace."

"Mannu." Rehaan thanked him and as he left, and had to ask, "You are from Hyderabad, Sir?"

"Yes, yes, my family lives in Jubilee Hills. Small row house bunglaow we have. Happy."

The non-sequiturs were getting to Rehaan. He thanked the ACP with a handshake. Jung's grip was so firm that it said, "Don't think I'm a weak old man." Next stop - Mannu Sharma of Noida. It wouldn't be feasible to airdash to Delhi, but he could dangle the carrot before Noor. She had to come to Mumbai, to take care of Fayazi Nani who had tired him with her pleas, "Call her here! I don't want to die blind while you're at that office of yours. Everyone gets a month off. You never take a day off. You don't spend time with me at all."

Noor, bless her, without any persuasion was on her way to Mumbai by Rajdhani Express, chair-car. "After all, your ma is my ma," is all she said over the phone.

"Thank you, Baaji. I will reimburse your to-and fro fare," Rehaan promised, grateful that the baby-sitter hadn't brought up the treacherous Mannu Sharma.

Till the cataract surgery, Fayazi Ma would return to watch television, in the company of Noor. Their laughter brought some relief when Rehaan crawled back home, after an average of 12–14 hours in the newsroom.

On a Saturday, he returned home early, shaving off his hours at the office. Noor seemed to be cheerful in her additional role of Fayazi Ma's nurse. She would cajole her into eating fruit, feed her small portions of hafshi halwa which needed no chewing. Najma, the household help who would be rudely rebuffed, was relieved. The cataract operation was underway. Laser surgery would cost but make the ordeal easier. The surgeon wasn't closed to the idea of performing the surgery on both the eyes simultaneously. "That's not the ideal way of going about it," he warned. "But the reports show that she isn't sufferering from blood pressure, cholestrol or diabetes. Can be done."

Noor agreed with Rehaan. Fayazi Ma would have brought the house down if she had to endure two separate sessions. Noor repeated the age-old Aladia chant, "Allah maalik hai. He will take care of her."

For a fortnight during the post-operative care, Fayazi Ma had to be kept calm and steady. Eye-drops had to be administered every two hours, Noor would sponge her with warm water, morning-evening.

Fayazi Ma's sight became sharper, but no TV allowed. Not for a month at least. The neighbours visited her regularly, morning-evening. As her condition improved, Noor became withdrawn, morose. Understandable, she had to go back to Kucha Lattu Shah to play nurse to Jameela Begum. No respite for her.

"I don't have a life of my own, never did," Noor turned to Rehaan during an after-dinner conversation. Fayazi Ma was asleep. Rehaan had waited for the apt moment to express his gratitude to Noor, with words and the fare reimbursement. He offered her the money sealed in an envelope. She wouldn't accept it, she was talking to herself now, "I have nothing to live for. I am alone."

"I am always there for you," Rehaan hugged her, a counterfeit hug. He didn't care enough to mean what he was saying. Now that Fayazi Ma was on the mend, he couldn't wait for Noor to leave. She would have to accept the envelope.

"I will not, Rehaan. I have sold the diamond pendant for Rs 10 lakhs."

Rehaan was offended, "But that was a decision for Jameela Nani...or my ma to take, not yours. You had no right to do that. You have done that without asking us..." he said insultingly, adding injury with, "You must have sold the cat also. You're a selfish woman, Noor."

"I will never sell the cat," she retaliated.

"Thank god for small mercies."

"Rehaan, you will never understand the sisters. They didn't have it easy. My ammi has suffered all through her life. I have inherited that sufferance."

The night was lengthening, but for Noor, it seemed as if a new day had begun. She would give back the diamond's worth, to the last rupee. Rehaan wanted her to talk, she would.

Her narration streamed as if on a high-speed Internet drive. To begin with, "What you might know about Jameela Begum could be false. If you have been told that her singing career was cut short by Rana Nihal Singh, a benefactor with ulterior motives, it wasn't. He made her voice heard, he groomed her, he didn't bind her to any contract. Neither did he ever lay a hand on her.

"Ammi wasn't interested in her career. She realised she was mediocre. Apart from her two renditions – ghazals by Mir Mohammed Mir – which were released on both sides of one 78 rpm record, she wasn't making much headway. If Zainab Nani hadn't been pushy, if she hadn't made her a golden goose with the complicity of Nizam-ul-haque Nana, who knows she could have scaled great heights. Talent or no talent, my mother's career was nipped in the bud. Sardari Khatoon was signed up by the record company. Her voice had a range, depth. What else could Nihal Singh do? He was so weary of the interventions, the demands for more money by the parents, foster parents as you know. And they wouldn't allow her to perform at radio shows or at mehfils hosted by the nawabi sorts for the British lords. The career had to end, as it did. Ammi's voice, for whatever it was worth, was strangled. Did she put up a fight? To an extent, she did.

"Not by tears, but by rebellion. She would disappear for days…imagine days… Hamid Abba would just sit at home. To report her disappearance at a police chowki would have brought shame to the little honour left of a disintegrating family. Ammi had fallen in love…what else could it have been? When she quit singing, the coach…that Ustad Shaandar Khan was out of work and returned to his wife and children in Meerut. No one recognised Jameela Begum there. They would meet at lodges in Meerut at times, in Delhi at times… Even those days, there were places with six to seven rooms, where lovers could meet. No questions asked.

"The lover, the ustad...was doomed to spend his life holding on to women who entered and quit his life. Once, he even had the cheek to come home and announce that they had been performing at mehfils secretly. Ammi had thrown the ace up her sleeve. Her foster parents had created a monster beyond control, they had no alternative but to turn a blind eye to her affairs. Whenever Hamid Abba attempted to bring his begum back on track, she would lash back at him, that I, Noor, wasn't his daughter. I was Ustad Shaandar Khan's daughter, conceived in a lodge. That was a horrible lie. I was born with Hamid Abba's light eyes as you might have – noticed. I'm fair-complexioned, a Kashmiri like my abba. Ustad Shaandar Khan was anything but. For me, there's no doubt that I'm my father's daughter, not of my mother's lover. Too late for a DNA test. That gawaiya, ustad...the lord alone knows what he was...must be dead and gone. Did anyone tell you this? They wouldn't dare to."

Noor was unmoved. She looked wronged, subverted at that moment. Then the streaming of her storytelling stopped. She said she was tired. Rehaan agreed that she should get some rest. He was feeling restless about Fayazi Ma being alone in her room. Would Noor go and sleep on the mattress by the bedside as she had for weeks?

"Don't worry. She doesn't get up in the middle of the night," Noor restarted. "Rehaan, like all families, we are dysfunctional, as they say. Do you think the Kapoors and Aghas living next door are happy? They may wear smiles, own cars and take off for holidays abroad, but like us, they are acting. Only we're bad actors. Ammi could have been an outstanding singer, double-tasking even as a successful actress like Noor Jehan and Suraiya did. She couldn't because she didn't have a killer instinct. Neither would she do riyaaz to improve her voice, or at least retain whatever quality it had. About the only support she ever received was from you Fayazi Ma, who would send her gifts, money-orders and once that...that diamond pendant which she handed over personally when she visited us for the first time. The pendant was our savings bank, Rehaan. I came here to look after her because I will always be under your obligation. Rightfully, the pendant should have been yours. What else can I say? What else do you wish to know?"

"Do you hate your mother?"

"Hate! Not at all. Jameela Begum made something special of her life. She could have become a star who'd be remembered to this day as an icon."

Rehaan asked with caution, "Aren't you resentful that she coerced you to annul your marriage to Mannu?"

"Who told you that? My parents were more than okay with him. It was I who saw through the bastard, excuse my language. He had promised to convert to Islam, change his name. We had even picked one, Niyamat, but he backed out. He said we could follow our different faiths. Our children would be brought up as both Hindus and Muslims."

Rehaan, a believer in his faith, but not an avowedly practising one – he didn't keep rozas or perform the namaaz – sided with Mannu at the moment, "Frankly, I see nothing wrong in that, Noor Baaji."

"You aren't a pukka Aladia. Far from it. Do you even pray, keep rozas? I certainly hope you don't eat pork."

"Never."

"Wah, how noble of you. Still, you're a Muslim by name only. Let me tell you, our ancestors were tempted by Jesuits to convert. It would be a joke to keep switching religions as if they were clothes which can be worn, discarded and worn again. No, I could never be happy with someone from another faith. You know how Muslims... and as a journalist you should know how we are treated better than I do."

Her face contorted, turned ugly, "Expecting you to be a Muslim is asking for the moon. You don't have it in you. We are blamed for riots, the madness in politics. Every other Muslim is considered a potential terrorist. If we don't defend our faith, who will? Ever thought about this? You don't have the passionate faith of a Muslim."

To that tirade, Rehaan laughed, "Your marriage to a Hindu wouldn't have changed the world."

"It wouldn't have changed *my* world, and that's what matters."

They were getting into superficial polemics. Rehaan was as disturbed by the deepening Hindu-Muslim divide as Noor was. He had majored in Political Thought. On occasion, he had written editorials on the urgency of secularism. He could whip out theories at random. It would have been pointless to tell Noor about his minute contribution to the faith. Intrigued by her civil registrar marriage to a Hindu and then its annulment, he asked, "Do you want to meet

Mannu Sharma because you want to bring that episode in your life to a closure? Feel…noble?"

"There can be no closures, Rehaan," she said. "I don't know why I want to meet him but it could help me. I'm sick of medication, tranquillisers, useless weekly meetings with a counsellor. There are days when I don't think about Mannu at all, like Jameela Begum doesn't think about her days of brief glory. And there are days when I can't get Mannu out of my system. Ammi at least has her Paksitan radio to listen to, and who knows, for that she could be called an anti-national if someone tries to rake up trouble. I have no one I can listen to or look up to. I have always been fond of you, Rehaan. But you are in your own world. I requested you to find the whereabouts about that man. Did you even try?"

"I did, Noor Baaji. I might just have a lead. I'll follow it up as soon as Ma is alright. I'll come to Delhi and do what I can."

"What is the lead?"

"There's a certain Mannu Sharma who lives in Noida."

"You know the address, phone number?"

"No," he lied.

"Very well," Noor ended. "I will now sleep by your ma's side. I have come here to nurse her. It's my duty."

She moved to Fayazi Ma's room, spread out the jaan-namaaz, performed her prayers, switched off the lights, and slept. The next morning, Rehaan would drop Noor at the airport so she could take the noon flight for Delhi. It was an online discounted ticket, costing as much as a seat on the Rajdhani Express.

A seminar on Print versus Internet Journalism was coming up in New Delhi next month. Rehaan began lobbying for an invitation – air fare and hotel expenses paid. He wasn't much of a speaker, but heck, he could read out a prepared text. Would the newspaper's managing editor put in a word? "I'll see," the editor said gruffly. A fortnight later, the invitation came through, or else he would have had to break a fixed deposit. Expenses of Fayazi Ma's medical bills were on the incline.

The hotel turned out to be a basement room at the India International Centre, the habitat of journalists, columnists, politicians and academicians. He would surely accost his Badshah, Anikendranath Sen there, who was by now editing an online portal for a media group in Nepal. The reporting and editing were done on the Internet from his home in upscale Saket. Badshah was ever gregarious, his spirits high on pre-lunch whisky sours. At his age-old corner in the bar, he raised a toast, "To you my friend. I believe you were quite a hit at the seminar. The audience was laughing at your hilarious speech."

"The hilarity, unfortunately, was unintended," Rehaan said, modestly.

"Go on, you can be very funny with your play on words."

"Badshah, I need some help."

"You're not touching me for a loan are you, old chap?"

"You're the funny one. I need to find someone in Noida."

"So what's your problem, take a good ol' taxi chum. Those Ambassador taxis are houses on wheels."

Rehaan subtracted the details, outlined the story of Noor and Mannu Sharma. He needed a friend to accompany him. Would he?

"Hey, you're not a kid. I can't hold your hand through this. Sounds like personal shit."

"Please."

"Nopes."

"Badshah, I've never asked you for a favour. When you were in Mumbai, I'd fill in for you on night shifts at the newsroom?"

"Tchah, this is sheer blackmail. Done, old chap. Let's see, maybe I'll drive you there in my chariot tomorrow. Let's start early. After 9 a.m. the traffic is a killer."

"Thank you, we can start at 7 a.m. if you can."

"Fuck, what am I getting myself into? Right, the drinks are on you tonight," Sen called out to a waiter, asked for the bill, signed it with a flourish, and grinned, "You're in my city. No need to reimburse me. I was just kidding, buddy. What's a little bill between friends?"

Noida is an acronym for the New Okhla Industrial Development Authority, as impersonal as Delhi, the National Capital Region of India, can get. Developed as an urbanisation thrust during the Emergency era of 1975-'77, it's said to have a 50 percent green cover, the highest of any city. It has emeged as a hotspot for IT service industries, banking, media groups, corporate conglomerates in proximity to the inevitable malls and mulitplexes.

Noida is also the address of mid-income housing complexes, with a bewildering array of slash-numbered sectors. Badshah, the man about any town, drove Rehaan in his trusty old Maruti 800 within an hour from the India International Centre to Mannu Sharma's slashed sector home, not without grumbling, "The things you make me do. I couldn't even have my toast-omelette breakfast, no yolks, only white. Healthy, I'm told. Proteins! Let's hope this Varma has the decency to offer us some food...for thought, eh?"

"It's Sharma, not Varma."

At 8 a.m., the roadway before the apartment of the Sharmas on the first floor of a two-storey blandly distempered structure, was busy with school buses, vendors and milkmen delivering tetrapacks. Badshah stayed put in the car. Rehaan could go up and do his number, "If he bashes you up, just holler, mate!"

The phantom Mannu Sharma answered the Swan Lake-chiming doorbell, handling a newspaper and a ribbed glass of tea, expertly. Perhaps he was used to morning bells. Of medium-height and build, his fortune was his movie-starrish face. He could have modelled for pressure cookers, flanked by an ecstastic wife and puppet-like children. He guessed Rehaan's identity straight-off, invited him to occupy a cane chair in the narrow verandah dotted with wilting potted plants. His wife called out, "Who is it?"

"A friend from Mumbai," he informed her. The pleasant, cotton-sari clad wife sized up Rehaan from top to toe, suspiciously, "From Mumbai? How would you like your cup of tea? Black or regular with milk and sugar."

"Black is good," Rehaan nodded gratefully, hoping she'd make a quick exit. She did, instructing her husband, "The kids have tests today. I'm worried, the poor things could barely eat their eggs…they need proteins."

"They'll be fine," Mannu consoled her. "They always pull through the tests, don't they? Did they reach the school bus in time?"

"Obviously," the wife said. "Have they ever missed the bus?"

As soon as she was out of sight, Mannu began, "Noor would talk about you all the time."

"Complimentary things, I hope!" Rehaan said.

"What brings you here today? Is Noor okay? Please convey my warm wishes to her."

"I don't know why but she would like to meet you."

"It's too late for that, Rehaan. I've got the name right? Whatever happened was for the best."

"For you, not for her."

"Agreed. Do me a favour, please tell her to forget that I ever existed."

Rehaan wasn't going to let him get away, "Does your wife know about her?"

"Please, speak slowly."

"You mean speak softly. I won't, unless you agree to meet her."

"Very well then. I run a hosiery shop in the colony's market from 10 in the morning to 10 at night. During the lunch break, I could make some time."

"Day after's Sunday. You could meet her at Volga restaurant, Connaught Place, around noon. Noida is too far for her."

"Will you be with her?"

"No, I'm leaving for Mumbai tomorrow."

"I see. This will be difficult. What if someone sees me with her?"

"Too bad, Mr Sharma. At most, I can request a friend of mine to accompany her. He'll sit at a different table."

"No, no. That's worse. I'll meet her alone."

"Sunday noon it is. May we exchange our cellphone numbers?"

Mannu was about to decline when his wife announced his number out loud, placed a mug of tea in Rehaan's hand, and left with the parting shot, "Sharmaji, I have no objections if you meet Noor one more time…in a public place."

Embarrassed, Mannu said, "My Mrs knows all. I'm sorry I didn't wish to get her involved in any of this."

"That makes things simpler, then. Noor will be at Volga at noon, Sunday. Thank you."

Badshah had been chain-smoking in the car which smelt like the IIC bar did before the clampdown of non-smoking zones. "All cool?" he grinned and drove off from Noida at hurricane speed.

Noor smiled one of her rare dazzlers on being informed about the Volga tryst. But she wouldn't keep the appointment if Rehaan didn't accompany her. "It's the last favour I ask of you," she entreated.

Damn, his air ticket would have to be rescheduled, his pockets were getting shallower by the hour. A favour, she had said. Weighing the odds, Rehaan assented. It had to be done for his Baaji who had so doted on him in the past. She had given him a tenner once to buy himself a copy of Lewis Caroll's *Alice in Wonderland* off a pavement book vendor. The wonderland words returned, "Have I gone mad?" and its answer, "I'm afraid so, but let me tell you something, the best people usually are."

Badshah seconded that, "You're going loony tunes. Take care buddy," leaving him at the IIC, where despite himself, Rehaan hit the bar way before sunset. The next day, he would wander around perhaps, or maybe it would be wiser to stay in the Centre's room doing nothing, a luxury for a journalist wedded to the newsroom.

Rehaan reached Connaught Place, at 11 a.m., apportioning himself an hour to browse around ED Galgotia & Sons, one of his favourite book shops. As the rickshaw puttered around the plaza, he saw that Volga was closed. The rickshaw driver said all-knowingly, "Oh, that happened in 2010. Volga had lost its clientele. Aajkal toh fast-food selling only. No taste, no lazzat. Where should I drop you?"

Rehaan, his hold-all in tow since he intended to taxi to the airport soon after the meeting, broke into a sweat. Now what? He would have to hang around closeby and pick another restaurant at walking distance.

Perhaps Wimpy's. Feverishly he called up Noor on her landline to tell her about the change of venue, giving her directions.

Mannu's wife answered Rehaan's call, saying he had left a while ago, forgetting his cell phone at home. Rehaan would just have to wait outside the dead Volga. Fortuitously, Mannu was punctual. They walked without exchanging a word towards Wimpy's. Noor was seated at the most inconspicuous table. Garbed in a burqa, her composed face shone like a light. The two men joined her. A round of cold coffees was ordered. A young crowd was trickling in, to use the wi-fi.

Mannu was more nervous than Noor. Rehaan blushed. The two were looking at each other shyly as if they were out on a first date. Neither was about to say anything. Rehaan, never the diplomat, hissed, "Come on, I don't have all the time in the world. I have to catch a flight."

Mannu began, fiddling with the cold coffee, "Salaam alaikum, Noor."

"Walaikum salaam. I am not here to say much. I want to stop thinking about you…dreaming about you. I can only do that by returning things which keep reminding me of you."

Quickly, she handed over a bunch of letters, held together by a red string. Mannu accepted them expressionlessly. He looked at Rehaan to explain, "These letters I wrote to her. I was foolish."

"Was it foolishness or deceit? You damaged me," Noor murmured. She then handed him a cardboard jewellery box, containing six gold bangles.

"Noor, they are yours. I bought them for you."

"You can give them to your wife. I have no use for them."

Rehaan's eyes were smarting – a love story with an unhappy ending. How he hated those. Noor and Mannu had lapsed into silence.

Assuming the role of a lawyer in a courtroom, Rehaan said, "Is that all, Noor? Mannu do you want to say anything?"

"Yes, that's all," Noor spoke up. "Now, please ask him to leave."

"Let him finish the coffee at least, Baaji."

"He hates coffee," Noor said.

Mannu placed his hand on Rehaan's shoulder and left, walking briskly towards the metro station.

Barely a quarter of an hour had elapsed. Noor asked Rehaan to see her off in a rickshaw. Before he could, she removed two boxes from a mirrorwork satchel. The smaller one contained spools of Jameela Begum's unreleased recordings. She said, "I don't know what to do with them. One of her best renditions but least appreciated recordings could be there – 'Hasrat Mohani's Phir bhi hai tumko mashihai ka dawaa dekho / Mujh ko dekho mere marne ki tamanna dekho…'"

He couldn't grasp the meaning of the verse. She didn't expect him to and said helpfully, "It means, can you still claim to be a messiah? Watch my state, my death wish… Maybe you could check if it's on the tapes…if it hasn't been erased by time."

The second handful of a box contained the sleeping porcelain cat. Noor said, "Handle it with care." She put a finger on her lips to say, "My apologies, about the pendant. The cat is yours, always was."

Humbled to the core, Rehaan saw Noor off at the autorickshaw stand. She waved, "Don't ever think badly of me. Allah haafiz."

In the broad noonlight, Rehaan broke into tears. He was gaped at curiously. It was just another Sunday at Connaught Place. He placed the tapes and the cat in his hold-all carefully, hailed a taxi to the airport and was back home late evening.

He kept the spools of the unreleased songs in the drawer of his desk. He unpacked the cat, placed it on his bedside table, looked at it lovingly, and wept again. He wanted to be a man with qualities. He wasn't. He was just another self-centred asshole, acquisitive about every material thing which belonged to him, always tense, like a wave before it breaks.

Fayazi Ma couldn't hear him. He had closed the door tight. The cat, he would have to hide, from her post-cataract-surgery eyes. Rehaan had done wrong. He had disrespected the bond between Jameela Begum and his Ma. Why? Why had he been so petty?

He had failed Ma. She was large-hearted; he had no heart at all.

Don't think like that Rehaan. That's not the way to be, if you are to continue excavating the Humshira story. Be detached - the first lesson once tattooed on him in the newsroom.

17

In the Realm of Anxiety

There was this game he played – of colours. He would close his eyes tight in a dark room and determine the drizzle of shades. Greens and browns came easy. To reach a red or blue screen behind the shuttered eyes, impossible. Abstract patterns would revolve and vanish. No faces, no figures, only solid colours and intricate patterns. Dream, Rehaan would, the recurring one being of an unrelieved field of green.

The game could be played no longer now. Scenes formed themselves. If he could recall them, they were only end images: Rehaan hiding behind a brown pillar from a battalion of invaders with no faces; women carrying baskets of stolen fruit, boarding buses to nowhere; a shopping centre with its mannequins disintergrating to rubble; pigeons unfurling their wings to applaud a stand-up comedian's jokes on the prevention of cruelty to his feathered friends. And there was the recurring one, Dr Abhay Mehta's couch, black against white walls.

Sigmund Freud's The Interpretation of Dreams *has held forth, "(A) Dream's evenascence, the way in which, on awakening, our thoughts thrust it aside as something bizarre, and our reminscences mutilating or rejecting it – all these and many other problems have, for many hundred years demanded answers, which up till now could never have been satisfactory."*

There could be no explication. His will power, his inner strength if he possessed one, had to extinguish the dreams with some help. Though the psychoanalyst was unwilling to take him on as a patient, Rehaan still had to make an appointment. He had to talk. Friends had stopped listening. His three buddies, he had concluded, were much too exploitative. They had used him. Agreed, he was viewing friendship from a narrow prism – his own. Yet one would never offer to pay a bill when they hung out at bars, Chinese restaurants and junk-food outlets. Another would persuade him to ghost-write his movie reviews for as many as the last 12 years. Another would answer his calls depending on his priorities of the day. If the friend was busy, "Sorry Rehaan, let's think of next week maybe."

Hey, get off his cloud friends, never there in his hours of need. None had volunteered to come over and see his grandmother after the fall. She was pleasant enough with them. They gushed, said she was a charmer. He didn't need hoax comfort. A college benchmate now into real-estate business had come over from Jaipur, claiming that he had to ask after her well-being. He did, for what seemed like a nanosecond, and cadged a loan from Rehaan, payable when able.

With a little help from his friends, he would have been more composed, collected, but then the world didn't owe him any favours. Friends were decimating in number; colleagues had their own professional and personal upheavals. Retrenchment was seeping in. The trade union body which looked after the employees' rights, was doing all the wrong things: ordering closures. A lay-off was on. Only the essential staff would be called in to work surreptitiously, ceiling lights off in the newsroom, to cobble together the next morning's edition.

By a whisker, Rehaan was among the essentials, sneaking in and out of The Daily Chronicle's *backdoors which had strangely escaped the attention of the trade union. Or were the doors allowed to open and close by the union by some covert agreement? The union leaders were in cohorts with the management, it was conjectured. Before the conspiracy theories multiplied, the strike was called off. Back to normal. The message was clear – accept the status quo or take a long walk.*

The novel wasn't inching forward. Fayazi Ma was becoming crankier by the day. His love for her though was intensifying. He would carry home apples, mash them and serve her the purée. She wouldn't accept lunch or dinner. She would pretend to swallow vitamin capsules, spitting them out as soon as Rehaan's back turned. He needed to talk to her. She wouldn't, staring at him with dead eyes. He was losing his sole precious possession. How could he ever live without her? Unthinkable, don't go there, Rehaan. We all have to go some day – remember – but not Fayazi Ma, he would deny her that pleasure. "You have to live for me Ma, me me me, and you know that," his thoughts would run amok, then stop. So many 'me's'... Is it all about yourself, about the aloneness you dread like solitary confinement for eternity in a maximum-security prison?

Even paranoids have enemies. In Rehaan's case, he had created them. The demons would slap him hard across the cheek

– a recurring bit of masochism this, a resonance of the never deciphered Tweedle slaps at Qalayat's Super Hotel. He would be attacked by blood-drooling zombies – vampires were so civilised in comparison. He would see himself being buried alive in a grave, hollering, "Reduce me to ashes in an electric crematorium, instead. Please, it's faster."

The appointment with Dr Abhay Mehta was firmed by the clinic's irreplaceable secretary. He wouldn't curl up on the couch in that sea-sound chamber of his. He selected a foamed chair with arm rests, and narrated fragments of his disorder to the analyst. Cussedly, the good doctor concluded again that analyis wouldn't be the panacea. If Rehaan insisted on being treated, he could be referred to a pyschiatrist who would put him on medication. Nothing serious – tranquillisers which would serve in mitigating panic attacks.

'Panic attacks', a new-fangled terminology, just as 'virus' and 'infections' have become buzzwords in medical diagnoses. The patient who wasn't a patient wouldn't leave without paying the hourly fee, and without apologising for having walked out of the dinner rudely. "Understandable! Understandable!" the analyst echoed as if repeating 'understandable' would convince Rehaan that he was stable, and all was right with the world.

Surfing Facebook, he messaged Murad Aladia's son Nauman Ali in Dubai once again. Just as he was about to log off, Nauman keyed back, "Salaam alaikum. All well with you, sir?"

"Walaikum salaam, Nauman. Am not well," Rehaan shot back. "Why doesn't anyone tell me about Murad saab, your father? Why?"

The reply came right back over cyber-space, "Why go into that zone now? No one can turn back the clock. I am busy at the store, peak hour. May we connect tomorrow?"

"Tomorrow around 10 a.m., your time."

"Can we make it 9 a.m. please, Nauman?"

"Done."

At 9 a.m., Rehaan logged in anxiously. Nauman had left an inboxed message which said, "Salaams, I hope you don't mind. I sincerely request you not to ask me about my father. I know little about him except that he was a good man. As you know, he wasn't liked by your nani and her sisters, for no wrong except that he was born male. I can neither forgive them nor forget. I am sorry I have 'unfriended' you. Please do not reply to this or I will have to block you."

Rehaan wasn't taken aback. Nauman, bald and turret creases on his face, looked older than his age in his display profile picture. Other posts showed him grinning in selfies with his two daughters and a wife at the Al-Jumeira beach in Dubai. The wife never smiled. She looked sullen, as if she didn't like being photographed.

Rehaan could intrude no further on Nauman. The first impulse was to call up Dr Mehta's office for another appointment. He had to talk to someone, anyone. No point, he corrected himself. He didn't want to go on a recommended psychiatrist's medication. He was already on a heavy course of vitamins, anti-cholestrol and pills to prevent another attack of epilepsy. Nearly a decade ago, he'd had a seizure at the office; he'd fallen unconscious. The newspaper's chief reporter, who was in his room then to plan the day's edition, informed him,

"You convulsed badly. We were about to call in an ambulance to rush you to a hospital when you came to. You were laughing uproariously. I took off one of my shoes, made you smell it, and you seemed to be delighted. Take care."

Scans showed that Rehaan would have to be placed on anti-epilepsy pills for the rest of his life, supplemented with vitamin tablets. He had to be careful; he couldn't get hyper, overwrought. Daily yoga exercises would put him on the mend. He tried but couldn't match the regimen. A yoga teacher, tentatively hired for bi-weekly two-hour sessions, was useless, treating Rehaan as if he was made of rubber. Lift a leg there, bend your back here. Yoga worked magic for others. He was hopelessly resistant to its healing powers. Instead, long walks, taking deep breaths whenever he felt queasy, worked. Rehaan had kept the epilepsy attack a secret from Fayazi Ma. She would have fretted, adding to his discomfort.

Nauman's message revived the memory of that attack. He would have to deal with the knot he felt within. No one could untie it for him except himself. How?

He couldn't push Fayazi Ma, aggravate her. He could have but wouldn't, above all in deference to a tragedy, his biological mother's death soon after childbirth. "The hurt of a mother who is alive when her child is no more…you will never know how I die every moment I breathe," Fayazi Ma had said to ward off his curiosity about the death of her beloved, never-hurt-a-fly Zahira.

Fayazi Ma could be mercurial. She appeared to be on the mend. She had begun to accept the apple purée and foot massage. To bring up the phantom Murad now would have been insensitive, cruel.

He couldn't attempt to read the shadow cast by Murad on the sisters, a shadow with no contours at all. Stonewalled by Nauman, he shelved the story, the book, or whatever there was emerging from it. There were more urgent matters to handle. At the workplace, journalism had become a trap from which he couldn't break out.

The scion of the family group which owned the newspaper was based in Indore but had begun to visit the Mumbai flagship office with alarming regularity. A taciturn young man dressed most often in white linen pants, a white shirt and Kolhapuri chappals, had summoned him to his chamber, and suggested that he should write a two-page feature on the aesthetics behind producing a perfect pair of running shoes, Keds. Rehaan had nodded, "Excellent idea" to which the scion had said, "We must think more out of the box, don't you think?" The article was done, never mind if it was ghastly gobbledygook about the brilliance of new trends in footgear. It was printed prominently on the Media centrepage, next to a half-page advertisement for a Japanese brand of Keds. The scion wasn't interested in 'aesthetics'. He was interested in the ad revenue. No quarrels with that. The paper has to survive. But Rehaan could no longer be a part of this. Something wasn't right – the ideals of journalism were in tatters. He couldn't possibly continue to be a "yes" man.

Frequently he had been told he could come up with catchy headlines and captions. Move over to advertising, give it another go, more money there. Pause, think, no way, he was much too senior. Next option: move to a web portal, doctor film scripts, freelance for other publications. Dicey, very dicey. Those would amount to great leaps backward. Think, think. Got it, stay rooted to the newsroom, that's where you belong, Rehaan. If they don't want you anymore, they'll send you three months' notice. Till then Zen, read, look after Ma, count your tender mercies. Distraction from the everyday beat might do you a world of good. Forge new friendships. Where? No dearth of dating sites, idiot, go there. What! Quickie sex or its polar opposite, commitment – what the fuck are you looking for? No, someone to chat with, share confidences, meet up for a coffee, or slyly suggest a drink (make that beer or wine, no hard drinks please) and go with the flow. Hell, masturbation after midnight – to Internet porn – would have to suffice.

Right. In any case, whom would he want to chat with? A stranger? Sure, why not? Someone ha-ha, fun, like-minded, out of the box. Wait, better still, he would strike up an anonymous friendship with the one person he would like to chat with right at this moment. Nauman Ali. Easy. Create a fake account, pose as a woman, and see if he bites the bait. No harm in trying. Devious? Slimy? Sure, so what?

18

Woman in the Box

The fake Facebook account was on. Name: Shaheen Siraj. Studied: B.B.S., Gitanjali Public School, Home Science diploma, Vijayadevi Insitute. Lives in Hyderabad. From: Delhi. No display profile picture. Posts comprised about 20 love couplets in English, accompanied by visuals of misty mountains, bubbling brooks, skies in placid and menacing moods. Reproductions of Van Gogh's Sunflowers. Within a day, there were 100 followers, escalating to 500 within a week. Bubbling brooks are perfect, poetic and cheery. A friend request was shot to Nauman Ali, with the message, "Salaams. I would like to be your friend, warm wishes, Shaheen."

The request was ignored. The ruse didn't work, till a week later…an inboxed message asked Shaheen, "Why me?"

Right off, Rehaan replied, "Why not?"

"Who are you, mystery woman?"

"Someone special, like your sweet face. There is a sadness in your eyes which I can relate to."

"Can I see your face pic?"

Rehaan was ready for that. He had clicked photographs of his friends in college, among them of the classic delicate beauty, Roshanara, daughter of the Chief Fire Brigade Officer of Mumbai. She would wear a hijaab to college but removed it as soon as the car left her at the entrance. Her smile was to die for. Her face could have launched a thousand movies. Rehaan inboxed a close-up of Roshanara, her face partially covered with a striped dupatta.

"Wow, mashallah" came Nauman's message. "Are you for real?"

"Yes. I like you. Can we be friends?"

"What do you like about me? I'm an average, simple person."

"You are not. Nauman, I chanced upon your photograph among suggested friends, and it was…"

"It was what?"

"Love at first sight."

"Do not try to play the fool with me, lady. I will block you."

Rehaan replied with a dozen emoticons of a crying face, and as many broken hearts.

"As you wish Nauman, my jaan. Your children are beautiful, your wife also."

"Yes, my children are beautiful. The less said about my wife, the better."

"How mean is that."

"Lady, who are you?"

"I live in Hyderabad. Divorced at age 25, no children. Not happy. Am searching for a soulmate."

"Sorry Shaheen, am married, two children…not possible."

"You are not attracted to me?"

Rehaan inboxed a picture of Roshanara in a clinging tee and a clingier pair of jeans.

"You are lovely. Am attracted. Sorry busy at work now."

"Do you love your wife?"

"Can't chat. Will ping you later."

"When?"

"I will let you know. Going offline now dearest."

Nauman was easy prey, desperate for romance and a chat relationship. Shaheen's inbox pinged within an hour, "Are you there?"

Rehaan went offline, thoroughly chuffed at assuming the identity of an Eve who had dozens of apples in the basket. If the victim wouldn't open up about his father, Murad, it would be thrilling to pay him back by going silent.

The prey kept pinging throughout the day, "I need to speak to you Shaheen", "This is not fair", "I am thinking about you", "There's no harm in chatting", "I am also looking for a soulmate", "My wife doesn't understand me", "It's over between us", "This is no way to live", "Shaheen where are youuuuu?"

Rehaan replied late at night, "Sorry jaan, your Shaheen could not respond earlier. Guests at home. Will chat ASAP."

Nauman begged, "When?? I need to chat now."

This was going way too fast, but that mother of chat clinchers had to be used, "Love you, Nauman. Sweet dreams, dream of me in your arms, my love."

"Sweet dreams. I want to kiss you."

Woah, what could Shaheen say to that but, "I want to kiss you too, all night and day"?

Rehaan logged off. That night, he slept restfully. No dreams. He had become Shaheen and Shaheen didn't dream.

The Nauman-Shaheen correspondence continued without any let-up for a week. Love assumed sexual overtones. Both confessed their fantasies in bed. Nauman longed to make her his bride – his second. It was about time, he pleaded. He would leave his family if need be. He wanted out. Rehaan had guessed that his marriage was loveless from the very start.

Shamelessly, Rehaan's fantasy creation wanted Nauman to make love to her again and again. She would massage him with almond oil, breathe on the nape of his neck, stroke him, squeeze him in her arms till he couldn't breathe. She wanted to make love in public places, by moonlight in hill-towns, in forests, hold hands and caress each other in multiplexes. The chats became explicitly pornographic.

Nauman wouldn't be able to leave Dubai for another six months. The job was like that. Neither could Shaheen leave Hyderabad even if he sent her an air-ticket. Her parents would never allow her to travel alone. He would make "some arrangement in Dubai. It would be difficult but come to me. I'm counting every minute."

"Impossible."

"Why the fuck not?" Nauman asked belligerently. "You're a grown-up woman. You can take your own decisions."

"What arragement can you make? Where would I stay?" Shaheen countered.

"In my heart, darling," the besotted patsy wrote. "Will work something out. Can get good discounted rate at five-stars. I will

handle, will find a way without using credit card. Just come. Can mail you e-ticket."

Come to the point, Rehaan, this is where you can get the dope you want.

Shaheen said, "My father is strict, a tyrant. How are your parents? Will they let you take a second wife?"

"No worries, darling. They are no more."

"My father has a horrible temper. He would kill me if he even knew I was chatting with you, jaan. All fathers are like that."

"No, they are not. My father was a saint."

"Unlike me, you must have had a wonderful childhood. Tell me about those days, jaanam."

"Why?"

Tough one this. Rehaan had to play it cool, write, "'Coz I want to know every little thing, every little moment of your life, darling. I long to make love with you again and again. I want to be yours, body and soul. Tell me all about you."

"Long story, my darling Shaheen. I will tell you everything when we meet."

Smartly, Rehaan brought up what he had been avoiding, "Can you tell me everything on videocam? I want to see you naked, make sure you love me."

The cam proposal was a dare. Nauman would have wanted to see Shaheen face to face but wasn't quite ready to take the risk.

"No, no. My kids have access to the laptop. Can't take chances," the bait was rejected.

"Coward!" cried Shaheen.

"I want to be your hero. Please be patient, love."

"Are you a good lover? Passionate?"

"Madly passionate for you, my beloved."

"You don't even agree to audio calls, love. You don't trust me, you don't share your cell phone number," the Shaheen in Rehaan moaned.

"My sweetheart, cannot do that. Who knows what happens on these calls. They could be recorded."

"I do hope you delete every chat, Nauman…this is torture. How long can we go on like this?"

"I delete, don't worry."

"Kay, gotta go. My father is screaming his head off."

"This father of yours will come around."

"Would your father have?"

"Absolutely."

"Tell me about him some day, jaan…bye now. Shabba khair."

"Shabba khair, jaan."

"Remember to tell me about your dad. Mine is a tyrant. All men, all fathers are tyrants."

"You keep saying that. They're not, believe me. Will tell you about mine."

"His name?"

"Murad. I thought you had to go…"

"Yes. Kissses."

"Make them wet kisses…kisses like rainfall on my lips."

"Mmmmm, you're so hot and horneeee."

19

Of Our Fathers

Over the next week, the Nauman-Shaheen correspondence was stuck in the groove of kisses, embraces and unspeakable intimacies. Whenever Shaheen brought up his father, her cyber paramour avoided answers till he had to ask, "Why so curious about my abba?"

Rehaan soft-pedalled, "I have always longed for a kind father, that's all. If you don't want to talk about him, it's your wish. No worries."

"Do you know anyone in my family?" Nauman asked.

"No, I wish I did. My own family is such a mess. Very dominating. Hyderabad is such a conservative place."

"Swear on my dead body, there's no other reason. Kasam khao."

"It is wrong to swear. Kasams are only for people you don't trust, my jaan, isn't it?"

"Yes. It has been so many days. Now I want to hear your voice."

"Can't take risks…it's okay…it seems you don't love me anymore."

"I love you more than my own life, Shaheen, and you know that."

"Are you hiding your past?"

"Not at all. I will tell you whatever you want. Have to work now. Chat later. Bye, my princess."

"Bye, my emperor."

Rehaan had to play hard to get. He wouldn't answer Nauman's messages again and kept up the charade for five weekdays. Over the weekend, he answered Nauman's entreaties, saying, "Sorry, my father has found a groom for me. He's a civil engineer. I will have to remarry in a month or two. My loss, jaan. I will always cherish our friendship."

The besotted one was distraught, "Shaheen, I will come to Hyderabad ASAP…my job be damned…and ask for your hand in marriage. There will be a proper nikaah."

Shaheen messaged dryly, "Abba will want to know about your parents."

Now or never, if Nauman didn't open up, he never would. Rehaan didn't feel diabolical at all. He was enjoying being a woman, and his behaviour was noticed by his office colleague Karmarkar, "You better watch it, buddy. Don't know what you're doing at the comp, but you look like a girl at times, all pouty and sexy. When you walk, you swing your arse. See your wrist is lame. Are you a closet gay or what?"

Thereon, Rehaan had to be careful, walked straight, and kept a poker, even rough face whenever he was online with Nauman. He was seducing a man. He saw himself as Shaheen, her face straight out of a Rembrandt painting, and to his horror, she was stark naked, a woman with a nubile girl's breasts, with

Nauman in bed. If Rehaan had been a woman, he would have behaved shamelessly.

What if he were to tell Dr Abhay Mehta this? The analyst would have probably told him, it was normal. He was doing what he was, with a reason. Terrific, makes sense. But don't forget you're a man, Rehaan. Take it easy. You're play-acting, and if you're deriving pleasure, fantastic. You're not as uptight as you thought you were. Be a man though in your body language, keep your face expressionless at the office. The affair is about to come to a close, anyway.

On a Sunday, Nauman said they could chat for an hour at least. The store remained closed only on Fridays, but on Sundays, the footfalls were low during the lunch hour. This chat had to be the finale.

"Jaan, salaams," Rehaan cooed.

"Salaams, my lovely. You can tell your father this about me. It's the honest truth. I come from a farming family. Abba Murad was the only son of a large family and became a wrestler as they often do in villages in north India. His patron was a zamindar. Wrestlers are used for gambling purposes. Abba made lots of money at the outset but he was injured in a wrestling bout."

"Then?"

"He was paralysed. Ammi had to go to work as a sweeper in the zamindar's house. My grandparents had left us some money. We survived. I was educated in a convent school, boarding house, in Patna. I completed school.

"After the accident, Abba was never the same again. He suffered from deep depression. One day, he was found dead in

his sleep. We never came to know what happened, but village people gossiped that he had committed suicide."

"Oh no, why suicide?"

"Abba was like that, unpredictable. He was cheated of money, of his property by his sisters, with whom he didn't get along. The zamindar discarded him after the accident. I would agree with the rumours. No post-mortem was done. I suspect he must have taken an overdose of painkillers. Shaheen, I am telling you the honest truth. I don't want your past or mine to come between us, my love."

"Jaan, it breaks my heart. How can anyone commit suicide? It is forbidden by the Quran."

"I am sure the Almighty forgave Abba. Who doesn't break rules? I might as well tell you I have drinks…whisky…in moderation. Do you mind?"

"As long as your drinking is under control. My first husband was a drunkard and he would get physically abusive."

"I will give up drinking once we are together."

"You did nothing for your father? You could have fought for his property rights."

"That is forgotten, my love. I am a self-made man. I hope to start a store of my own some day. Who knows, it could even be in Hyderabad. Close to Banjara Hills, lots or rich people there… done some research. I am fed up of Dubai. Wife and children, I will provide for. I love my children."

"Wife. You love her?"

"No, never did. Arranged marriage."

"Your father. Did he keep in touch with his sisters at all?"

"Why are you asking me this?"

"Just."

"Shaheen. I may not be from a rich family, but we have always been God-fearing Muslims. I make enough money Alhamdolillah and will make more."

"Life has not treated you right."

"I would not say that. The only thing I cannot come to terms with is my father's suicide."

"I understand."

"Does this make any difference to our love?"

"I love you madly. But…"

"But?"

Think fast, think fast, you cannot get more out of this charade, think. Kill Shaheen right now.

"But I am not sure Abba will agree to my nikaah with you."

"We will elope then."

"I don't have the courage."

"You sound different."

"Nauman, give me a day or two to think…"

"As you wish."

Rehaan logged off. He had the missing piece of the Murad puzzle. He would soften the blow for Nauman Ali, send him a farewell message as soon as he could conjure one up. Shaheen Siraj would disappear from Facebook.

Do it right away, Rehaan. Do it right away, Shaheen. Don't prolong Nauman's agony. He rushed to the Press Club. Three large vodkas later, he went to his office cabin to send Nauman a farewell message.

"My love, at times what we desire cannot be fulfilled. I have nothing but admiration for you. I appreciate the warmth and

affection you have given me during so many of my lonely, wretched hours. There is one thing my father will never accept, me being a mother to your two children. Also, your kids would hate me for the rest of their lives. Let's forget each other, move on. I will have to marry the man of my abba's choice. That is what a daughter must do. Forgive me. Kisses."

Nauman Ali was unfriended and blocked. Shaheen Siraj's account was deleted.

20

"What can we do for you today?"

The birth-name of the sisters yielded quirky information on the net:

*An Aladia, a site claimed, was linked to the desire for the creative, artistic and musical expression in an "original way". An Aladia was self-confident, persevered in the face of obstacles, but was incapable of "harmonious relationships". Argumentative, an Aladia was vulnerable to skin and liver ailments, colds, sinus, headaches and hay fever.

*A lowcost chartered Aladia Airlines, in Mexico, had commenced in 2006 and packed up two years later, citing a financial crisis.

*Namespedia says Aladia is used as a first name 119 times in six different countries; the surname 10 times in four different countries. The gender of the first name Aladia is 100 percent feminine and 0 percent masculine.

*According to the John Doe search engine, there were 17 people named Allarakhi worldwide. The name's popularity rank: Not applicable.Top of Form

Bottom of FormAllarakhi Aladia was holding on to her isolation, from all accounts by Fayazi Ma, somewhere unknown. She had not married, she had no one to take care of but herself.

Fayazi Ma would not permit any investigation into the whereabouts of Allarakhi whose face returned, if at all, as a blur from childhood recall. She couldn't be on social media. She wouldn't be on the cyber-data of ACP Jung.

Allarakhi Aladia could have been dead and buried, but then Fayazi Ma had proclaimed, "All of us are alive still. More's the pity." If Allarakhi had passed away, his ma wouldn't have said that, or would she have? Mumtaz Chaudhran and Jameela Begum, Shuhaba and Noor didn't have any leads on Allarakhi.

So go ahead Rehaan, look for her. You're a reporter, but wait, you're not a detective. Google had yielded factoids about one Alla Rakhi, beneficiary of an India Earth trust. A short documentary on Vimeo showed her to be based in Ramzan Goth, Sindh Pakistan. She had been given a sewing machine and two goats. She was doing well. Much too young, in her 30s, like an Allarakhi on Facebook, based in Glasgow, U.K.

Should he just subtract her from the story, then, reduct the six sisters to five? What difference would it make to the reader? Rehaan debated.

Fayazi Ma was playing in a mean-spirited way with his curiosity. Time and again came the warning that her sisters were a taboo topic. Mumtaz Chaudhran and Jameela Begum, she couldn't rescind. The others, she could.

Around 1995, Rehaan had located the Missing Persons Bureau at the Police Commissioner's headquarters, while inquiring about the repercussions of the December 1992 – January 1993 communal riots in Mumbai, in which 960 people perished according to official records. The riots were sparked by the Babri Masjid demolition by Hindu Karsevaks in Ayodhya.

One theory has it that the Hindu rioters in Mumbai had targeted the locations of homes and business areas predominantly occupied by Muslims. The police, according to a fusillade of reports, were spearheaded by Maharashtra's political party, Shiv Sena. The event has been described as an anti-Muslim pogrom.

In retaliation, followed the reprehensibly vengeful Bombay bomb blasts of 12 March 1993, coordinated by Dawood Ibrahim of the organised crime syndicate D-company. On record, there were 260 fatalities.

On the day of the serial bomb blasts, Rehaan was in the distant suburbs on an interview assignment at a movie studio. He had to stay over for three days at a film technician's apartment, a Hindu who kept emphasising his faith in secularism. "You are welcome to eat at my table. If my parents were here, no offence meant, I am sure they would have turned you out," he had said casually.

While the beneficiary of secularism was distraught, over a groggy phone line, Fayazi Ma had coolly told him to take his time, days if necessary, till the roads were clear of rioters. The neighbours were taking care of her, not to worry. She seemed unaffected, the way she would never express her remorse over the sub-continent's partition. She consoled him that *The Daily Chronicle*'s CEO had also called in to ask, in all earnest, if they could offer him any help. Political turbulence hadn't ever frazzled the Aladia sisters, it would have seemed. They had never played their Muslim card. They felt distanced from the passages of history and politics.

In the bomb blast spree, the lesser-privileged Muslim homes had faced tragedies, many of which remain untold. Hundreds of men went missing and over the years, were confirmed among the dead.

There must be a Missing Persons Bureau which could possibly have some records of the Partition as well. No chance. At most, there was a bureau comprising two empty desks in an abandoned shed of the police commissioner's headquarters bang opposite the shop-for-all-your needs Crawford Market. A constable outside had informed him wryly, "No one comes here for inquiry. Officers don't have time to waste with answers they don't know themselves. If you ask me, all Muslims missing in the riots must have become terrorists."

Muslims by and large were being ghettoised as potential terrorists, an extension of the canards which had simmered ever since the sub-continent's partition.

At school he would be teased as katela – the cirumcised one. Decades after, whenever there was a cricket match between India and Pakistani, he would be mocked, "Bet you're siding with the katelas." Muslims were a vote bank which couldn't be ignored by the politicians. This bank had come to be regarded as a necessary evil. "Go back to Pakistan" – graffiti on the walls of the Muslim mohallas would threaten. Inclusion and assmilation into the social fabric had become thorns in the flesh.

At this rate, the police couldn't possibly help in tracing a young Muslim woman who had left Qalayat in pre-independent India. If there were any records of deaths pre- or post-Partition, the certificates, if any, must have been junked.

Rehaan couldn't see himself as a sleuth in search of a lost era. Maybe a detective agency could drum up leads. On Googling the best-known agencies of their kind in Mumbai, he was instructed to tick a box first and then proceed. Detective agencies are into speciality cases: Corporate, Cyber Crime, Forensic and Personal.

Got it, he'd contact the Personal agency. Maybe the detectives there would think of him as a nut job. Fine, their problem, not his. He had never met a real-life detective. This could be an adventure or a disaster. It was neither. It was another shot in the dark.

Rehaan dropped by at the Kothari and Sons Detective Agency, lodged in a warren of rooms above a convenience store, close to his office. A cherubic, pony-tailed girl in her late teens, speaking simultaneously into a switchboard and a cellphone, looked up at him, "What can we do for you today?" He asked to meet someone who could help him locate a missing woman.

"Oh," she placed a call on hold, said, "Wait a sec. Hold on," returned to the cellphone and quizzed happily, "So what can we do for you today?" Quick jabs at the switchboard, later, a detective as festive as a Santa Claus cut-out materialised, looked at the visitor with urgency, and said, "I am K.P. Kothari. Come, come, come...always a pleasure, great pleasure. Sejal, send a couple of coffees to my room. In pot, sugar and milk...hot milk on the side."

Sejal nodded, "Yes, K.P. Uncle."

Santa Claus nodded back as if an important armistice had been signed, "Only you're allowed to call me Uncle," and then addressed Rehaan. "She's my niece, brother's sister you know. We're Kotharis, second generation, proper gentlemen. We're a family concern since the last 50 years...half a century! No shady business here."

As it turned out, the cabin was shady, letting in lean columns of the sun through retractable window shades. A bunch of fresh marigolds in a brass pot sat on a circular desk. Kothari plonked himself on a straight-backed rattan chair. Rehaan was welcomed to occupy a chair with arms ending in lion heads which he shuffled into awkwardly. "Don't mind, don't mind, Sejal baby presented it to me on my 59th birthday. The lions are so Versace, no? Clients like them."

"They are not lions, they are Medusa's head," Rehaan said superciliously.

"Who's Medusa? According to me, the clients are always right. They ask which shop they can buy lions from. Not real lions, fake ones. Right, Sir, your good name and occupation?"

The preamble – an exchange of business cards and coffee poured from the pot accepted – Kothari gaped at Rehaan as if he had escaped from a zoo. "You're not serious, are you?" the detective's smiley contorted into a frowney. "This is not a matter for Kotharis and Sons. Even if we were to take up the case of this missing lady, who's to fight with the tides of time? We would like to help you. You are a known journalist and all, but sorry, good luck. Finish coffee please, sorry we can't do anything for you today. By the way, what do you think of the government...at centre, not state-level?"

Rehaan was mildly amused by K.P. Kothari. Squirming out of the Versace chair, he said, "You're quite a character. Are all detectives like you?"

"I don't get you."

"Never mind, thanks for your time."

"On your way out, you can pay Sejal 2,500 rupees for consultation at the reception. Cash will be better. No tax headache."

"Rubbish. This was not a consultation. It was a joke."

Rehaan left the building as fast as his feet could carry him. The hurry he knew was irrational, a symptom of his obsession of squashing a confrontation. Back at the office, in the whirl of deadlines, he would have switched off Kothari's call but didn't, and asked brusquely, "What is it?"

Kothari's jabberwocky began, "Money is the root of all evil, sir. But we have to charge for our time. We are very busy people here, so many cases of personal variety to investigate.

After thinking and thinking, since you are a journalist, we will not carry this demand further. A single tweet of complaint from you I admit will be like a tax headache. You are an intelligent, educated person. I'm B.A. pass also. Take a tip from me, Bhaijaan. Detectives cannot locate the missing lady. You lost your way, coming here. I can only tell you – family is best, most reliable. Chit-chat with all your family members. Someone will talk. Free advice I am giving. Take it or leave it. Good day. And remember please, if you suspect your wife is having an affair, if she is not behaving decently with you, our doors are open for you. Our motto is, so what can we do for you today. Happy? We Kotharis want people to be happy. So how are your wife and children. No problems, no?"

Rehaan disconnected the line. Detective Agency – what a farce. Just like the story he had to edit within the next half hour on a movie personality who was missing in action. The superstar had flown overseas with a mysterious companion, destination unknown, a scoop which would entice the newspaper's management to send him a note of congratulations. The search for Allarakhi could wait. Decades had elapsed. Maybe Kothari was right. Family is best...someone with a loose tongue. How about Abu Bakr, the loser of a journalist, Mumtaz Chaudhran's son? He would talk for money. He had said that it was high time he had received a payback.

Abu Bakr was expecting the call, and said in a professional tone, "I know about Allarakhi. You won't be able to digest what happened to her. If you are ready to, if you don't think I am making it up, I will write it for you as I would write an article. You are employed, I am not. You have been sitting on a high horse, you are a byline. I am not."

"But who knows how long I will be employed?" Rehaan said, straining every nerve to be polite.

"Even if you are not, you will be able to publish the book...hear my warning, you don't have the exclusive rights to the story."

"I don't know what you mean by that. Anyway, tell me what you know."

"Give me co-authorship and half the money you will be paid."

"There's hardly any money in books, please understand."

"That's what all you fancy writers say. Don't bother me, then."

"What happened to Allarakhi Nani?"

"Let's come to a settlement," Abu Bakr haggled. "I will write what happened to her in my own words. You have to include it in this book of yours without any changes, editing."

"Let me think about it. May I get back to you?"

"When?"

"Give me two or three days. How about Monday...at say 11 a.m.? Would you be free then?"

"I'm always free. Monday it is. What I write you can corroborate with your beloved Fayazi Ma. She won't have the guts to contradict a word. Anything else?"

Nothing else at that moment, but the recourse of ending the call with a Khuda haafiz which demands a Khuda haafiz in response. Abu Bakr didn't respond. He didn't believe in Khuda.

Rehaan couldn't wait till Monday. Within an hour, he called Abu Bakr to negotiate, "Salaam, here's what I can offer. Your information on Allarakhi will be given due credit, but it will have to be edited to go with the style of the rest of the book. As for money, we will have to wait to see how the book sells. If I get any royalties, I will pay you whatever I can. Allah kasam."

Surprisingly, Abu Bakr agreed right away, "You will get my Allarakhi story in a week, maybe two. Text me your postal address. I do not have computer, email and cyber cafés are not for me. As for the money part, 25,000 rupees is all I ask. Agreed?"

21

God of all Tragedies

The story came via snail mail a month later. Its fractured, rambling prose had to be cleaned up. It read:

Allarakhi was ditched.

She was ditchedby her sisters. No other reason. They did not care for Allarakhi. They cared only about saving their own skin. They did ungodly things...if you believe in God, that is.

Because of their ungodliness, we, the children of the sisters, have suffered. It doesn't matter if I do not have faith in any god. Never did. We were cursed to be born to them. They were cursed that we were born to them. My brother Abu Fazl and I tried to earn an honest living. We learnt a lesson – honesty gets you nothing but damnation.

Allarakhi died during the partition days of 1947. She was exiled by the sisters to Pakistan. Collective decision it was. Allarakhi must have been gullible. I remember her fasting throughout the roza month, soaking jalebis in milk for sehri, sleeping for the rest of the day, waking up for her prayers. When the sun set, she would break her fast with two dates, two almonds and a dry roti. She didn't ever have an appetite. How could she? She would be cheated at her shop. Children can be cruel. Abu Fazl and I were children then. We would steal sweets from her. She knew about this, but never said a word. If my great mother Mumtaz Chaudhran was a sinner, her sister was a saint.

I know the tragedy of Allarakhi. Abu Fazl also did, but no longer. He has lost his head. I have lost my head too. My sister Shuhaba's sons Sameer and Saagar were just like us – they lost their faculties. Once, like us, they had sense. The Aladia women took on the roles of fathers in all our lives. We were afraid of our mother, just like you are of your grandmother…she is more of a father than a grandmother to you. She has no right to be, but it's your life, you enjoy being sheltered, pampered.

Somehere within us, we are all aware of what the sisters did to Allarakhi, but only I am not afraid to defy them today and will continue to do so till my dying day. The Chaudhran will outlive me. She will outlive my brother who drinks and does drugs more than I do. Difference in quantity is an important difference. His brain has deteriorated to a point of no return. I have some of my brain intact.

My mother Mumtaz Chaudhran could not give Allarakhi shelter at the Kennedy Bridge kotha. Allarakhi was mentally backward. She could not sing, dance, procreate. She watched women being sold night after night. Who knows the Chaudhran would have sold her sister if she could, but out of pity, kept her away from harm's way, I would like to think. Or it could be because Allarakhi was slowly but steadily going mental. She would sleep under Kennedy Bridge, a derelict. There was no roof above her head. She must have felt safer, purer, outside the kotha.

Fayazibai was upper class, a capitalist's wife. Capitalists and those feeding on their filthy lucre do not care for the common people. Allarakhi was common.

Jameela Begum could not accommodate a mental case in Chandni Chowk either. She was with foster parents. There was no reason for them to take on one more outsider. I have not met them personally but Ameena and Ferozi must have had no compassion either, like the Chaudhran does not have any for Abu Fazl and myself. We are of no use to her. Allarakhi was of no use to anyone. She had become a liability, an embarrassment.

She could not beg on the streets. She could only beg for her sisters's mercy. Allarakhi began to have seizures. She suffered from epilpetic fits, a genetic curse maybe. She was in and out of hospitals, charitable hospitals. Hospitals may say they are treating patients for free. They do not. Hefty bills would have to be paid by the Chaudhran and Fayazibai. They did for a few years till the great Chaudhran came up with a great plan – send her away to Pakistan. As a Musalman, she would receive kindness and find a home there.

Chaudhran consulted Fayazibai. Capitalist Sir Osman Baksh Mitha, a toady of the British, played a double game. He had secretly supported the struggle for Indian Independence. He was an expert at buttering the right side of the toast. He had silver trophies from the goras. He had more cash than he could handle, but he was shrewd. The whites were about to be evicted.

Every Ramzan and Bakr Eid, there would be a line-up of poor women to get zakaat. Clever man. The British depended on him. Secretly, the Quit India Movement also received funds from him to free the nation. Muslims regarded him as a man of faith. He could arrange for the mad Allarakhi to cross the border and live with some distant family connections of his in Multan. These connections depended on his handouts. They could not refuse. Since he was entranced by Fayazibai, he could be persuaded to find a home for Allarakhi. That was that.

History books do not have to be re-opened to remind anyone. Hindus and Sikhs fled from Pakistan, a country that would be Muslim-controlled. Who knows how many Muslims of no means fled with whatever they could carry – clothes and utensils mainly? Allarakhi was one of them.

At 25 percent of the population, Muslims were British India's largest religious minority. Under imperial rule, they had grown accustomed to their minority status. The British system of political control hinged on identifying interest groups willing to collaborate, a governing style that you should know was described as "divide and rule".

To bring this up in the context of Allarakhi may sound irrelevant. It does not to me (note: the para above and this cannot be deleted). Karl Marx is not wholly relevant today for some. Vis-à-vis Allarakhi's condition, his beliefs are relevant: "Social progress can be measured by the social position of the female sex" and "The only antidote to mental suffering is physical pain."

Allarakhi suffered mentally, physically. I go back to her story for you today simply because of yet another Marxist belief, "The writer must earn money in order to be able to live and write, but he must by no means live and write for the purpose of making money" (note: my reason for not demanding money beyond the sum stipulated).

It was agreed, Sir Osman would donate a handsome sum of money for Allarakhi's stay and mental cure in Multan, somewhere on the banks of the Chenab River. An exorcist with an unblemished success record could remove the shaitaan from her system. Her flight across the border would be carried out with professional stealth.

There are so many stories about the carnage wrought by Partition. Who has not heard of the story of a woman who was carrying her two newborn infants while fleeing? The heart of one of the infants stopped out of sheer exhaustion during the flight to Pakistan. The woman had to leave the infant in a river before she was attacked. In the chaos, she left the infant whose heart was still beating in the river. This is one of the heart-rending stories so many writers have claimed to be as theirs. Was it any writer's imagination or was it real? If it was real, how can any writer claim that he has the rights to the tragedy?

(Note: neither you nor I have the exclusive right to Allarakhi's story, another reason why I am sharing it now for a price.) So during Partition, Allarakhi did not have any clue that she was being betrayed by her sisters. Once she had run away from Qalayat with them, next she was being coerced to run away from them. I cannot forgive the Chaudhran and Fayazibai – they knew what they were doing.

Allarakhi was accompanied by about 20 to 30 women and their children. They were sent by train from Bombay to Delhi from where they would make the crossover to Jalandhar, under the protection of an Afghan mercenary.

The mercenary left them just about at the border, close to the Dera Baba Murad Shah dargah, sweet-talking them into taking shelter in the dargah if need be. Allah would protect them. When there's no one else, Allah makes his entry, a genie from a lamp.

The mercenary was to return within an hour with some form of transport. He did not. The women did not have the guts to enter the dargah right away. Allarakhi and a few others did. It was deserted. They returned from the dargah to ask the rest of the flock to join them. The women were no longer there. Where had they disappeared? Whether they had been fooled, transported to some distance and slaughtered, is anyone's guess.

The dargah was ominously quiet. There are no details about what exactly happened to Allarakhi and the group she was attached to, except for the supposition that they hid there for a day or two. Do I really have to say what did happen or could have happened next? I might as well. The group Allarakhi was with, which included a 60-year-old grandmother, were most probably raped, their heads chopped off with swords.

Let's say Allarakhi was one of the victims of Partition. According to estimates, around one to two million people died during the partition of British India. One million, or two – as if it's the same thing. Allarakhi was one among the millions, one, or two millions. Her body was never found. Her sisters have never acknowledged the fact that she was raped and killed. In their heads, she is somewhere still in Multan. They have lost her and think they will find her some day. Lost-and-found theory. In their heart they believe, if they possess one that is, what their mind wants to. Convenient, isn't it? Their hearts are far more treacherous than yours or mine.

The Aladia women have reasons which are not reasonable. Nothing can be done about this. They could have mourned the death of Allarakhi which they haven't right to this day, though they are now on the doorstep of death themselves.

The account, with its obtuse Marxist sub-text, begged for disbelief. Rehaan didn't believe a word of it. Granted, Abu Bakr could have listened in on the Chaudhran's conversations, which must have been loose-tongued. The images conjured by Mumtaz Chaudhran's embittered son were strictly stock-in-trade. A mentally unhinged sister exiled to another land, was raped and slaughtered by faceless villains brandishing swords. He couldn't subject Fayazi Ma and the Chaudhran to the charges of abandonment and guilt by association.

Thus far, all the updated information he had tapped was from within the family itself. No option, there could be no other route to his quest for redemption. Still Allarakhi wasn't traceable, swinging the vote towards Abu Bakr's version.

22

The Little Shop

Rehaan couldn't look Fayazi Ma in the eye for days. Quick on the uptake, she remarked, "As always, something is bothering you." He couldn't contain himself anymore, and thundered, "Allarakhi Nani was slaughtered during Partition. Chaudhran and you are guilty."

To that, she turned her back to him and wept, "You are right. What are you going to do about it? Hand over an old woman to the police? Rather than being a crutch to me in my old age, you're tormenting me. I will throw myself into the sea, if you bring this up again."

Once there was Allarakhi's tiny sweets-and-biscuits shop, bang opposite Kennedy Bridge, gifted to her probably as charity in a combined gesture by the Chaudhran and Fayazi Ma. Extinct, it had been replaced by Smart Services, which had taken over the neighbouring teashop as well, and now repaired cellphones and computers.

The Smart Services proprietor could be talked to. The salesman at the Smart Services counter, in the midst of attending to a dozen or more customers, pointed towards Ideal Café on the next block, saying quickly, "You'll find my boss there. Ask for Nishant Agarwal...just ask for Agarwalji."

Agarwalji, a prosperous-looking 60-ish man was solving a crossword in an afternoon English newspaper, alone at a round marble-topped table in the café specializing in peppermint chai – indeed, every second home and lane in the city has its flavoured brew of tea. His was the only table that had two unoccupied chairs. Rehaan asked if it was okay to join him. Without looking up, Agarwalji said, "Why not?" Taking off his thick spectacles, he squinted, "I am stuck. Do you know a seven-letter word for a river in China?"

"Yangtze?"

"Let me see if it fits. It does. I should have known the longest river in Asia. Thanks," he returned to the crossword saying, "Myself Nishant Agarwal, also seven-seven letters. You believe in numerology?"

"I'm here to meet you," Rehaan said politely.

"Your good name?"

"Rehaan Salamat Siddiqi, writer...actually journalist."

Gratifyingly, Agarwal didn't clam up. "Welcome, welcome." He folded the newspaper with a flourish, bellowed out to whoever could hear him, "Two more cups of chai and cream pastry."

Fast on the draw, he curved his right thumb to the bend across the street to Smart Services, "So someone is finally here to ask about my shop. No problem, no problem. All is legal. You're a family member of Allarakhiji. I was told by my father always good, God-fearing lady she was."

From his narration, which was clear as the day he could recall it was on the auspicious Gudi Padwa, the springtime festival which marks the beginning of the New Year according to the lunisolar Hindu calendar. Agarwal had been told by his foster father that the shop had been acquired from a Muslim woman.

The property had been attached. Its owner (presumably Allarakhi) had crossed over to Pakistan. With the tacit consent of her relatives who had stayed back, and of the municipal authorities, it was auctioned to the highest bidder for a sum of a few thousand rupees. The legal papers had been preserved by the Agarwal family in a bank'ssafe-deposit vault.

"My father…may his soul rest in peace…felt the little shop was lucky for him. His business flourished. After vending a variety of goods – you know electrical parts and household essentials – we now have to live with the times. Technology, I tell you, is advancing by leaps and bounds. Cellphones are hot. There's no end to the new handsets coming in. Extra features, cameras…selfies ka craze is going *crazy*. Mind you, we don't sell cheap Chinese brands, only genuine goods. My father would be glad to see his son doing well."

Nishant Agarwal seemed to be in no hurry to return to the shop, explaining, "My sons look after it. I drop by once or twice a week. Anything else?"

"Yes, if you don't mind, could you tell me a bit about yourself. How come you said 'foster'? You were adopted?"

"Arre you know about the Yangtze, but can't guess why I'm an adopted son," Agarwal answered. "Simple, my parents back in Alwar had four sons. His elder brother had none; confirmed bachelor he was. So I was handed over…like a toy to my uncle. No hassles. After a few months, Uncle got married to a widow. We are practical people. Marrying a widow was much better than paying an ayah to look after me. Uncle and his wife pampered me, sent me to A-1 school, A-1 college. I completed B.Com. and looked after the shop even while studying. Life is beautiful, brother."

The happy, loquacious Agarwal had to be asked, "For you, everything has been smooth-going?"

"Yes, yes. Be positive, I say. I go by what Bhagwan Osho said, 'You feel good, you feel bad, and these feelings are bubbling from your own unconsciousness, from your own past. Nobody is responsible except you. Nobody can make you angry, and nobody can make you happy.' You can buy Osho books anywhere. Tell me, Rehaan, is something bothering you?"

"The owner of that little shop was my relative, Allarakhi. I am told she was killed during Partition."

"That cannot be," Agarwal assuaged Rehaan. "Father would tell me that she settled in Multan…who knows she could still be alive. Chalo, I will take your leave." He paid the bill at the counter and smiled at his visitor, "Drop in any time. Tell you what! I will talk to my auntyji. She's confined to bed, but her memory is stronger than any gymming equipment. I will call you in a day or two." They exchanged cellphone numbers. Agarwal clicked a selfie with his guest, ending with, "If your cell ever needs repair, you know where to come. No charge. Our shop is your shop. I take your leave, dear."

The dots weren't connecting. The ebullient Agarwal believed Allarakhi was a survivor; the embittered Abu Bakr had outlined a story to the contrary. Agarwal called as he had promised, "My auntyji doesn't remember anything about Allarakhiji. Gymming equipment also grows old, she's only human. We all have to go some day, no? Sorry. I wish I could have been of some more service. Must be difficult for you."

23

Fall Among the Pigeons

Shaken by Fayazi Ma's acceptance of her guilt by association, Rehaan's love for her was contaminated. He stopped speaking to her; she sulked. This mutual punishment by silence pained him. She wouldn't ask him whether he had warmed his dinner from the fridge. The next morning, it would be binned.

He returned home from work later than he would. He would notice her keeping a vigil from the balcony when he zipped past her room. She would pretend to be unconcerned. This wasn't the first time. Often, they had gone silent on trivial matters. She wouldn't utter a word for days, particularly when she suspected that he hadn't handed over every rupee from his monthly pay packet, which would at the time be given in cash. Even as the money increased, he would still be given 'pocket money', with a bonus on Ramzan Eid.

He didn't object to the money rationing. He would be overjoyed to see her content with a grandson who had done right by her. When he handed over his first pay, amounting to about 350 rupees, the stipend for the temporary job of a tutor at the St Xavier's College, she had touched him on the forehead, blessing him with, "May you rise higher and higher in life." He had, but not sufficiently to become independent. The apartment they lived in was bought with Fayazi Ma's money. She paid the bills with the interest accruing from bank fixed deposits. Journalism was a luxury, not a necessity. Unlike his peers, he didn't have to house-hunt, or crucially, succumb to expensive presents – bribes – to favour any worthy or unworthy person in print.

The silent warfare would last for a couple of days at the most. This time it had lasted close to a week. Probably, she had resolved to call a truce on Sunday. "Stop this, we have to speak." He was relieved. He nodded, "If you wish. After lunch, if that's okay with you."

Sunday mornings, he'd be scanning the papers in bed. Fayazi Ma hadn't insisted on the truce right away. She left to feed the pigeons grain and diced bread in the narrow corridor outside the apartment. The pigeons would gather there for the habitual feed. She would talk to them. They'd peck away at the grain, avoid the bread which would be later beaked away by the crows, less choosy about their diet. Then lunch would be served to the fussy grandson.

That Sunday was different. Jolted by her scream, Rehaan rushed to the corridor. Ma had slipped on a puddle left by a morning rainfall. She had to be taxied to the emergency section of the St Elizabeth's hospital. An X-ray confirmed a fracture of the right hip. She would have to be admitted for tests which could be carried out only the next day. The presiding doctor was away for the weekend. If Fayazi Ma was in pain, she endured it with silence except for the remark, "This is what you wanted, Papu." She rarely called him by the pet-name his birth mother had given him.

She was in hospital for a week. Despite her resistance, a one-hour surgery was performed, the bone was re-set. She could walk again perhaps after a month or two of intensive physiotherapy at home. Rehaan was ashamed. If only they had spoken when she wanted him to. If only he had not allowed her to venture out in the corridor on a wet morning, Ma and he would have exchanged recriminations at most. She would have spent the afternoon lolling on the drawing room's sofa, watching the afternoon movie on television.

If only he hadn't behaved churlishly, Ma wouldn't have had to go through unendurable pain. He requested his year's month of privilege leave from office. He would nurse Ma back to normal.

A part-time nurse had to be employed to be by her side, diaper her bed sores, complete her ablutions on a bedpan, feed her soups and soft fruit. The neighbours would take turns to drop by, and to keep her in good humour. The physiotherapist Roda Engineer, a young woman, would cajole her into a five-minute walk in the drawing room, its furniture re-arranged so there would be an empty lane for the patient to limp through with Herculean effort. From Delhi, Noor called to ask if she was needed. Rehaan said he would let her know if his ma's condition didn't improve.

Courtesy Roda, Fayazi Ma could walk again, first with the help of a handler and then with a medlar wood walking stick.

Forget the Aladia story, the wretched book. Rehaan could quit the pursuit of unhappiness. Ma, in his eyes, had suffered more than a hundred mothers could. Let life run its course. There was the newspaper he could re-immerse himself in. Abu Bakr was straining at the leash for his 25,000 rupees. The medical expenses had burnt a hole in the fixed deposit account. Pay off that Bakr, be done with it.

Fayazi Ma hadn't changed perceptibly. She asked Rehaan to resume massaging her feet. He pressed her toes gently, she looked at him gratefully. He got up to smell her hair which she would oil herself. Cautiously, he lifted her chin and drew her into an embrace. Ma would never permit that, she would never ever hug him. About the only overt signs of affection she would display was a peck on his forehead, and the tearful command whenever he had to catch an airflight, "You had better come back soon. I'll be counting the hours."

Restricted in her movement, dependent on spoonfed meals, Fayazi Ma had shrunk in size, her collar bones accentuated, her rib cage visible. She was gazing into the eye of a needle; she couldn't quite thread it. Her tongue curled up on her upper lip. Rehaan offered to help. For once, she surrendered, sighing, "Imagine, a seamstress now cannot handle a needle to mend her blouse. I was so good at it, but that was so long ago..." she trailed off.

Ma was determined to wear patched-up blouses and petticoats, topped by white cotton saris, bordered and occasional design printed, the pallu flung over the right shoulder carelessly. The grandson loved the sari which had flaming yellow cornstalks printed on white cotton. The prints she favoured would kill him – there was one showing repeated images of a boy fishing in a pond against the backdrop of a sunsrise. "That boy is you, fishing for his ma," she had told him. Immediately his eyes welled over. She had the talent to loosen his tear ducts.

As was his wont, Rehaanwas crying now, dabbing away the briny tears with the pallu of her cornstalk sari. She selected a key from a bunch, the key to her wooden cupboard which she guarded with her life. "Take out an envelope, the airmail envelope from the drawer there," she said sadly. "Bring it to me, and you can decide whether I'm guilty or not."

The unaddressed envelope contained a single English newspaper cutting. She asked him to take it to his room. Under the headline, "Homeless woman found dead on railway tracks", the cutting went on to add that her identity was unknown. No relatives had come forward to claim her body at the morgue of the J.J. Hospital. A small, cavalier news report tucked away in an inside page, it had been preserved in a Manila airmail envelope.

"That homeless woman was Allarakhi, my sister," she began to narrate as he sat at her feet on a withering carpet, which, like Ma's blouses and petticoats, should have been replaced ages ago. "She died right here, not at any Pakistani border. Abu Bakr was fed with lies by that bloody Chaudhran. Those are the lies which Bakr has taken as the truth, and which I suppose, you have swallowed as the truth."

Her eyes were a flood, her face crumpled. The grandson didn't want her to talk at that moment, he could do without the truth. He said, "Ma, let it be...rest now."

"I will rest only after I'm dead and gone, and you know that," her voice waned. "Allarakhi Aapa wished to cross over to Pakistan. The situation in Bombay troubled her. She was attacked with acid when she was sitting in her shop. She had covered her face just in the nick of time; her right arm and palm were a mess.

"The shop was torched to ashes. She hid at our house, the bungalow. Sir Osman offered her the choice of staying with us forever, as long as she was agreeable to occupying a room in the servants' quarters in the backyard. She was fine with that, but she wouldn't come out of the room – which was quite neat and comfortable I might tell you, shaded by the branches of a mango tree. She must have felt she wasn't an equal, a sister, anymore but what could I do? I couldn't have her lurking around in the fronthouse, visited as it was by high-society people. Sir Osman was even embarrassed of me. I would be introduced to the burra log. I would have to excuse myself and disappear. The butlers would serve them drinks – beer, gin, whisky – it wasn't correct for a Muslim woman to be in the company of men and women who smoked and drank. Neither did I know a word of English. I'd smile, say hello, how do you do? Retreat, go and sit with Allarakhi in her room till I was summoned back by the saab.

"Aapa became more hostile and withdrawn by the day. When she asked if she could go away to be with people of our faith, frankly I was relieved. I wouldn't have to deal with her presence in my house every day. I appealed for her safe passage to Multan, where Sir Osman had delegated his business interests to his less fortunate relatives. They would look after Allarakhi. Sir could be kind when it came to the rescue of Musalman people who were in turmoil all over the country. At our home in Bombay, there was no disturbance at all, except for the alarming radio broadcasts. I told Allarakhi she could wait for some months and then decide. Her shop was still there. We would get it repaired for her, she could return there when the madness stopped. And you know what she said, 'I don't want your sir's charity. I wish to leave immediately. I will find my own way.'

"That Mumtaz Chaudhran couldn't do anything. She was keeping a low profile. If she went out, it was with sindoor in her maang to convey that she was a Hindu woman. She's clever, you know; she can survive any catastrophe. Meanwhile, Allarakhi was becoming more and more restless, beyond control. She would crash Sir's parties, curse him and his guests. She would have to be pulled back and locked up in her room by the butlers. My heart bled for her. I wanted to keep her with us; for her that wasn't good enough. She was always soft in the head, poor poor Aapa. God's own child she was, innocent and fragile."

Rehaan intervened, "Ma, stop crying. We can talk about this later."

"Later or now, what's the difference? Allarakhi Aapa wouldn't touch a drop of water, a morsel of food. She would gape at the walls of her room as if we had imprisoned her. Chief Butler Hashim Nabi Khan had been with the Osman

Baksh Mitha family ever since he was a boy. So faithful, so loyal, we all thought. But he was the devil. He would unlock Aapa's little room and express his sympathy with her. He would speak bad things about me, about Seth; he convinced her that we wanted her out of our lives. To be honest, Sir Osman did. After all, which wealthy man will tolerate a mental case barging into his evening parties?"

"Please don't tell me what I dread to hear, Ma."

"Dread is another word for fear. Who doesn't have fears, child? When you were a child...you still are...didn't I tell you that you shouldn't dread those school and college examinations of yours. You just had to concentrate on the correct questions and answers, top every examination you did. That worked for you, didn't it?"

"It wasn't easy Ma. I felt horribly pressured...about emerging the topper, every month at the tests, every year at the examinations."

"Nothing comes easy. In any case, I wasn't asking Allarakhi to top anything. I was begging her to overcome her fears."

"If she wasn't in her senses, how could she?"

"She wasn't, and her condition was aggravated by that swine Hashim. He could seduce a stone. A rugged, well-spoken Pathan, I may tell you he was easy on the eyes, even beautiful. Any woman would have mistaken him to be an aristocrat if it wasn't for his butler's white uniform with a red cummerbund. For me, Sir Osman was my saviour. Despite his short height and bald head, he had a certain glow on his face which comes with good food and drink – he would sip pomegranate juice while his guests drowned themselves in liquor. To be honest, on occasion, it would seem Hashim was Sir Osman's master. His attraction stemmed from his perfect manners and the beauty he was born with. Do you know once Hashim had the nerve to touch me inappropriately? I slapped him across the face but didn't have the courage to tell on him. Sir could have taken it badly, he would have blamed me for encouraging Hashim. That fucker didn't dare to try his tricks out on me again. I would have beaten up the maadarchod with a stick till he begged for mercy. Allarakhi Aapa, I'm afraid, wasn't as strong-willed as me. She was like a child. He would narrate stories to her, he would keep her amused. She took to him. But she would never let him touch her. I think, she wouldn't let anyone touch her as if she would break into pieces. I like to think that swine Hashim must have kept his distance. I hope he did."

"Ma, that man should have been taken to the police."

The newspaper report about Allarakhi was the affirmation of Fayazi Ma's story.

Hashim had connived in Allarakhi's move to Pakistan. A fellow Pathan had been brought in by the butler to Sir Osman who trusted Hashim with his own life.

"The money given to the Pathan was divided between the contracted transporter and Hashim who had a plan of his own. He would set up his own business in the land of his faith. Hashim would cross over to Multan, persuade the mentally askew Allarakhi into marriage, or just barter her to the highest bidder. Women were easy prey for him. Do you remember Sakina Bano at all, the woman who would dust and sweep the bungalow during your schooldays? The fellow had got her pregnant...she had told me that, but Hashim denied that outright. Sakina Bano had a husband in Kolsa Mohalla. He would vend boiled eggs on streetsides. She didn't get along with him and had stayed on with me at the bungalow for four or five years, taking leave on Sundays to check on the eggwalla of hers. Sir Osman was furious when he heard of Sakina Bano's condition. She was sacked on the spot, she left cursing Hashim. After that, we never heard of her again. I should have listened to her. Allarakhi should never have been confined to the servants' quarters. He must have told her that he would protect her like a brother would.

"Allarakhi Aapa had never let me know of what was going on," Fayazi Ma continued. "Then that awful, awful news came. When her body was sent for post-mortem, the reports said there was evidence of violence and traces of a sedative...I can't say more child, whether it was..."

"I don't want to hear more."

"Rehaan, since you've been after my blood, about the truth, truth, truth, let me say what I have to. Hashim disappeared into the night. Sir Osman used all his influence with the police, the collector. He even claimed to have writtten a letter to Pandit Nehru, but at that time, Sir's influence had become nothing more than a formality. The nation had more important things to do than to spare time and effort to do justice to my sweet, naïve Aapa. According to the cursory inquiry made by the police, Allarakhi was strangled and left to be found on the railway tracks between the Charni Road and Grant Road railway stations. Whatever jewellery, money and clothes she had were missing except for the salwar kameez and dupatta she was wearing. Do you want to see her clothes? They're right below my saris in the cupboard."

She insisted that the clothes be brought to her. Rehaan had to. Fayazi Ma smelt them, wept into them, dried her eyes with the fold of her cornstalk sari and said, "Go and put them back properly where you found them."

Rehaan felt he was carrying her, his Allarakhi Nani, back to her grave.

Fayazi Ma implored, "Now leave me alone. I would like to get some sleep."

Rehaan said she needed to have her dinner, which he would warm up, and administer her, her round of medicines. He would have to add a mild transquilliser. She would sleep soundly.

"No medicines for me today, Rehaan bache," she called him over, and gave him the trademark peck on her forehead. He helped to complete her ablutions for the night, tucked her into bed after a round of vigorous mutthi.

Soon Fayazi Ma was snoring lightly, as she always did. He slept early that night, too.

In the morning, she was still sleeping. Fearing the worst, he shook her shoulder lightly. She did not stir. He crouched by her side, checked her pulse. She opened her eyes and grinned toothlessly, "I'm alive bache. What did you think? There's no chance of this old woman ever leaving you alone so soon."

She didn't resist his embrace, and asked, "That bungalow of ours, will you take me there one more time…when you can find the time?"

"You won't like what you see."

She had never returned to 35, Land's End Road where the seven islands of the city ended. The bungalow, a colonial Edwardian marvel with a never-ending row of chambers, a three-storey apartment building which was used to accommodate guests, a kitchen as large as the front-garden divided into three sections – for a lawn with bursts of flower beds, chickoo and papaya trees and vegetable patches – two garages for a Dodge and Wolseley, and the one-storey servants' quarters, had been demolished.

When Sir Osman passed away, Rehaan was just out of school. The ISC results were awaited. The will was a cat's cradle of confusion. The trustee appointed from the upper-crust Bhabha family had not been consulted. J.C. Bhabha backed out as the will's trustee. He managed a bank, he had enough on his plate. The Estate Duty department took over the marvel, where three nondescript towers stand now. Grade-1 government officials live there, clueless about the estate's history, or of the existence of Fayazi Ma who had once kept the bungalow spotless, the grass manicured, the flowers and trees watered and nourished twice a day. The tall wrought-iron gates, now mottled green, were still there.

Allarakhi died by strangulation. Whether Rehaan liked it or not, Fayazi Ma was guilty for being cavalier. Unpardonable but a mother cannot be held guilty by a son, a grandson.

Ma was lapsing into poorer health. Rehaan had to hang on to her. Like a biased judge, he declared his ma not guilty.

24

She's Gone

Naa yeh chand hoga naa tare rahenge
Magar hum hamesha tumhare rahenge

Bicchadkar chale jaayen tumse kahin
Toh yeh naa samajhna mohabbat nahin
Jahaan bhi rahen hum tumhare rahenge

Na yeh chand hoga…

The moon and the stars won't be the same anymore
Yet I will always be yours

If I go away
It's not because I do not love you
Whevever I may be
I will always be yours

The moon and stars won't be the same anymore…

That song, lyrics by S.H. Bihari and composed by Hemant Kumar, from the 1954 film Shart, *Fayazi Ma would hum far too frequently in her tremulous voice, to remind him of her mortality. Rehaan would be alone, but she would never leave him.*

That song was playing on the radio, on its early morning slot, a day or two ago. On 10 May, she passed away in her sleep, her face placid, her eyes shut like a walkie-talkie doll's, her mouth partially open as if she wanted him to close her lips for the last time. No more medication, no more enforced meals, no more spoons of glucose water.

Rehaan had rushed to her room, on waking up early, to receive his birthday peck on the cheek and the brush of her right hand on his hair, her blessings as he always would. She would pick at her prayer beads, ask for the moon and stars for her boy, and maybe there would be a box of chocolates for him to distribute among the colleagues he got along with at the office.

The box of chocolates was there. Ma wasn't breathing. She had gone. He didn't feel numb; he was floating, crying himself a river. The doorbell rang. The trusty domestic help, Najma, who'd been detected with arthritis, was reporting for work on the dot of 8 a.m. She read his face; she howled, "No, Bai cannot do this." Neighbours gathered. One of them informed his office, flipped through the telephone diary by the landline for the relatives to be informed about the last rites which would be performed after the late afternoon salat-al-asrnamaaz. The burial couldn't wait till Noor could catch the first flight out of Delhi. Mumtaz Chaudhran and Shuhaba shouldn't be informed, that was Ma's express instruction. They showed up, nevertheless. The Chaudhran shuffled into a chair, looked on beady-eyed. Shubaba took charge of the last rites.

Rehaan was not there, as if he had injected himself with local anaethesia. He saw without seeing; he heard without hearing. He didn't care about the condolences. Six mullahs from the closest mosque chanted passages from the Quran for her safe journey to another plane. Najma, reciting an inaudible prayer, gave his ma her last bath, covered her body with a white sheet, starched without a crease. Lillies, roses and chunky jasmine garlands materialised in the home where there had never been any before. The aroma of sandalwood incense sticks evaporated, columns of ash fell on the apology of a floral carpet. Rehaan was told to take a last look at her before the body was transported in an ambulance to the Bada Qabrastan for interrment. The money had been kept for the rituals in a white envelope marked "For Ma". He asked Najma if she could get him a lock of his mother's hair to keep with him forever. She had done that without his asking.

For the last time, he kissed Ma's forehead, smelt her hair – the shampoo it had been washed with was overpowering, chemicaled. He strode around the room to see her from different angles, the way he would at a painting in an art gallery. She looked radiant, beautiful; no indication of regret that she was leaving him. The moon and the stars…who needed them?

The crowd was unexpectedly large. Only males are permitted to enter the graveyard. The women stayed back home, their faces appropriately grim, their conversation underscoring her virtues – she was kind, she was God-fearing, look how she cared for her grandson, and look how he cared for her. Let's hope he doesn't have a breakdown. Dr Abhay Mehta SMS'd, "Sorry to hear about your irreparable loss. Be strong." Yes sure, Doc, as if strength implied indifference.

The stretcher was light, she had become a former shadow of herself. At the qabrastan, he was told there was no more room for an exclusive grave for her. She would have to share it, the qabrastan's caretaker announced, with other souls departed in the last few months. If Rehaan wanted a tombstone, he would have to use influence, pay money under the table to the municipal ward officers. It would take a week or two, but it could be done. Fayazi Ma wouldn't have approved. Rehaan didn't say a word, neither 'yes' nor 'no', which meant 'no'. Ma would be buried with the others. He hoped there was no afterlife. He hoped this was the end. He couldn't imagine her mingling with the dead. She didn't take to strangers; she could be condescending, querulous. Rehaan let the qabrastan's soil fall from between his fingers slowly onto the body...it was covered before he could throw more flowers into the pit. He excused himself from the mourners whose faces were a blur – the few celebrities, the doctors who had attended to her, her physiotherapist Roda, his office colleagues, the neighbours who turned up in large numbers to guage how much he was crying, or how much he wasn't. Grief is measured by the volume of tears shed.

At home, Mumtaz Chaudhran and Shuhaba were joined by Noor in the evening. Jameela Begum was far too ill and lost in her transistor to make the trip. Abu Bakr and Abu Fazl were conspicuous by their presence. What were they doing there? Forget it, Rehaan. Remember Ma had said, "Do not allow anyone to attend my funeral." Did she mean it? Unlikely.

Float he did, through the chautha, the fourth-day lunch, prepared by specialist funeral caterers, served to priests and whoever came to the house that afternoon. He wouldn't have gone through the ritual if Ma hadn't been a stickler for Islamic tenets. This is what she would have wanted.

Her will, on stamp paper, left him all her property, jewellery and assets. The lawyer grinned stupidly, "You and your next two generations can live the rest of your lives in peace now. She was a rich lady." The lawyer was shushed up by his assisant, "Sir, he is single. No more generations." The lawyer grinned some more, "Great! You can lead a rich man's life now. Congratulations!" Bastard, shut up.

Rehaan shut himself in his room. He felt her absence in the room separated from his by a wall, the emptiness. Najma had to leave for her village in sync with her yearly month's leave. She could delay that by a few days if need be. No need Najma, he gave her a packet of money and one of his mother's gold bangles which she never wore. Najma nodded with gratitude. He embraced her and was ashamed of himself – all he could register at that moment was that she was stinking. "You can have a bath here," he blurted out loud. Najma said it was kind of him to think of a help bathing in the house, but she would bathe only after returning to the village. She ran her hand through his hair, like his ma would have.

The Oshiwara and Delhi relatives left as quickly as they had arrived. They had fulfilled their duty. Najma said, "Bai would have been glad...they came and prayed for her. I'm surprised Ferozi and Ameena didn't bother. After all, they could have also caught a train to Bombay."

Najma was aware that Ferozi and Ameena had cut off all ties with the Humshira, their sisters. Before she left for the village, Najma was curious. Why hadn't Rehaan attempted to contact them? They were settled in Ajmer for the longest time. How come he wasn't curious about them at all.

"I am, Najma," the writer in Rehaan spoke up. "But they seem to have guarded their privacy fiercely. Are they alive? I don't even know they are in Ajmer."

"Nothing can be hidden forever, baba," Najma said. "Bai told me that you were talking to all her sisters...for a book or something. She wasn't happy about this, but she said she couldn't stop you either. It was when she was delirious that she told me about her sisters in Ajmer, but she could have been just imagining. Whether they are alive or not, go, go there…you can visit the Ajmer Sharif dargah at least…you need a holiday from what you have gone through."

Holiday? Just what he didn't need. He had to keep the Aladia sisters far-removed from him. Ma gone, and he still felt imprisoned. He needed her to be there, he needed to be answerable to someone but to himself. He saw Najma off to the door, and said politely, "Yes, I will take a holiday."

The stories of Ameena and Ferozi didn't interest him sufficiently. They had no secrets. Simple women who wouldn't add any drama to his novel. He shut the door, logged on to his computer after a week. There was a message from Nauman Ali on his email, "Sincere condolences for your loss. And thank you for a making a fool of me, Shaheen. You are a disgusting person. Allah haafiz."

Nauman's message made him feel lighter. A distraction from his loss. The departure of Ma weighed on his mind. He logged on to the moon-stars song on YouTube. It sounded ridiculous.

He wasn't the first or the last person to lose his mother, he reasoned. Get real. Only, he had lost two mothers. Forget them, forget Fayazi Ma if you can; you must. He smelt the lock of her hair, her clothes, the armchair she sat in, the plate she ate from. He was living in the museum of his savior mother. He had to alter the apartment, break down the walls between his room and hers. He would live in her room as well as his. The restructuring of the house was assigned to an interior decorator of his acquaintance. It would take a month or two, some more, to make it habitable.

He moved into a rented room close to his office, wandered the streets of Flora Fountain, ate at mid-rung cafés, slaved away at the office. There was a still a fortnight to complete the apartment. So Ajmer it was. Ameena and Ferozi wouldn't be welcoming or polite. That would have to be handled. A reporter's religion was to get an attainable version of the truth. If the truth of these sisters was inadequate, he could scrap their story from the novel or whatever there was of it. Instead of six sisters, he'd make them into four sisters, revise the earlier chapters. A writer can be the executioner of his characters, and no one would be the wiser.

On second thoughts, journalism meant sticking to facts. He could neither be an executioner nor a life-giver. Be objective, don't impose your opinions (unless it was one of those 'thought' pieces on the edit page); the newspaper had become a load to carry for the writer – it was the polar opposite of his creative impulses. Whether he was capable of being creative was another story. He re-read the first few chapters of the novel. He wasn't sure if it was the absolute truth. Clearly, there was empathy for the sisters. He couldn't imagine a pack of brothers who would have done what the sisters had. The girls' escape from Qalayat was novel. Published or not, their story had to reach a point of closure.

Rehaan explained this to the newspaper's chief editor, whose terse answer was, "You may write what you wish in your spare time. However, I cannot give you any more leave. As it is, I'm not happy with your output."

His proposal for a six-month sabbatical was shot down. "The print medium is going through a paradigm shift," the editor editorialised. "We need all hands on deck."

Rehaan resigned from the newspaper after a stint of 12 years. A farewell function on a restaurant rooftop, a going away gift of a wall-clock and a carton of crystal whisky glasses later, his colleagues and the Sphinx-faced editor raised a toast, "Here's to a jolly good fellow."

Jolly? He was dying inside. Karmarkar sidled up to him, "You lucky devil. You don't need your pittance of a salary. You can do any shit you want. I'm telling you, it's never too late. Get yourself a woman. Haven't you ever fallen in love? Even if you haven't, doesn't matter. Just go out and get laid."

Rehaan tried to laugh, he couldn't. The farewell party was a farce, no one was going to miss him. Karmarkar heckled, "If you leave now, it won't be noticed. Go man, get a life. I'll give you the address of the most discreet hotel in Colaba, in a lane, kind of a lodge, to go to right now. I'll send your farewell gifts home tomorrow, not to worry. Mention my name to the man at the counter there, he'll give you a discount. Nice girls there, clean. If Shabnam is free, she'll make your night."

Karmarkar prattled on, edging Rehaan to leave the terrace where the bar was just about to run dry. The editor had left. A clutch of colleagues was requesting the jitterbugging deejay to switch to Bollywood tracks. They were about to dance as if their hips had come unhinged, as they always did at the newspaper's annual celebrations. A remix of "Mehbooba Mehbooba" from Sholay *was blaring. The night to bid farewell to a senior colleague underlined Rehaan's conviction that it was time for him to pack up for the night, and from journalism.*

He told the middle-aged taxi driver to take him to Kennedy Bridge, without knowing what he would do there once he reached the compound which was once the turf of Mumtaz Chaudhran, his beloved ma's sister and mentor.

The taxi driver halted outside the rusting iron gate of the compound, and said, "I can take you to a better place. The brothels here are not good enough for you. You seem to be from a decent family."

The passenger said hazily, "What makes you say that?"

The taxi driver shrugged," Just saying. I know where you can get any kind of girl, A to Z quality," read the fare from the metre, and on receiving a tip, said happily, "Have a good time, mister."

Enrircled by a group of touts, Rehaan with dazed eyes, scanned the brightly lit red and green windows. When they offered to get him a woman – will it be for an hour or a whole night? – he was nauseous. He despised himself at that moment, he felt depraved. He was led by the most enthusiastic tout towards a mosque in the compound, up the stairs towards a room with a bed, a table with a plastic bottle of mineral water, and agarbattis smoking the scent of sandalwood, as they had done by the side of his Fayazi Ma's lifeless body. He sat at the foot of the bed, a calendar showing the image of poet Omar Khayyam with a jug of wine and a woman entwined around him, hung crookedly above the bed. He straightened it, a neatnik habit. The tout returned with half-a-dozen women, thickly powdered and nylon sari-clad, who were lined up before him. "Take your time," he said seriously. "You can select the one you want. No charge for looking. Decide, all same rate. Let me know if you want for two hours or for full night. If you haven't brought protection, I will arrange."

Rehaan felt a surge of independence. He was free to make love like he never had, without guilt or remorse. The women waited, as if they had been drained of life. He couldn't look at them. He left the room, the bed, casting an eye at the bottle of mineral water. Did anyone drink from that bottle? This world is not for you. You're too damned confused about your sexuality, he told himself. Get out of here, or you'll never forgive yourself. The tout grinned, "All clean, there's no illness-villness here." The women looked on expressionlessly. They would be paraded like criminals at an identification procedure. They were used to it.

Running into the night, Rehaan finally stood at a distance from the compound. He was afraid. He was being watched by his Ma. She would know that he was losing his balance. He walked on, down the bridge, towards his home. He would keep walking. It would take an hour, two maybe.

He was tired of himself, spent. As he rested his head on the pillow, he went blank. His ma's voice rose, sepulchral, and addressed him, "Bache, have you loved anyone?"

"Love?" he crossed his heart. "I have only loved you, Ma, and always will. The moon and the stars won't be the same anymore. Yet I will always be yours."

25

Ameena, Eye, Ferozi, Short

In his redesigned apartment, he felt asphyxiated, cooped up, windows clamped shut to muffle the hammering at the apartment being renovated next door. He had subjected the neighbours to the noise himself. He had no right to get tetchy.

The months – must be three or four – after Ma's interrment, were a formal exercise in self-improvement, change. He'd take off for two-hour-long walks through Mumbai's Lamington Road precinct. He'd click photographs of the fast-vanishing monuments, and the deteriorating ones, in main the cinema theatres – Naaz, Swastik, Apsara, Novelty, Shalimar – where Ma would take him, bellowing at anyone tall, who dared to obstruct her boy's clear view of the screen. "We didn't pay good money to see your big fat head," she'd storm. The offender would sink into his seat.

Rehaan needed to talk, work, write, read. He couldn't. Detachment from his surroundings would help. He was told it usually does. Childhood can't be exhumed, a watchdog called it Banquo's ghost who stays within. But but but, a holiday from what? He had to catch up with two absentees, Amina of the one blind eye, and Ferozi, the short, and he hoped, the likeable one. Whether the rest of the Humshira had boycotted the twins, or whether the twins had boycotted them, hadn't ever been discussed in detail before him.

All he could now suspect was that they were alive in Ajmer somewhere. The Aladia family lore had claimed they had achieved a semblance of notoriety as joint authors of pulp detective paperbacks in Urdu, commonly known as jasoosi novels. Perhaps they didn't wish to belong to the Aladia clan. They had meshed their names into a male's – Afroz. After all, women couldn't be sleuth storytellers. Afroz had become a best-seller during the 1960s and 1970s. Their detective hero went by the name of Jasoos Habib Chacha, a senior citizen presumably modelled after Agatha Christie's Hercule Poirot.

They'd be some pair, probably way more stable than their sisters. Rehaan allowed himself an affectionate smile. Evidently, they'd been educated in Urdu. Perhaps they would be civil to him, even glad to receive a long-lost nephew – technically a grand-nephew, but then he still saw his ma's sisters as his aunts...quite simply a generational adjustment.

A bad traveller complains about delayed flights, train connections, hotels with paper-thin walls, burping plumbing systems and micro-ovened buffets. The trip had to be an endeavour at self-improvement: to seek new opportunities, revive his self-esteem, find a new version of himself, stop being so feeble...a morose frog in the well. Rubbish. Just go Rehaan, go, to the unusual suspects in your Aladia story. Get to Ajmer right away. If the temperatures are soaring there at 38° at the outset of June, it couldn't be worse than the humidity of Mumbai, still in suspense about the onset of the monsoon. The rains will have arrived by the time you return. Plan a four or five-day get away.

He had passed through Ajmer, encircled by the Aravalli mountain range, on a drive from Jaipur to New Delhi. He had stopped at the Ajmer Sharif dargah, where he could stop again. His ma and Najma would have wanted him to. And it wouldn't be too crowded either. The annual Pushkar Camel Fair in November, photographed by travel magazines, swarming with tourists, was far away on the calendar. The surviving flower children – hippies they were once known as – wouldn't be there. The unseasonal ones would be hanging around the Pink Floyd Café. Maybe Rehaan could try out a chillum, go for grass. Hell, he had to unwind, and more importantly, renew the novel, that's if the Afroz detective twosome would allow him to...if they existed.

The memory of visiting Ajmer as a child with Sir Osman Baksh Mitha and Fayazi Ma were indistinct. They had stayed overnight at a serai, an inn run by a local family. It probably wasn't there anymore. Used to an economy budget, he would book himself online at a three-star, The Swan. It had to be an improvement on Qalayat's strange Super Hotel. As for locating the Afroz pair, it could be difficult but not impossible. He requested a Mumbai-based trustee of the waqf of the Ajmer Sharif dargah to message the clergy there, to lead him to the aunts, grand-aunts.

Surely, they would know of the two ageing Muslim women who must be visiting the dargah regularly. The dargah is the shrine of the Sufi saint, Moinuddin Chishti. There are so many stories related to the shrine. One of them was about a water-bearer, Nizam Sikka, who had saved the life of the 16th-century

Mughal emperor Humayun. As a reward, he was appointed sovereign of the empire for a day. The tomb of the water-bearer was located inside the dargah.

Dargahs attracted Rehaan. The incalculable number of beggars, the hustlers outside the shrine, the young khadims trained in the calligraphy of recording donations in a voluminous ledger, wouldn't allow him a moment with himself. He accepted that. There would be a quiet spot where he could sit on the marble floor, sway to the impromptu qawwalis, watch the devout, wonder what was going on in their minds. Were they as restless as him? Of course, they were. He looked forward to assimilating into the crowd.

The roadway to the dargah is a long and winding one, thick with stalls, shops and instant meals from pot-bellied degchis. Shoes deposited with a caretaker outside, he inched forward in the melee to find a khadim, one of the attendants appointed by the trustees. An apple-cheeked, rotund young man was expecting him, "I recognise you. You have come from Mumbai. We are at your service." He sounded as programmed as a voicemail. "My name is Munnawar. You can call me Munna if you like. Take care of your cellphone and wallet, sir. Even at sacred places, thieves are at work. They are poor…they have to steal." A flower chaddar had to be picked first and then a cover of thin synthetic green cloth with gold thread trimmings, which could be bought at rates varying from 100 rupees to 5,000 rupees. Rehaan chose a chaddar for 500 rupees and donated 1,000 rupees to the ledger. The khadim was disappointed, "You have come from so far, sir. Open your heart and your every wish will be granted." The sum of the donation was doubled.

Rehaan was pressed into the shrine. He placed his head on the flower-bedecked mausoleum. He wished his ma well. She must have found a comfortable perch under Allah's protection. In the low-ceilinged limestone office of the trust, which belonged to a lost century, he saw a wooden chest serving as the desk, a modest chandelier tinkling above and a whirring fan which was dangerously close to smashing a couple of naked light bulbs which were on even though the room was bathed by the afternoon's ochre rays.

Munna suggested that Rehaan meet the senior mullahs of the dargah, but they would grant him audience only after the sun had set. There was something shifty about the khadim. He asked for a selfie, a flash of smilies, and then Munnawar came right down to the nitty gritty, "Saab, I know you are searching for two old ladies, the Afroz mohataramas. I don't have the permission to take on such a responsibility, but if you wish, I could arrange this tomorrow morning. Does 9 suit you? I will be in the lobby of the Swan Hotel, on the dot of time. Please don't be late."

In effect, the khadim was offering a short-cut to the search. The senior mullahs could be skipped. Munnawar nodded conspiratorially, "This will remain between us only. I beg your pardon, but I am poor too. I could do with some charity. English mein education toh huyi nahin...didn't acquire an education in English. I lead an honest life, helping the needy such as you."

Needy, right. Rehaan gave him 500 rupees in advance. The khadim's face fell. He was promised more, once he had taken him to the doorstep of the mohataramas. The address was withheld. Naturally. Every search has a price. This wasn't especially taxing on Rehaan's wallet, his ma's will had seen that he would never have to think of money again. Neither would he squander the nest-egg, nor multiply the money's bank interest rates by investing in mutual funds. His profile at the bank was 'conservative'. They had quit offering him special investment deals. Mutual funds? No, thank you.

"How do you know I am at The Swan?" the visitor inquired.

The khadim pumped his right hand and said, "At the dargah, we know about every visitor who comes from a big city, sir." Wary that he was sounding like a know-all, Munna corrected himself, "Just joking, sir. We were informed from Mumbai by our trustee saab when to expect you and at which hotel you could be found. I hope they gave you a good rate. Or I can organise a more suitable hotel."

The Swan was as good as it gets. Rehaan took leave of the khadim and said he would be waiting for him at the foyer the next morning. The journalist within him was near-extinct, or he would have checked out the Pink Floyd Café. Maybe he would hear the Floyd lines, "Run, rabbit, run / Dig that hole, forget the sun / And when at last, the work is done / Don't sit down, it's time to dig another one." Or he could have cabbed it to the Adhai Din ka Jhopda mosque, believed to be constructed at the command of Muhammad Ghori of the Ghurid dynasty, by Hindu masons in two-and-a-half days, in the 12th century on the remains of a Sanskrit college.

Monuments in a state of neglect, with communal undertones, were ideal for a news story. Spiked with fresh facts, it could have made the front page of The Daily Chronicle, *if he was still employed there. The report would have to be non-partisan, omitting the Muslim-Hindu divide which reeled back to the forgotten centuries. "Idiot," Rehaan shut himself up. "Journalism is out of your blood. It's not the same anymore, is it? Reeelax."*

The hotel choc-a-bloc with plaster of Paris lopsided swans of all colours and dimensions, was oddly calming. He felt at ease in his suite, watched a soap on television, called room service for a chicken burger with fries and a beer. "But Sir," said the service voice, "beer not possible today. Dry day," and after a pause added covertly, "Cola we can send...with rum. Yes?"

Ajmer was no different from Mumbai. There were ploys to flout every rule. "Yes, please," the Swan guest reacted. The room service voice persisted, "Shall we send you two drinks or three?" He settled for two – a compromise. Swigging three at one go would have been so blasphemous after a visit to the dargah. Two made it less sinful.

Sleep wouldn't come easy. The banes of his travel, thin walls – an infant howled for hours in the next room – and the burping plumbing kept him wide awake. Quit complaining; it won't help. He counted sheep behind his shuttered eyes, which never worked. Around midnight, he dared to knock himself out by ordering one more rum and cola. It was sent over with an added surcharge. Unpleasantly high, Rehaan slept for a couple of hours. Then abandoning himself to a cold-water bath in a ceramic-tub festooned with swan stickers, he quacked idiotically. A buffet breakfast– scrambled eggs, toast, cut fruit, orange juice– in the dining hall, and time laboured towards 9 a.m.

An hour, two hours later, no show. Rehaan would have to return to the dargah. Perhaps the khadim couldn't get away from his daily chores. He looked through the courtyard for Munna. He inquired at the office. An elderly mullah told him that the khadim hadn't turned up, he was unreliable. Then he pulled out a ledger and asked if Rehaan wanted to make a donation. Befuddled, Rehaan said he had already made his donation. There was no notation, no record. "Achha," the mullah closed the ledger. "I will have to inquire into this. What can I do for you?" Rehaan mentioned the names, Ferozi, Ameena…Afroz… The mullah said gravely, "We cannot help you. They are dead for us. They wouldn't dare to come here, they wrote behuda novels. We do not approve of heathens."

Rehaan picked up his shoes. The caretaker waited for a tip. Looking at the pittance of a few rupees, he said, "That's all? Be more generous and I will show you the way. Munna is waiting for you there…" he said pointing towards a decrepit two-storey building down a narrow lane. A higher-denomination note handed over, Rehaan walked towards the lane, to be called out by Munna into a motor garage, "Sir, sir…sorry. I let you down. Mullah Hazrat Saab has forbidden me to help you. I cannot take you to meet Aminaji and Feroziji. They are considered to be kaafirs around here. They have been insulting our faith for years…long before I was born."

"What do you mean, Munna?" Rehaan felt his anger rise. "Don't speak in riddles."

"I can't say more, sir, but…"

"But what?"

Money would facilitate the answer. It did. Munna said, "I will WhatsApp you the address."

"Their address? Just tell it to me."

"It is the address of the man who would publish what they had been writing. No one knows where they are. Maybe he does."

The WhatsApp read Anand Sablok, Nayee Soch *Publishers, Purani Mandir, Chudi Market. Rehaan headed there to find that the publishing firm had stopped functioning at least a decade ago. Fortuitously, Neeraj Sablok, a shrivelled prune of a man, sat on a grimy, striped mattress amidst stacks of files, unsold copies of books which had mottled with age, bottles of homeopathy pills, steel containers, probably empty, and a dehydrated tulsi plant which grew out of a dusty beer pint bottle. Sablok was as small as the room. He looked at the visitor with resigned eyes and didn't say a word, as if he was used to strangers arriving for a random inspection. He unfurled the day's Hindi newspaper and folded the pages, noisily.*

The visitor announced his name. Again silence. This could have gone on forever. Sablok was either senile or speech-impaired, or both. Rehaan cleared his throat, self-consciously, hoping that the man would acknowledge his existence. Not a word. Perhaps he needed a password. Rehaan drew closer to him and said, "Ameena and Ferozi…Afroz."

The publisher looked at him with febrile eyes. He pressed a shrill electronic bell. A squat, grey-haired woman draped in a brinjal purple nylon sari bustled into the room, "What is it, Papa?", freezing on noticing the visitor. "What is it?" she said irritably. "Papa is not to be disturbed."

"I am sorry, ma'am," Rehaan said. "I just wanted to know about the two women whose books were published by Nayee Soch. *They are related to me."*

"What, how dare you come here?" the woman looked at Rehaan with as much hatred as she could summon up at that instant. "Those damn floozies…we should have never published

their rubbish. After years, we are still facing the consequences of those books they wrote, the work of infidels."

This was going too fast. He would have to placate the woman, convince her that he meant no harm. If he had come to dredge the past, it was because he had lost track of his grand-aunts. Politely he told her, "I have come here to make amends if I can, ma'am."

The woman hid Sablok from the visitor's view, flung out her right hand, and showed him the door. "Please, if there are any books of theirs, I would like to buy them," Rehaan said politely. Her anger was mounting, "Every copy has been burnt. All we have left are school mathematics books which no one wants anymore. What would you pay for those women's books even if there were any left?"

"I don't know," Rehaan said nonplussed. Just then, the father had a coughing fit. She rushed out to fetch a glass of water. Sablok muttered, "Sit, sit beside me. Don't mind Sir, my daughter has never understood books and publishing. If she had, we wouldn't be in this pitiful state today. Sit, sit, she shouldn't have been rude to you. Every guest is sent by Bhagwan."

Sablok had feigned the coughing fit. As soon as his daughter returned with a steel tumbler of water, he said benignly, "Come come, let's hear what our guest has to say. I was told by Munna about him. I've been expecting him."

The daughter eased up, she had to. The old man was far too fragile to be disobeyed. With fluency, for well over an hour – interrupted by the popping of homeopathy pills – he narrated the case of the two jasoos novelists, whom he had pseudonymed Afroz. Perfect, he had believed, for the two sisters were bright and would chatter away non-stop, "How they ate up my head till stuffed radish paranthas were cooked and ready for them. Both pretty little women. Ameena...aaah that Ameena it was to whom I had suggested that she wear dark glasses to hide her bad eye. And Ferozi was so petite and flirty. She would even call me handsome and desirable. Yes, desirable. Imagine. She made me feel like a man."

Rehaan switched on his cellphone recorder in his shirt pocket. Sablok was a raconteur. Every word of his had to be relished. The story by itself was ribald and racy. The sisters had arrived at the very same room with a manuscript, handwritten in Urdu, describing the exploits of a middle-aged Muslim detective, Jasoos Habib Chacha, who was facing a marital crisis. He neglected his begum to solve other marriages, sniff out affairs, and organised separations with incriminating photographs he would click on an Agfa Synchro Box camera.

The plot was as lurid as any 150-pager, bootlegged from the 1950s Olympia Press of Paris, which would be vended at railway stations, on pavement book shops and at Sablok's retail outlet which had once functioned beneath his home. The sisters had added a twist to the serial tales. Habib Chacha was conceived of as a god of sexuality, an avatar of the mythological Kamadeva. Pages would be devoted to the detective's libido which could be rarely satisfied by his begum. The detective frequented brothels, he seduced women who were into flaming affairs. If a woman client was chaste, he couldn't disappoint her either. To her delight, he would trap her into bedroom liaisons, click her stark naked and one more story would be complete. All the characters received their just desserts. Habib Chacha would have torrid affairs, only as a professional duty.

The affairs would be described in lascivious pornographic detail. Sisters Ameena and Ferozi were either gifted with a limitless imagination about sexual foreplay and repeated the phrase "the final sword-like plunge" or they had cleverly plagriarised the Olympia Press porn. It was emphasised that women wouldn't have to fake orgasms; with a compatible partner they could be taken to the heights of ecstasy. Detailed sexual positions, the sound effects, aahs-and-oohs, the smutty talk – where was this coming from? Sablok hadn't dared to question his best-selling duo. They weren't married as far as he knew, and their behaviour in public was exemplary. They would show up at his publishing firm in burqas, and keep their faces veiled till they reached his room.

Nayee Soch *flourished. The sisters were paid their dues, even if they periodically asked for a quantum hike in royalties. The orders placed for Habib Chacha's sexual exploits were especially high from Delhi. Pirated copies began emerging from printing establishments in Ajmeri Gate. Sablok had never seen money rain in torrents. Books on poetry and romance had never been in demand, they would never be. The series which went with such double entendre titles as* Bistar ka Sukh *(Bedroom Pleasures),* Zaalim Balma*(Cruel Lover),* Saanson mein Saans *(His Breath on Mine),* Raat Bhar *(All Night Long), and* Madhosh Aahen *(Intoxicated Sighs), were released at the prolific rate of one new Jassoos Habib Chachanama a month…till a publisher sought to poach Afroz to their label. The writers, through letters addressed to Afroz at* Nayee Soch, *were offered far higher royalties. The mistresses of porn chose to be loyal to Sablok.*

And hell broke loose. The rival slapped a case of obscenity against the sisters and the publisher. Copies of Jasoos Habib Chacha's bedroom daredevilry were burnt outside Delhi's bookshops. The case was about to be argued in the High Court. Fearing ostracism, the sisters quit Ajmer, and Nayee Soch *went bankrupt. To hush up the case, the Delhi publisher and a battery of lawyers had to be paid off in sums ranging from thousands to lakhs, at a time when even hundreds were a staggering digit.*

Sablok's Nayee Soch – New Thoughts – *was derided as Nayee Thok – New Thrusts. His family was mortified. His only daughter Radhika, whom you called, 'ma'am', stuck by her father. She didn't marry. "No one wanted to marry the daughter of a disgraced publisher," Sablok concluded sadly. "Some men did give their nod for my only child, but do you think I could have shelled out the dowry they demanded?" The two rooms they lived in above the retail shop, had been under litigation. Decades had elapsed, the eviction notices hadn't. If they weren't on the street, the publisher admitted, that's because of the delays in the due process of law, which would last through his lifetime, if not more.*

Sablok hadn't preserved a single copy of the pornographic detective's exploits. That would have been inviting trouble. He quoted passages from memory. Rehaan's ears turned red, he requested him to stop.

"I know, you will ask me where your aunts are now, and if they are alive." Sablok, said. "And you know what?" He stopped, gulped down the water. With a flourish he declaimed, "Everyone knows where they are, but won't tell you unless they're paid. I'll save you the money. They are in Mount Abu."

"Do you have an address?" Rehaan asked, seeing himself taking the next means of transport to the hilltown, a three-to -four-hour trip from Ajmer.

"I don't have their address, son," Sablok looked at him squarely in the eye. "But they shouldn't be difficult to trace. Wahan bhi, they're quite notorious. Your aunts were involved in a scandal, even there. They used to live in with one man, probably someone like Jasoos Habib Chacha who could make them both happy. If you know what I mean."

The insinuation was ugly. Rehaan let it pass. Sablok returned to his newspaper. Ma'am banged the door shut, and thundered, "Those lowdown women, they destroyed us."

26

The Prodigal Sisters

Indian hill-towns, better known as hill-stations – because of their quaint, British-era railway platforms, preserved colonial architecture, the quality of being lost in time and blessed with relatively salubrious weather – are the nation's prime domestic holiday spots. Accessible by treacherously winding roads on which speeding monster trucks thunder, they offer views of deep forested valleys.

There was a time when Rehaan would feel he'd been transported, staying in the closer-to-Bombay hill-towns, particularly Matheran with its red earth and no vehicles permitted. A trip to Mount Abu could be like revisiting childhood. If his ma was with him, she would have propped him by the window seat, accompanied by the warning not to lean out, or his head could be crushed by electric poles or heaven knows, those terrible truckwallas. How they drive, the villains!

Fayazi Ma had never spoken about Mount Abu; it was too far from Mumbai. Lonavla, Mahabaleshwar, and Matheran were the reachable destinations. No hassles of an overnight journey. In hindsight, she must have been aware that the two prodigal sisters had moved there. They were alluded to in family conversations, but they had been left to their own devices. Could be because of the porn scandal. These Aladia sisters, closely knit in a way, had come unravelled, a patchwork quilt left incomplete.

Mount Abu looks as if it had been sculpted by the hand of god in the mountain range of the Aravallis. And it houses the spiritual headquarters of the Brahma Kumaris, the daughters of God Brahma, who teach meditation focussed on identity as souls, not bodies; race, nationality, religion and gender no bar. Oddly, he had been bombarded by emails from the Brahma Kumaris, till they had stopped completely. Meditation, Rehaan wasn't capable of. Whenever he tried to close his eyes and see "beyond", he gave up in a split second.

Ameena and Ferozi, he imagined them meditating. Not a chance, the Aladias weren't born to meditate. They had run helter-skelter after that great escape from Qalayat, hadn't they? Afroz was his last stop. Once he had the sisters' story, he would give meditation a go again. Yeah, yeah, dream on Rehaan Siddiqi. You're a circuit of nerves, as always.

The Fiat cab, which took him to the hilltown, was driven by an unusually silent driver, a middle-aged Rajasthani man, who would intermittenly slick his luxuriant handle-bar moustache. Rehaan was deposited outside the Guru Shikhar post-office, where a weathered clerk refused to look up at the intruder. A woman telegraphing a money order at a counter, asked in the voice of a cherub, "May I help you?"

He mentioned the names of the sisters, and her face lit up, "You mean the writer begums? They are a pair, interesting... interesting." Immediately, she gave him their address – Kothi No 211, Nakki Road. It wasn't too far away if he didn't mind a half-hour walk. He didn't. Now that was quite easily done, QED as the acronyms went below solved geometry riders.

The walk was a hike. The noon sun was merciless, the way it is during summer even in hill-towns at a high elevation. The tarred road gave way to a half-built stone-scattered lane leading to the kothi, which whooshed him back to Hansel and Gretel's confectionery house constructed of systematically piled gingerbread loaves.

He rang the bell to the wooden gate which came up to his waist. Not a peep. The gate was open in any case. He passed through a handkerchief-sized lawn sprinkled with rose bushes and framed by chestnut trees.

No one seemed to be at home besides a litter of cats which looked at him with jaundiced, non-committal eyes. Perhaps they were used to visitors, or else they wouldn't have turned their faces away.

The house was classic colonial. Not perhaps the classic colonial, but resolutely built, agreeably proportioned and with the look of architecture having grown organically out of its site. The mellow brick walls, festooned with creepers, gleamed richly. It was a welcoming house, but a heavy silence lay over it. The row of elegantly proportioned windows were empty eyes.

Right then, an autorickshaw stopped outside the gate. There they were, Ameena, wearing tortoise shell-rimmed shades and Ferozi, shielding her eyes from the sun with her right hand, to figure out who the visitor could be. Both carried jute bags overflowing with leafy vegetables. They were dressed in identical white cotton salwar kameezes and black cotton dupattas. Their complexion, the colour of cinnamon now, the most dimunitive of the Qalayat sisters were wearing chunky diamond bangles, and beaded amulets around their goose necks.

He just had to announce that he was the grandson of Fayazi Ma, and the two went berserk. How they squealed, as if they had finally discovered Alibaba's treasure. Both enveloped him in their arms, wept out loud and touched his face, Ameena pinching his cheeks to verify if he was real. "Zahira's orphan child," she gushed, removing her glares, revealing her black currant eye. "We never thought we'd ever see you during this lifetime." He was smothered with kisses on his chin, his forehead. They closed his eyes, outlined his face with their manicured fingers. Rehaan wished to call for a cut and okay the take.

They rushed him to the living room, neatly proportioned, draped and furnished with taste, a wall of shelves lined with Urdu, Hindi and English books. A huge fawn leather sofa and two armchairs surrounded a sooty bare fireplace. A heavy mahagony table, ornately carved and a bust of dancing angels lurching on a pedestal, occupied the centre of the large room. Photographs of the sisters, a man and a child, he noticed, were framed in antique silver and kept on a table whose legs resembled horses' hooves. This was the kind of place Rehaan could have never foreseen. If he had ever come close to such a house, it was a boutique hotel in Jaipur, owned by former royalty. The sisters had done well for themselves. Wonderful, wonderful, wonderful. He hoped they would ask him to stay. They did, without any ceremony, ushering him to a room with a brass bed covered by a mosquito net, handloom rugs spread on the grey kota stone floor, a potted money plant placed by the window. A gilt-edged print of Leonardo da Vinci's *The Last Supper* presided over the dining table. Ameena and Ferozi fussed that he must be tired. Tea and cheese sandwiches appeared in a flash from the kitchen at the back-end of the house. He was cajoled, "Freshen up, dear bache, we are so happy you are here. We haven't ever recovered from your ammi Zahira's death…tragic, she was a lovely girl. How did you find us?"

"That's a long story," he said, still not certain whether to be enthusiastic or keep a distance from them.

"Long story, wah," Ferozi exclaimed. "Those are the best. But who has the patience for them? I'll switch on the geyser for you. Have a shower, lie down for a while, think of this as your home."

The sisters flapped off, like agitated bats in a belfry. He shut the room's door, apprehensive that it would seem impolite. He was overwhelmed; the duo had accepted him without so much as a half a doubt. A stranger could have barged in there, killed the two darling women in cold blood. How could they be so trusting? He heard them gabbing away merrily in the living room. Next, they had phoned in for takeaway food – a Margherita pizza and potato wedges. He assumed that they didn't run a kitchen, no hot meals.

He was left alone in the room till he felt squeamish. It was stuffy. He waited, thumbed through the Gideon's Bible kept on the bureau. The sisters were probably dressing themselves appropriately for the family reunions of sorts.

The scent of the German No. 4711 eau de cologne wafted in before the sisters did, bedecked in chocolate brown ankle-length kaftans. Taking him by his hand, they said garden chairs had been laid out under the shade of a ring of trees. A kind breeze mitigated the harshness of the sunlight. The pizza had already been sliced for him, sprinkled with chilli flakes. The ice cubes in the tea frosted the glass, an adaptation of the American ice cream sundaes straight out of Pop Tate's soda shop in Archie comics. Rehaan, where are you drifting to? Focus on Ameena and Ferozi, they seem to want to tell you something. Some more fleshy skeletons are about to tumble out from the family cupboard.

These two Aladia sisters were the prodigal ones, decidedly different. Perhaps the most skilful method to prod them would be to let them do the talking. He could sense they merely needed a nudge.

"So," he said blandly. "How are you?"

"Decaying, counting the rest of our days," Ameena riposted.

"No, no, we're happy. Today, more so, because of your visit," countered Ferozi. "Don't pay any heed to Ameena, she sees half a glass even when it's completely full. We hope you like iced tea."

He didn't reach for his cellphone to record them. He was rapt as Ferozi chattered on, while Ameena would butt in, wheedling him to polish off the pizza, which he did without tasting it.

Ameena, through her glares, gaped at him without embarrassment. Possibly, she had written the smutty detective novels. Possibly, Ferozi had dotted the ps and qs. The talk meandered, commencing with the pleasures of living in a hilltown, bringing up their sisters in passing, and then amplifying the reason why, formally, they weren't Aladias anymore.

They had chosen to drop their surnamesbut hadn't altered their first names on embracing Christianity. The sisters, in particular Mumtaz Chaudhran and Fayazi Ma, could tolerate any sin but their conversion. If they hadn't followed the faith they were born into, they had committed sacrilege.

"So, here we are beta, Ameena and Ferozi, even if everyone we know likes to call us Amu and Rosy. We could have become nuns, you know, joined the order. That was not to be...we didn't have the discipline. So much like Julie Andrews in *The Sound of Music*! Our next path was to believe in the lord Jesus Christ. He personally sees to our needs. We all receive Jesus' care and protection. Or we wouldn't be alive today."

Blushing at the confession, Rehaan asked to be excused. Born to Islam, a believer, he was neither startled nor revulsed. He needed to sort himself out. He couldn't offend them either and said shortly, "I understand."

"Will you stay with us for a few days, at least? You are our only family. All that is ours is yours."

"Meaning?"

"We have willed this house and whatever we have to you," Ferozi smiled.

"Let's not get into all that," Ameena butted in. "You will scare him off."

"I couldn't possibly accept," Rehaan said decisively. "Ma would never forgive me."

Ameena's tone sharpened, "We did consider an alternative…to leave our assets to charity."

"That makes sense," Rehaan remarked.

"No, it doesn't," Ameena persisted. "We'll discuss this later. Now tell us, what would you like for dinner. Ferozi is a marvellous cook; we do run a kitchen, you know. We called for pizza only because it would have taken her majesty time to rustle up a meal. Ferozi's so fussy, silly goose."

Against what he thought was his better judgement, Rehaan spent a weekend at the villa. In a corner of the living room, there were crucifixes, images of Mother Mary and wicker candles burning through the day. By his bedside, the Bible summoned to be read. He turned to Psalm 23: "The Lord is my shepherd; I shall not want; He maketh me lie down in green pastures; He leadeth me beside the still waters; He restoreth my soul; He leadeth me in the paths of righteousness for His name's sake."

How different was this in essence from the surahs in the Quran?

"So verily with the hardship there is relief, verily with the hardship there is relief"…Allah does not burden a soul beyond what it can bear.

And the *Bhagvad Gita* has said, "Nothing is ever lost in following one's own dharma. But competition in another's dharma breeds fear and insecurity."

Stop Rehaan. The Holy Books, theology, faith are beyond your grasp. It is not for you to accept or reject anyone's faith or conversion. It is only those who are judgmental without knowing the cause and effect, who can see no other point of conviction but their own. Let it be. They are the Humshira for you, they are entitled to follow their path. And it's not as if you're a stickler of your faith, are you? Do you follow the rules of Islam yourself to the last letter? So believe and let believe. That should be your code. Stick to it. Don't waver or become bigoted the way your Fayazi Ma and Mumtaz Chaudhran must have become. They had their reasons, you have none.

Next morning, the sisters went off for Sunday mass at St Lawrence Church, without telling him. The house was empty save for the wiry gardener who trimmed the shrubbery and doffed a Gandhi cap to the visitor. Rehaan began packing to leave by the evening train. The sisters would have none of it, baiting him with a journalist's wish come true, "We have so much to tell you." He agreed to stay on for a couple of days more. They were pampering him with multi-cuisine meals, breakfast in bed, and coercing him to take afternoon naps. He couldn't sleep but the few hours of nothingness in his room had calmed him over the weekend. He would have to ask them to tell him their story. Simple.

"We write to taste life twice, in the moment and in retrospect," Anaïs Nin, the French-Cuban American author of *Delta of Venus* had said. Rehaan sensed Ameena would go with that. She wouldn't cavil. She didn't.

He could predict Ameena was the articulate one, Ferozi the assentor. They would take turns to tell their story. "We do have our differences, you know," both said happily. Ameena would go first, and she did.

27

Monday

So, Monday was reserved for Ameena, who emerged with a new pair of gold-framed glares. She had taken the trouble of talcum powdering her face, had added a strawberry shade of lipstick. After breakfast – poached eggs, toast, marmalade, Earl Grey tea, all very British – Rehaan and she remained at the table. Ferozi would ensure they would not be disturbed till lunch – leftovers from last night's chicken casserole, lettuce, baby tomatoes and radish salad, caramel custard. "You can leave us now, Ferozi, and you know what to do. Don't try to eavesdrop on us, will you?" The sister agreed solemnly and was off, rinsing the breakfast crockery and cutlery. Bugged by the clatter, Ameena shut the kitchen door with a bang. The sound stopped.

Ameena spoke as if every word of hers was the gospel truth. Rehaan didn't interrupt her. If he had, it would be at the risk of alienating her. That the Mount Abu sisters were fond of him was as apparent as Mumtaz Chaudhran's distaste for him. If Ameena ornamented the truth or didn't bring up any incidents from the past which showed her and Ferozi in a negative light, so be it. She gave him the permission to record her, with the proviso that she would like to see the transcript. Could he transcribe what she said by tonight? It wouldn't be easy, but he'd give it a go.

The transcript, when handed over to her the next morning, read:

Where do I start? My story, our story, Ferozi's and mine, was conditioned by our birth. We obeyed our parents, the darling souls. We obeyed our sisters about whom we have mixed feelings. Lord Jesus would want us to forgive. We have tried to. We do not hate anyone. That luxury is not permitted to women who have been guilty of so many trespasses, for which we have to give an account on our day of reckoning.

We have welcomed you with open arms, Rehaan. You are one good memory we have of our sisters and of your gentle mother. You have been a presence in our lives without knowing it. We heard you became a journalist; you did well at your job. We have read some of your articles in some newspaper from Bombay. There is a spirit of bravado in you which, I dare say, we once also possessed in ample measure.

You told us you have given up your job in pursuit of this novel you are writing about us sisters. That's your call to take. We would seriously suggest stop drifting. You seem to have a talent for writing which we didn't. Don't even think about those detective stories we wrote. They were trivial, sex for sex's sake. We aren't ashamed of them. Not in the least. We wrote because we enjoyed ourselves thoroughly. You may be shocked, but we were well-versed in sexuality. All the bedroom stuff, if you want to call it that, was real. Now see, your face has fallen. Why?

We weren't sluts, beta. It was just something natural to us... being loved by men, and the men leaving us. Ferozi was so much sweeter and attractive than me, but my bad eye made me... what's the correct word...desperate?...passionate? If you don't want to hear this, Rehaan, I will stop. Alright, I will take your silence for consent. Women are not meant to talk about sex right to this day and age. We didn't pay any heed to those not-meant-to's and imagine this was during the 1950s and 1960s, when girls had to submit to male desire and lust. Ferozi and I had our desires too, and if we could write about our sexuality, we felt released. I'm sorry I wouldn't use the word 'liberated' for that era. All this talk of feminism began way after we wrote our books. Correct me if I'm wrong.

I don't know whether I should be flattered or insulted. You are not contradicting me. You are not interrupting me with questions. Maybe that's a rule of journalism, though I see on TV, the interviewers talk more – pure bakbak – than the persons who have been placed in the dock to prove themselves as guilty or innocent. Ferozi and I are innocent, if I may say so. It doesn't matter if our books were burnt. We were described as 'witches' and 'whores' by the very people who had relished our writing. They were titillated, to put it politey...thanks to every word we wrote. Instead of praising us, they almost burnt us at the stake. Only the lord knows how we managed to leave Ajmer. If we had been caught at the railway station, there is no doubt we would have been killed on the spot. I'm not exaggerating.

As for that publisher you met, Neeraj Sablok, let me tell you he is crafty, a wolf in an old man's clothing. He made pots of money, never gave us the royalties we deserved. It's because we invested whatever little we got in land and property that we're comfortable. We own another place close to the town square which has been rented out to a hotel. If you found Sablok in a bad state, don't get taken in by it. He's a bloody miser, saving up the cash he has hoarded somewhere for that daughter of his. Did you meet her? Radhika, how she controls her wretched father. Why do you think she has stuck on with the old man? She's waiting for him to drop dead.

We do not harbour such ill thoughts for anyone, child. We wish that publisher and daughter well. They live according to their own beliefs, don't they? Why he's sitting on his savings, and I can bet he has plenty of the royalties owed to us, is beyond our logic. He's insecure.

It is written that the Day of Judgment will come as suddenly as the Flood of Noah's day, which swept away a wicked generation. Destruction of the ungodly will clear the way for a new earthly society in which righteousness will prevail.

Right or wrong, Ferozi and I were raised by nuns and released to face the world. Unlike our sisters, we were lettered in English. We picked up Urdu and Hindi on our own. Urdu came to us as the sea must to a shoreline. We taught at a school for a while. We did social work, helping and feeding the poor. We were untouched by the changes which our nation was going through. Independence, Partition, communal riots…believe it or not, nothing affected us. Allarakhi Aapa died during those

Partition days. There are so many conjectures about her. May her soul rest in peace.

We would pray for peace and harmony. We continue to every day, for the well-being of mankind and of our sisters. Your Fayazi Nani has gone. She must be so happy to be reunited with her daughter, the gorgeous Zahira…

I can sense that you don't care for my beliefs and dreams, child. That's alright. You are what you are. We hope you will agree to take what is ours when we are gone. We beseech you to. You can't deny us that. We feel no connection with Qalayat, with our sisters. If we do feel a connect with you, I cannot express it in words. Neither do I want your assent to the proposal right away.

Think about it, child, think about it. We know you will not squander it, you will do right by us. Ferozi was telling me that you intend to build a mosque in the name of Fayazi some day. Excellent. She couldn't have found a better grandson in the world. We don't expect a church in our memory, Rehaan.We only wish you would use our money to help people of our faith as well, Christians, in a way which will not come in the way of your faith.

Life's short, they say. We don't agree. We have lived long enough. We have experienced every facet of life, the good and the bad. Of the men who flew in and out of our lives, there is none we would like to remember – except for one. Daniel D'Sa and I were married at St Lawrence's Church. I must have been 35 or more, he was just a boy, 22 or 23. He repaired cars, washed cars. Unfortunately, he was quite a philanderer. I wasn't enough for him. I went into denial about his affairs, flings. I was at a breaking point. I'd pray and pray that he would return to the straight path.

For long, we have had no men in our lives, except for that gardener whom you might see, dumb as they come but efficient at his work. Rehaan, I feel lighter having told you this. But what I'm going to tell you now could well re-open my wounds. I would be grateful if you let Ferozi tell you why I suffered. We have talked it over. She will tell you how and why I was betrayed. I forgave Daniel D'Sa. I forgave the women who sinned with him. Let Ferozi tell you why. I won't, it wouldn't be proper.

28

Tuesday

Next morning, yet another English breakfast later, Rehaan handed over the transcript. Ameena had changed her mind. She didn't wish to read it; she trusted him. At the table, Ferozi was beside herself. Her eyes were dry, but she was dabbing her bleeding nose with a muslin handkerchief. "Nothing to be alarmed about," Ameena decreed. "She always has a nose-bleed when she's stressed. Come on Ferozi, the boy's our very own, our only family. Talk to him..."

"I'm not a good talker and you know that," the twin sister begged off.

"It's high time you talked..."

"I have promised you I will talk at the confession box at the church when I'm ready."

"You will never have the guts to do that. Take Rehaan away from the house. Find a quiet place somewhere. For once in your life, don't be a fusspot, Ferozi."

A journalist is expected to be quick on the uptake. Ameena had requested a transcript to check on distortions and then backtracked. Clever of her. She had cautioned him in her own way to stick to the facts, facts through her prism. If she didn't read it, he guessed that's because it didn't matter. He could have fudged the copy later. As a writer of scabrous detective novels, she had employed her and Ferozi's imaginations to advantage. Detective stories liberally sprinked with sex weren't the domain of female writers. The pen name Afroz had made them gender-less.

Rehaan woke up, bogged down by anxiety. It wasn't at all fair to extract stories from the two sisters who were so bonded. They were mutually dependent. They had erased all traces of their Qalayat origins, as if they had been immaculate conceptions.

He had this swirl of admiration alloyed with dismay for the smut writers. He liked them not for deracinating their oneness with the Humshira from the roots. He liked them for striking out. They had scripted their survival without looking back.

At the breakfast table, around 9 a.m., Ferozi absented herself, claiming that she had a high fever. Amused, Ameena promised Rehaan that the fever would abate by early evening. Not to worry.

"I'm not worried. It's just that I have to leave tomorrow," the guest left the table, as if it was his prescriptive right to extract a conversation. He wandered out into the garden. There were signs of rain. A drizzle had already started. The gardener hadn't shown up for the day. Easily affected by the vagaries of the weather anywhere, Rehaan sought shelter in his room – he could also run up a fever, couldn't he?

Lunch was served by Ameena on a tray to him in the room. Chicken soup, cheese and tomato sandwiches - they'd be good for his soul, she smiled wanly. He felt as if he had been incarcerated in that room. He wouldn't budge. He'd inflict solitary confinement on himself, if need be, till Ferozi consented to speak. *Will she? Won't she? Will she? Won't she?* His head throbbed. That what-the-fuck barbed wire head of his, don't get hyper now...he wouldn't be let down by his hostesses who had showered infinite affection on him. Their promise of legacy, he would have to refuse, no matter what. Ma wouldn't approve. She had left him sufficient wherewithal to last a lifetime, two lifetimes.

Ferozi's sulk didn't end. Tuesday, he marked off as a waste, a blank. He was fed and consoled by Ameena who waltzed into his room and out, without a word, as if to tell him, sorry if her sister doesn't wish to talk, that's the way it is.

29

Wednesday

A taxi was waiting for him at the villa at 6 a.m. Ameena had packed mooli paranthas and mango pickle. She saw him off with an embrace, saying, "We know you're disappointed. That's a pity really. We wish you all the happiness in the world. And you must have been told this often – get a girl who'll look after you, my dear boy. You need a companion."

Rehaan stiffened, thanked her for the stay mechanically. The driver was told to drive safely, and not to exceed the speed limit. The taxi bumped through the roads catatonically. Within half an hour, he was at the station, and sat on a bench. The platform was bare. He read a book without reading.

The train still had to pull into the platform. He fiddled with a cigarette without lighting it. That's when Ferozi walked up straight up to him, to say, "You can smoke if you want to, Rehaan. I'm sorry for my behaviour." Joining him on the asphalt bench, she continued, "I'm not a good speaker, not a good writer. I'm good for nothing. I should have killed myself long ago..."

Throwing away the cigarette which rolled down the platform to the tracks, Rehaan was nonplussed. His upbringing demanded that he shouldn't smoke or drink alcohol before elders. Incapable of formulating questions for his grand-aunt Ferozi, he looked away. And she began her story, almost as if she had rehearsed it for him last night.

The train had pulled into the platform. A group of passengers boarded the compartments. There was still an hour left before it left the platform. "Yes, I have even timed myself," Ferozi said guiltily. "I'll be done before you know it."

The platform began to crawl with passengers, hawkers and railway officials. Over the increasing din, Ferozi narrated swiftly, like a student trying to run through a viva voce test. Her sentences were garbled, incomplete. The editor in Rehaan was used to jumpy grammar.

The two sisters were put up for adoption in Delhi. They were accepted by a family of Muslims in Jaipur but abandoned. The family crossed the border to Pakistan.The adopted ones would have been excess baggage. Ameena and Ferozi spent a month, maybe more on the streets, hungry and hopeless, till there was "divine intervention". They had trekked aimlessly to a village near Makadwadi, and had reached Ajmer, their feet scabby, their spirits broken. There, they were rescued by a junior British officer, a bachelor, who employed them as househelps.

A benign man, he taught them basic English and treated them like his surrogate daughters, till he passed away of ailments related to advanced age.

They were expected to join the nunnery. They did. After two years they were considered too impetuous and rebellious. With their savings, they rented a room in Ajmer, attended mass regularly, and as they grew up, were considered a catch. Unbeknownst to the town, they wrote those novels. Ameena was the creative one, Ferozi was superior in concising, editing the tales. She also had a talent for falling in love. A series of young and elderly paramours were captivated by her delicate demeanour, but none promised commitment.

"We must have been 25 or so," Ferozi cut to the chase, "when I made the worst mistake of my life. I refused to marry Daniel, Daniel D'Sa…well because I thought I deserved more than a car mechanic. No, I'm lying…I was also aware that Ameena had a soft corner for him, but he had a problem about her bad eye. Or that's what he said. After all, when I turned him down, he proposed to Ameena and she accepted. I was livid, the lord pardon me. The devil in me surfaced, and…and…Icontinued to have an affair with him, while he was married to Ameena. She will never forgive me for that. After that, we were cursed. Our books were banned, the money stopped coming. That Sablok fellow gypped us royally.

"Daniel had always been a liability. I had to get him out of our lives. I made sure Amina would catch us together. It was as if I had stabbed her with a dagger. To avoid a riproaring scandal in Ajmer of all places, Daniel had to be packed off. Separation…not divorce mind you…was inevitable. The church would have railed against that.

"Daniel must have remarried or jumped into a well for all we care. We have never seen his face again...and at least I pray that we never do."

The train was getting packed to the gills now. Rehaan hugged her tight, again with admiration and disgust. You have no right to feel disgusted, he corrected himself. She gave him a gift-wrapped package which she requested that he should open only after the train had left. She kissed him on the forehead, and said plaintively, "Do visit us again...and... and do think about that will of ours, will you? Goodbye and good luck, child. God bless."

30

A Novel

Extravagantly, he had booked himself a coupé in the train, paying the fare of two passengers, a quirk of his. Fellow passengers irritated him and the trip would take close to 24 hours. As the train gathered speed, he opened the package to find a copy of a lurid novel by Amroz and a neatly handwritten note from Ferozi on ruled paper, saying, "This is the only copy left of the Hindi translation. Read it only if you wish to. Don't be harsh on us."

Leafing through the book, *Nasheeli Raatein* (*Intoxicating Nights*) published in 1958, he found it tame, the pornography being more girlish than adult. Clichés abounded, with the detective plunging his sword deep into one maiden after another, kisses wetter than a flood, vulvas throbbing with pleasure, bodies palpitating with repeated copulation. The plot, if there was one, concerned Jasoos Habib Chacha checking out an impotent aristocrat – a nawab from nowhere – who indulged in sado-masochism and bestial acts to hide his "paralysed manhood."

And then a paragraph, suddenly, turned reflective, "Men are such foolish creatures. The beauteous belle faked pleasure night after night with the Nawab who brutalised her with hot iron rods. The beauteous one suffered. She would wait for the detective to enter her chamber close to dawn, when she would feel like a woman again...and again, their bodies soldered into one body and soul."

Nothing new about this, he tittered to himself. If he updated this into a contemporary setting – the beauty replaced by a Bollywood starlet, the nawab into a Harvey Weinstein-like movie moghul and the detective into a struggling actor, titled it *Bollywood Night after Night*, the publisher would snap it up; he'd have a bestseller on those airport racks. Rehaan could borrow a sexual feat or two from *50 Shades of Grey*, and for an element of gravitas, bung in rephrased vintage erotica from Anaïs Nin's *Delta of Venus* if need be.

Afroz's brand of porn was lowbrow, yet didn't *Nasheeli Raatein* echo Anaïs Nin's credo? On his cellphone, he googled a brainy Nin quote, "When she closed her eyes, she felt he had many hands, which touched her everywhere, and many mouths, which passed so swiftly over her, and with a wolflike sharpness, his teeth sank into her fleshiest parts. Naked now, he lay his full length over her. She enjoyed his weight on her, enjoyed being crushed under his body. She wanted him soldered to her, from mouth to feet. Shivers passed through her body."

Come on Rehaan, desist. You've always had an appetite for pornography. The excommunicated Aladia sisters had consumed theirs boldly. You could never do that. Whatever remains of your track record would go down the drain. Switch off, you'll be home tomorrow.

Four days later, Shuhaba called to inform him that Mumtaz Chaudhran had passed away on Sunday in her sleep peacefully. She had been buried at the Bada Qabrastan. Efforts to contact Rehaan had proved to be futile; his cellphone had been switched off.

He headed for the qabrastan. The grave was covered with dead rose petals, marigold and chameli strings. He placed a chaddar embossed with gold thread calligraphy. The Chaudhran's grave, by design or accident, was at a considerable distance from Fayazi Ma's.

The qabrastan is an oasis of greenery and swaying trees right opposite Marine Lines railway station, the stop where he had disembarked for four years to walk to St Xavier's College. Once in a while, he would stop by at the qabrastan to confirm if the marble makbara of Mariam Begum, the first wife of Sir Osman Baksh MithaCassum, was still there.

From the Chaudhran's mudbound grave, he saw the makbara sat there proudly. Who was paying for the tombstone's upkeep, the watering of plants and rose bushes around it, for over half a century, intrigued him. Fayazi Ma's grave was anonymous, as the Chaudhran's would be in a few months from now.

Mariam Baksh Mitha lived on, enshrined in marble, browning with age, but devoid of any cracks, the breathing roses taunting the dead petals on the less celebrated graves.

31

Ashes and Diamonds

He had saved Fayazi Ma's role in the Humshira drama for the last, afraid that his bias would topple the story over in her favour, unfairly. His sense of aloneness was gnawing at him. On being asked by friends, rather acquaintances, what exactly his novel was about, he would say, it's about six Muslim sisters, who were a reflection of their times. It wasn't a satisfactory explanation, but he couldn't amplify the statement. The novel wasn't pre-structured. First impressions were edited and rewritten as he read them again over time, realising that when some writers said they had expended years to reach the first draft, they weren't lying.

There is no scale to weigh the balance between the truth and secrets. The writer must find his own code of justice. There at the qabrastan, he could visualise his ma calling out from the grave, directing him all over again as she had done forever – don't go into that lane; let our story be ours, untold, if you respect me.

Characters, minor and major, stood accusingly before him. Those he couldn't deal with so far, he had either sidelined or expunged. Mariambi Mitha was one such. Although Sir Osman Baksh had been knighted, neither of his wives would be called Lady. They were too homely, too unsociable. Imagine, a Lady Mariambi or a Lady Fayazi would have sounded high falutin' even for a prosperous Memon family.

Back home now, pretending that his novel is his companion, he's still altering words, sentences, glaring harder at the computer screen. He's mistrustful of the picture that's emerging. It's his way of seeing, his way of juggling the people who have determined the course of his life. Mariambi Mitha he had never seen. She had succumbed to breast cancer and who knows, heartache when Sir Osman had brought home another woman, younger than them by decades, more attractive than she had ever been. The seth had remarried without so much as warning his wife, who had borne him five sons and an equal number of daughters. The new bride was neither a Memon nor did she have any family back-up to boast of. Sir Osman's roving eye had chanced upon her at the madrassa. The seemingly timid girl had agreed to a nikaah and had entered the house which Mariambi had preserved with fortitude and care ever since her marriage as a girl who had just entered her teens. A woman who hadn't ever owned so much as a brass ring would have been an imbecile to reject solitaires. Fayazi Ma, whether Rehaan was ready to accept this or not, was the proverbial homebreaker.

Mariambi, the rule-keeper at the Mitha bungalow, spent her last years in a separate apartment, a short distance from 35, Lands End Road. And from his ma's account, she had sent for her, to emphasise that her sympathies lay with her. Whether this two-women meeting did happen, couldn't be verified. His ma would bring it up often, and on every Ramzan and Bakri Eid, garland the deceased Mariambi's portrait – wearing a Chantilly lace sari and diamonds – and do zakaat in her name. A queue of women from the mohallas would receive 50 rupees from Fayazi Ma's hands, in the name of the true haqdaar of the Mitha wealth. Ma saw herself as a protector of the realm, not the destructor.

As for the customs of the successful mercantile Memon social strata of Bombay then, she blended in with alacrity, smattering her Urdu with the appropriate Kutchi Gujarati. Marriage into the Mitha household wasn't complicated. The 10 children were all married; three of them had moved to Pakistan. The others were in Bombay and would visit their father regularly for handouts. When Fayazi Ma handled the keys to the ration godown – wheat grains, potatoes, onions, corn flour – and to the dozens of mirror-faced cupboards and a monster-sized safe which stored the family jewels, there were protests, especially from the eldest son Ilyas Mitha of Karachi. The Mitha children were placated with their share of cash, property, and jewellery. Ilyas demanded the two magnifcent Ming vases in the bungalow's living room. The demand was rejected with a telegram from his father, saying, "No -(Stop)- Not while am alive -(Stop)-."

The birth of Zahira was a surprise. That Sir Osman Baksh Mitha could sire a child was a surprise to himself. She had the Aladia features. As she grew up, she was regarded as an ublemished beauty who would slay every male who cast so much as a glance at her. The seth wasn't fond of children; he'd had enough. The child was despatched to a boarding school in Panchgani – the Kimmins High School founded in 1898, despite Fayazi Ma's howls of grief. Zahira would be educated in English, was the consolation, and she would be away from the lecherous eyes of the endless stream of elderly visitors. Moroever, she would be back at the bungalow during the protracted summer and Christmas holidays.

On learning there would be horse-riding lessons, Zahira was glad to go. She was sporty, and longed to watch the derby at the Mahalaxmi Racecourse. She saw herself in a hat, a white, layered summer frock and maybe a string of pearls around her swan-like neck. She dreamt, too, of going to shikars with the British and of becoming a movie star.

A flunkey of the Sir Osman, Kantibhai Chimanlal, who was paid a monthly stipend to spend his evenings at the bungalow, gossiping and updating the seth on his rival business leaders, was as oily as his brilliantined head. Fayazi Ma had seen him touching Zahira inappropriately. The British – who had stayed behind in Bombay or had settled in Poona – would fawn over her, claiming that she looked as gora as them. A fair complexion meant to a manor born.

Zahira didn't protest against her exile to the boarding school. She would be one with the children of parents, many of whom had separated or were about to. As soon as she completed school, at the age of 15, the seth had a groom ready for her. The girl had revealed a gift for drawing and watercolours; she aspired to become a painter. She played the lead in school plays, once enacting Ophelia in an abridged version of *Othello*. She was an expert hockey player and a horserider and aspired to become the first woman jockey of India. The seth wouldn't entertain such trifles. A girl was born to be given away in marriage. He had done that in the case of his daughters with Mariambi, and he wasn't about to permit his youngest daughter to make her own decisions. Fayazi Ma had to be grateful, too, now that she ruled over the Mitha household, where she was cloistered safely, away from the influence of Mumtaz Chaudhran and Jameela Begum whom Sir Osman would call "samras…they are not women, they are witches. Your ties with them are severed. Don't bring up their names in this house, if you know what's good for you."

Notwithstanding his hatred for Fayazi Ma's sisters, Sir Osman would relish playing the part of a godfather. Whenever there was a crisis, he did whatever he could, partially to prevent a public scandal. Fayazi Ma would meet her sisters in secret, escorted by the bungalow's secret-keeper, Hashim. If need be, the butler would drive Fayazi Ma, burqa-cloaked, in a lumbering black Dodge, to the Chaudhran's kotha on Kennedy Bridge.

Zahira's nikaah to Shafaque Siddiqi, the only son of a Memon family, was soleminised on a low key at a Pydhonie wedding hall. Rather than blowing up money on a lavish party, it was thought judicious to hike the charity dole to the madrassa, where Fayazi Ma had once found refuge. Zahira, petrified of her father, walked into the marriage without a whimper. Girls at the school would talk of marrying the man they loved. She didn't have the luxury of giving a second thought to romance, a dream-boy who would whisk her away on horseback, from the Mitha bungalow.

The Siddiqis owned a flourishing business in import-exports – an euphemism for smuggling contraband goods, be it bringing in made-in-England whisky to Indian shores or organising ivory antiques for European collectors. Sir Osman was aware that their business was irrevocably under board. So was his; he had dealt in exporting salt and spices, underwriting their market value. Besides, the Siddiqis had made enough money to be regarded as legitimate traders. The meher marked for Zahira, in the event of a separation, was 2 lakhs rupees, a more than handsome sum in those days.

Rehaan had pieced together his mother Zahira's stories by keeping his eyes and ears open right from the time he became conscious of his near-orphaned status in the Mitha bungalow. He'd listen in on conversations between Chimanlal and Sir Osman, giving the impression that he didn't understand a word of what they were talking about.

Sir Osman considered Rehaan a jinx, born under a bad star. He had devoured his mother, who had died because of him, and him alone. Shafaque Sidiqui's family had claimed the child as theirs, but feebly so. The meher amount and another lakh was given so that the Siddiqis, right then under pressure of illegal transactions, could migrate to the U.K. Their migration would be arranged, no problem. "Throw some bones before the goras there, like the babus here, and they'll chew the haddis up happily." Chimanlal was the facilitator, he needed bones to chew on too. He'd pretend to be strictly vegetarian at home. At the Mitha bungalow, he'd tear a tandoori chicken to its last scrap.

No speedbreakers. These can be fixed, yesterday or today, Rehaan would tell himself. Throw a bone of flesh before a person of authority, and your job's done. Not that he needed to. As a teenager, he'd travelled to London four times over to meet his father Shafaque, who lived in an Edwardian two-storey house in Chiswick, by a meander of the Thames. The ruddy-faced stocky, balding father, most often in blazers of different shades of blue, would brag that his immediate neighbours were British. He was snobbish about Indian and Pakistani immigrants, comprising a thick percentage of the Chiswick population. Asians were taking over England, creating a mess, he would grumble. Rehaan would cringe. His father wasn't exactly to the soil born.

How his mother, the ever-ethereal Zahira, could have ever agreed to marry this podgy specimen baffled him. But then he had seen such ill-matched marriages forever. Sandra, the British woman his father had married next, was large as their house, bursting with life and laughing as robustly as a paid audience at a TV reality show. They had two boys, angelically blond, but hostile, staring at their half-brother glumly as if he had arrived to snatch their porridge.

Rehaan loathed his father, a loathing exacerbated by Fayazi Ma. On returning from his third trip to London, she had suggested, "Break off all contact with that swine. I am all you need." He couldn't agree more. He wouldn't take any more phone calls, answer letters from either Abba Shafaque or Aunty Sandra. Birthday parcels were returned. They got the message. They didn't bother him any more.

Shafaque Siddiqi, given to the good life – pubbing, clubbing, womanising – did not live beyond the age of 42. Rehaan didn't condole his death. He did send a letter to Sandra with words to the effect, "Sorry to hear about your irreparable loss." She replied with a card, "Thank you, dear." No hint that she wished him to keep in touch, perhaps apprehensive that he could claim his share in the Siddiqi assets, if he had left any. On later trips to London, on professional assignments, the black cab would pass by the highway from Heathrow, offering a view of Chiswick on the right. He made it a point to look towards the left, at the advertisements of the benefits of drinking milk, the upcoming rock concert at Hammersmith, women in Marks & Spencer lingerie. If Sandra Siddiqi and her sons were still in Chiswick, it was none of his concern, never was.

He had exorcised the family males, be it his biological father or his half-brothers, from his system. For him, they were execrable supporting players. Grandfather Osman Baksh Mitha was possibly bipolar at a time when the term was unknown. Nana was capable of affection and indifference. Rehaan had never touched him, embraced him. Warmth, if ever, was granted to the boy when he topped his school examinations, especially when he was given a 'double promotion' – he went from the fifth standard directly to the seventh, throwing Fayazi Ma into a tizzy. *No*, he had to climb the stairs of education *rung by rung,* no tricks, no shortcuts. She compelled Sir Osman to show up at the school to convey her theory to the principal. The boy prayed for the ground to open up, and swallow him, as the seventh-standard boys tittered at the man wearing a maroon fez and outmoded leather boots over his achkan. The Anglo-Scottish principal, Mr Gunnery, pleasantly, assuaged the visitor's fears. The boy was bright, he'd still top the class, given his killer instinct to excel. Just go away weirdo, the boy prayed, and sought to look as if the man in the fez cap was a rank stranger.

As his childhood rolled on, Sir Osman's health deteriorated. Into his 90s, overnight he had a paralytic attack, rendering him immobile, and insecure. Dependent on his wife, and the growing collection of domestic helps, now led by a meekly Murari Bhai, he'd sit by a radiogram during the day, listening to news bulletins, the weather forecast, and for some reason, lamented the rise in prices of food grains, though he could buy up a granary by just instructing Chimanlal to set up a deal.

Chimanlal became the seth's companion. Meanwhile Fayazi Ma was desperate that she and her grandson's future should be guaranteed in writing. After much ado, an undisclosed portion was earmarked for them in the dying man's will. The rest, to Ma's dismay, would be distributed among his ten chidren. "See, that Mariambi's ghost won't leave him," she wept, while pleading that she be given her share of the family's jewellery right away. "What if you die tomorrow? Do you expect me to go running to my sisters?" was her double-edged argument, which would go ignored.

Sir Osman was wily; he would listen to no one but himself when it came to his will, which was kept in a bank's locker. Chimanlal slyly suggested J.B. Bhabha's name as the executor of the will. Ma's equity in the Mitha domain was plummeting; Chimanlal's was escalating. Paralysis aggravated by senility was making Sir – a meaningless title by this point – spiteful by the day. Worse, the dying sir had Mariambi's portrait shifted closer to his bed, and could be heard muttering, "You were the finest woman in my life. This Fayazi is a witch like her sisters; she will grab everything I possess…everything."

With the complicity of Mumtaz Chaudhran, Fayazi Ma pawned the silverware, clockpieces, Persian carpets, and oil paintings dating back to the early days of the Raj. The Chaudhran pocketed a commission, of course. Rehaan's wails – he was attached especially to the paintings – amounted to screaming in the wilderness. Fayazi Ma was trying to ensure that they wouldn't be on the streets or have to move in to Mumtaz Chaudhran's rooms at Kennedy Bridge. What had to be done would have to be done. Quite rashly, that porcelain cat and diamond pendant were gifted to Jameela Begum.

Rehaan mourned the loss of the objets d'art, and to his surprise, was shaken by the inevitable end of Sir Osman. He'd see the radiogram, the brass bell to summon Fayazi Ma or Murari Bhai. The creepy old man died after a fortnight in hospital, where he made the lives of the nurses miserable, cursing, and chucking his meal trays straight out of the window overlooking the sea by Breach Candy.

The Mitha family descended on the bungalow. At the burial, Rehaan was allowed to pour a fistful of earth into his grave, next to Mariambi's makbara. A separate tombstone was denied to Sir Osman. The Mitha progeny were in a hurry to grab their inheritance. Bhabha backed off from being the executor, Chimanlal took over – he was left a sum of 1 lakh rupees in the will. Fayazi Ma and Rehaan's share would have to wait. "Just look at them, just look," Ma wept into the pallu of her white sari. "Do you know that fucker Ilyas Mitha had even smuggled in a cobra to strike at sir once. It was I who had grabbed that saanp and raised such an alarm that it could be heard right across the city. They're glad the old man's gone now; they've always wished their father dead, the haraamis."

With Estate Duty on during the time, the expansive bungalow was appropriated by the state government. Two tall, ugly structures came up there, an official housing colony for income-tax officers. Denied the 25 lakh rupees marked for them in the will, Fayazi Ma and Rehaan shifted to the Saidunissa chawl opposite Grant Road railway station. Their neighbours, all Parsis, were baffled by the arrival on the fourth floor of an ageing woman and a boy just about to finish school. No elevator, Fayazi Ma could climb up the steep stairwell without stopping for breath, and found an immediate friend in Alamai, a few years older than her.

Alamai's son, Adi, a bachelor, read paperbacks of Erle Stanley Gardner, Pearl S. Buck and Ellery Queen. Adi, secretly married to a colleague in his office, led a double life. It was years later, that the mamma's boy brought the woman and their two sons, home. Alamai curled up in her bed and refused to touch meals cooked by her daughter-in-law. A tiffin from a Parsi food service would be left outside her door.

Most of the Parsi families worked at the Godrej factory as mid-level adminstrators. They were generous to the grandmother and boy, sending them meals on festive Navroz days, and lending money to Fayazi Ma whenever she was cash-strapped which was often. The Aladia sisters could now meet up with Fayazi. She was grateful for their company, but never asked for a loan, in a bid to assert that she was the sister who had struck a bigger fortune than they could ever imagine. Also, unlike them, she had remained a one-man woman. She hadn't sinned. Banish the very idea.

Five years winged by. FayaziMa was ready to explode. Grabbing Rehaan by his hand, she rung the doorbell of Chimanlal's home in an Art Deco building on Marine Drive. She made it clear to Chimanal's wife and daughter that an orphan was being cheated of his money. Chimanlal repeated his usual excuse that nothing was in his control. Ilyas Mitha from Karachi had been appointed co-executor of the will, after all.

Ma played her trump card, "I have had enough. I will go straight to the Prime Minister if need be. I will spill the beans. You think I never noticed the radio wireless set Ilyas would use whenever he was at the bungalow. He is nothing but a Pakistani spy. Just you wait. I'll raise such a storm now that he will be shamed. He will never ever get a visa to enter this country. Tell him that."

Silence hit the Marine Drive house. Chimanlal was speechless. He led Fayazi Ma and Rehaan to a taxi and saw them off. The inheritance was cleared within a week. Two apartments had already been reserved by Ma in an upcoming apartment colony on Napean Sea Road on Malabar Hill. The deposit had been paid from the silverware money left untouched, even during crises. One home they would stay in, the other would be rented out. Rehaan's college fees would be a priority, and who knows, perhaps he could even get himself a scholarship for higher studies abroad. "Oxford? Cambridge? That's where you should be, right?" she'd ask with sparkling eyes, which would dim in a split second. "But what would I do without you, child? I cannot live without you." She would be assuaged by the ever-amazed grandson, "You're my Oxford and Cambridge, Ma."

Losing a support was a common bugbear for Sir Osman and Fayazi Ma. If she had left him on his wheelchair, he would have been devastated. Similarly, if Rehaan on reaching adulthood had brought a woman, a wife, home, Ma would have been devastated. She had tried to reconcile herself to the prospect but thumbed down every marriage proposal. Every girl from the workplace he brought home for tea, would send her into a sulk. He would have to be her boy, no one else's. He couldn't be an Adi who had driven Alamai into a lifelong silence.

Rehaan reconciled himself to that pervading isolation, couldn't fight it, immersing himself in work till the onset of middle-age set which like rust can never be done and dusted with. That was the reason, when work became a grind, he had sought to investigate the Aladia sisters' story. There it was with him now. Relief or catharsis would never be his. No purgation, no purification. Those palliatives advanced by Aristotle were fine in his Political Science textbooks. Catharsis is supposed to be a moral lesson in which fear and pity inflicted by fate warn the spectator not to defy providence.

He was incapable of defiance.

32

"Your place is not here...not among us Musalmans"

There was an element of defiance, perhaps, in the bid to publish the book, get it done with, but move on to what? A thousand worders, articles he would continue to write on being solicited. These were getting to be a drag: nostalgic anecdotes about the show-business personalities whenever there was a death, birth or death anniversay. A glorified obit writer he had become. If he had something to write which didn't delve into the past, the response of the editors was stabbing, "We will skip this one."

Rehaan was in a quandary. Nowhere near the retirement age, journalists don't go off to smell the roses anyway. They regurgigate the material, in the style they've been branded with, involving either a light punny touch or sombre gravitas. Invariably, he would be flattered and insulted by his readers of yore, "We used to read you every weekend, turn to to your column the first day in the morning. So where are you writing nowadays?"

"Nowhere," he'd try not to be offensive.

"So, what are you doing then?"

"I've just about completed a novel," he'd say, only to receive indifference or at most, "Hope, it's a tell-all on Bollywood. That will sell like hot cakes." Fuck, where did this cake of a simile come from? From the U.S. it seems and has gone undocumented.

Touchy, touchy, take it easy Rehaan. Get yourself a pet, a dog, a cat, a parakeet. Ha, you're ready to be an old maid. Reconnect with Latika, the woman you thought you loved and wished to marry. Naaa, she's married, unhappily it seems. Takes care of a grown-up son. Too damn complicated. Get involved with a guy from one of those cybersex sites – Grindr is just a mouse click away – na, not interested. Sexuality had been sublimated, had to be. Can't make up for lost time by going sexually profligate, satisfying the mutual physical needs of strangers rather than his own.

Just be content that your novel's reaching endpoint. It interests you, but will it interest others? Won't you be accused of feeding off the lives of the Humshira, the women whose stories were their secrets, not yours. Wouldn't it be a stab in the back of let's say Noor Baaji? Do you need to grind the knife in her wounds? You should have thought of that before taking off on this irresponsible search. You think you're upright; you're as crooked as a scamster, a cheat.

Too late for self-questioning, you creep. Get on with it. Consult Dr Abhay Mehta? Send the draft to your publisher, wait for interminable months for a reaction? If rejected, try another publisher. Don't sell it for a pittance, but don't let them browbeat you with the condition of getting a celebrity to launch your book. Wait, how about talking to Noor? Get a go-ahead for the book from her? You could do with a trip to Delhi in November. Winter would have set in. The gardens would be blooming with snapdragons, petunias and orchids, sprayed with artificial colour, displayed in steel buckets at housing colony markets.

Jameela Begum was alive. Maybe she still listened to that transistor of hers heaving in her cleavage. She wasn't likely to recognise him anymore, which was just as well.

He phoned Noor to ask if he could meet her in a week or two. Uncertainly she said, "I don't know. Ammi's health is sinking by the day. But I can't say 'no' to you. Why ask? In any case, you'll be staying at Gulmohar Park with your fancy friends I suppose."

He said he would like to spend a few days with them at Kucha Lattu Shah, the way he used to as a schoolboy. Noor ended the phone call, "Very well. It's high time you did. The place is in a mess, but I will get the ground floor ready for you. The tenants for this winter will be arriving next month. Allah haafiz."

The scene was bleak. Jameela Begum no longer listened to Pakistan Radio. She had been admitted to hospital since a couple of months; she was in a comatose condition. Noor's Abba Hamid, infirm but in control of his faculties, would spend days and nights in the corridors, dozing off hunched at a crooked angle on a bench. The hospital authorities didn't approve but had quit telling him to go home and get some rest because he wouldn't. Noor seldom visited her mother, explaining, "It breaks my heart to see her like that. All I can do is relieve Abba during the nights to be with her. She doesn't recognise either of us."

Rehaan offered to help out with the medical expenses. Noor refused flatly, "Shukriya but no, and I beg you to not offer any help again." She had turned hostile towards him. Whenever he mentioned the novel, if she didn't wish to read it, he could at least synopsise the story for her. In vain again. She was a woman who wouldn't budge when her mind was made up. The haveli was getting oppressive. Its sanitary facilities may have been updated, but the structure was disintegrating, the paint cracked, the pillars and the filigreed ceiling rusty beyond repair. The noise levels of the mohalla had risen. Finicky as he was, Rehaan considered himself fortunate if he could grab three to four hours of restless sleep a night.

A week floated by. At long last, Noor spoke up during lunch which he was finishing desultorily. Apologies had become her mantra, "You came here for nothing, sorry. You're not comfortable here. I suggest you leave…you will not get a yes from me for your book."

"But I have to meet the publishers and hand over the manuscript," he pleaded.

"Do what you will then."

"Could I come with you to see Jameela Nani at the hospital tonight. I would like to."

"No need for that, Rehaan. By the way, the tenants have asked to come ahead of their schedule. I must ask you to leave."

He called up his trusted friend, Badshah. If he could get him a room at the IIC. His friends, the Guptas were overseas.

"Let me see what I can do," the friend's resigned voice said. After an hour, he reverted, "Only suites available. Can you afford one?"

He checked into a suite, which offered a view of the Centre's gushing fountains, and swaying trees. Badshah would meet up at the bar as soon as the sun set – deviating from his rule that any hour is happy drinking hour. He looked gaunt. He had been diagnosed with gluten allergy.

"Have to take it easy with booze too," he frowned, ordering himself a glass of red wine, which he said, "…is piss. Now don't tell me you're still stuck with that book of yours. Where's it at?"

"It's done, Badshah," Rehaan shrugged, "but I feel there's still something missing."

To his "Like what?" Rehaan went into a diatribe about obtaining Noor's go-ahead. At the end of the evening, Badshah had switched to rum, sighing, "It's okay once in a while." Then he added, "You're in a spot old chap. Just remember the classic journalist's dictum – you have to do what you have to. Truth must prevail and all that jazz. Noor or no Noor. She sounds terrible."

"On the contrary," Rehaan was about to describe Noor's upright qualities in detail. Badshah called a halt with the sagely advice, "Confront her, even if it gets unpleasant. Get it? Go to that hospital this night, and get it done with. Cheers!"

Moolchand Hospital at Lajpat Nagar was a hop away from the metro station. As forbidding as any hospital, its security guard said sternly, "No visitors allowed." Rehaan pulled out an old card, crediting him as a journalist. Didn't work. Only those with a 'special' card from the hospital's superintendent were permitted to enter. Could he get one? Rules are rules, the guard said fiercely, "Come back tomorrow. Visits between 10 a.m. and noon, and 5 p.m. to 7 p.m. Aur yeh bhi samajh lo...let me make it clear, no drunken visitors allowed." Rehaan's breath was reeking of vodka. The guard was right, he had to return sober.

He did during the visiting hours, for the next two days, spending the rest of the time wandering around Chandni Chowk, and taxiing to the publishing office at Noida. Yes, they would like to have a look at the manuscript and then take a call. The publisher was evasive; he was scheduled to leave for a book fair in Europe. No hurry, no hurry, take your time, the writer was told, which translated as, "Hey buddy, we can offer you an MOU, but no contract, not yet." Memorandum of understanding, a rung above a rejection slip.

At Moolchand Hospital, Jameela Begum was far gone, a lifeless figure in the ICU unit. Hamid Abba and Noor took turns, he by day now and she by night, waiting and grabbing snatches of sleep till the end came. Both kept busy with their prayer beads. Rehaan was permitted to go inside, have a look at Jameela Begum. He did, and recited the kalima 11 times over, 11 because he believed it was an auspicious number, in the manner 101 rupees and with time 1001 rupees had become the cash gifts in an envelope for birthdays, weddings and anniversaries.

On a Sunday morning, Jameela Begum passed away in her sleep. By the time Rehaan reached Kucha Lattu Shah, the haveli was spinning with men and women in mourning, outfitted either in white or black. Dressed in white for the occasion, Rehaan cut through the crowd to embrace Hamid Abba and Noor, who accepted his condolences. Noor's eyes were dry. She looked at Rehaan hesitantly. Before he could offer to be one of the pallbearers, it had been decided that an ambulance would transport the flower-covered coffin at a considerable distance away, at Batla House in Jamia. Mourners had already left by autorickshaws and buses.

In accordance with custom, Noor stayed home with the other mourners. Rehaan asked Hamid Abba if he could accompany him in the ambulance. He said, "There's no need. Return to your home in Mumbai, your place is not here... not among us Musalmans." Noor turned her face away, as if in agreement with her father telling Rehaan he wasn't needed, he was a nuisance. He was not one of them.

Before he could recover from the snub and talk back, Rehaan wept uncontrollably. He ran as fast as his feet could carry him outside the Chandni Chowk gullies, checked out of the IIC, caught the next available flight and was back home. He suspected the worst behind the reason for his rejection, but he wouldn't think about it. What if his suspicion were to come true? If this one did – the cornerstone of the novel – he wouldn't be able to take it.

The Quran says, "Allah does not change the situation of a people until they change what is in themselves." He would have to change by confirming the suspicion which he knew was true. And it didn't require much effort to get the family to break its silence over its secret – a compassionately guarded secret.

33

The Last Call

He felt protected by the Humshira, then caviled. He didn't need the protection. Ostensibly, Mumtaz Chaudhran had hated the sight of him, Jameela Begum had resided in her own transistor sing-song world, Allarakhi if she had lived, would have doted on him excessively, perhaps. Ameena and Ferozi were blissfully unaware; they had never been participants in a chain of secrets and lies, and Fayazi Ma had lived in denial.

Abu Bakr and Abu Fazl, did they know? Shuhaba must have, but she had adhered to the uncontracted family code. Noor's Hamid Abba wasn't the sort to be a harbinger of news, good or bad. Noor had vacillated. Spitefully she hadn't allowed him to be her mother's pallbearer.

The suspicion festered for days, weeks and months. It was pointless to blame Noor. She was in the throes of selling the Kucha Lattu Shah haveli to move to Delhi's Malaviya Nagar. Two apartments had been bought, one for herself and her father. The other one was rented out for a sum substantially higher than the lean amounts paid by Kashmiri rug-sellers in winter. The Aladias had a talent for acquiring and leasing property.

Rehaan would be updated by Shuhaba about Noor. She would keep her phone conversations with him cut and dried, till he had to say with as much politesse as he could, "There is something about me that has bothered all of you. We're adults. I'd like to think we are. Could we talk?"

"Talk to Noor," Shuhaba had said drily. "Vows taken in our family are sacrosanct, they cannot be broken. It's up to Noor to decide whether she will go against the oath taken on the Quran by the Aladias, a vow that their children and grandchildren have respected."

"What respect are you talking about?" Rehaan had had enough. "I have the right to know."

The cellphone went dead in Rehaan's hand.

He couldn't keep dashing to and fro from Mumbai to Delhi. Noor now seemed to be a consummate actress, impersonating an executioner about to deliver the final blow. He would grant her that privilege. He sensed she would like nothing better than to steal the show from the Aladia family's only paragon of virtue.

He would wait for Noor to re-establish contact. No, that could mean the rest of his lifetime. He would call her himself, at the right time, which would be on his birthday, May 10, a month away. The wait would be agonising, but he begged Allah to give him strength and patience – the first benediction he had ever asked for purely for himself.

Selecting a Sunday morning, he called Noor on her preferred landline. It wouldn't connect. On dialling her cell phone, she picked it up at the first ring. She was expecting the call and said, "Hello. Salaam alaikum."

"Walaikum salaam," Rehaan replied automatically. "Noor Baaji, it's high time..."

"High time for what?"

The line crackled; his heart sank. The cellphone network wasn't reliable in his neighbourhood. He leaned out of a window.

"Can you hear me clearly?"

"Yes. I'm listening."

"You, everyone has been hiding something from me. It's high time..."

"You have no right to tell me what's the right time, the high time, Rehaan. I'm busy, have to get lunch going. Abba isn't keeping well."

"Stop it," Rehaan's voice grew shrill. "I have the right to know why I was treated like an outsider at Jameela Nani's burial."

No pause from Noor, no holding back. Clearly she was as exasperated as he was, and said firmly, "Because you are an outsider."

"I have been treated like one. May I know the reason?"

"Rehaan, the reason is because you're not a Musalman. You do not belong to our faith. I can no longer pretend that you are one of us."

"You, you, a woman who slept around with a Hindu man. Fantastic! You have the nerve to tell me that I am not a Musalman. Have you lost your mind completely?"

He expected her to hang up. She didn't. Her answer was on target. Said she, "I have never been saner, thank you. The pretence has to an end. Your father was a Hindu, a Brahmin, a racehorse jockey Harsh Sharma whom you mother was enamoured of. After completing school, Zahirabi met him at the racecourse. They had an affair. She wasn't as pure as driven snow like your great Fayazi Ma led you to believe. To prevent a scandal, she was married off in a hurry to Siddiqi saab, who was more than aware that she was three months pregnant. If that doesn't make you a bastard, a kafir, I don't know what else does? That's your story Rehaan. The rest, I hope you are intelligent enough to piece together. I won't say Allah haafiz any more to you."

She hung up. He called her back repeatedly. The distended recorded voice droned, "The number you are dialling is unavailable." No request to leave a voice message.

34

Epilogue

That was the closure. He saw 'The End' appearing on the last page of his novel.

Rehaan's faith in the religion, bestowed on him by Fayazi Ma, strengthened. "I'm a Muslim and always will be," he heard his voice echoing in the Sunday quiet of his room."

"Allah is my only God. Zahira is my mother, Fayazi is my mother. My dear mothers, hear me as I say Islam means submit, and I do so with pride and gratitude."

He travelled to Qalayat, bought over the ice factory, had it demolished, and had a mosque constructed there. Money could wake up the most somnolent of traders in the Haryana township. The mosque maintained by a trust today, draws the devout from within the state and outside it.

The Super Hotel, the railway station, the tongawalla and his horse Chabook, the desolation, are still there in the unmapped Qalayat.

The mosque he dedicated to Iddanbi and Saunda Bhai Aladia. He would return there every year to oversee its upkeep.

He had a tombstone, a copy of Mariambi's, built for Fayazi Ma's grave. The qabrastan's caretaker reminded him that the grave wasn't hers exclusively. For want of space, others had been buried there too. It didn't matter. The tombstone would last like Mariambi's had.

Of the Humshira sisters, the ones alive, Ameena and Ferozi, would approve of any step he had taken. They would hope he would construct a church after they were gone.

The rest were no more; he wouldn't let them haunt him. If they re-entered his dreams, he'd deal with them.

His next sentence was: Allah has found you lost, and he has guided you.

Those were the words inscribed on the last page of his novel. He had loved only his Fayazi Ma, at the expense of sublimating the core of his very being.

Go on Rehaan, rebel. It's May 10, your birthday today. Publish the story and either be damned, or reborn.

Acknowledgements

As my age advances, friendship and mutual concern – to my consternation – shrink in number and intensity. Besides being separated by geographical distances, there are separate, round-the-clock busy lives to be led.

Admittedly, there have been unresolvable arguments, differences in values and ideology, culminating in the squelching of friendships and relationships. For this, I blame myself far more than those whom I have lost, hopefully not forever.

For my first foray into a novel, as against collections of short stories and biographies, permit me to shout out loud for the undiminished support of my abiding friends: Suman, Deepak and Sumi Gupta, Farouq Rattonsey, Tanuj and his mother Bharti Garg, Rafique Baghdadi, Sooni Taraporevala, Meher Pestonji, Nilufer Qureshi, Anil Tejani, Sabir Masani, Rohit Sharma, Tawheed Sofia, Nupur Nerurkar Kapoor and Vajir Singh.

Shyam Benegal, Raakhee Gulzar, Rishi and Neetu Kapoor, Asha Parekh, Sunita and Anil Kapoor, and Sonam Kapoor Ahuja, Karan Johar, Hrithik Roshan, Arjun Rampal, Manoj and Shabana Bajpai, Richa Chadda,

Achint Kaur and Santosh Sivan have been my go-to support systems.

Shukriyas to Shivani Bafna and photographer Vatsal Shah for their cover inputs.

Without them, and without the lessons learnt at the feet of Maqbool Fida Husain, and of Gautam Rajadhyaksha, I couldn't have dared to venture out on a novel journey.

My gratitude goes, fulsomely, to publisher Ajay Mago who has borne my mood swings like a way younger brother would. And to Dipa Chaudhuri for being there, just a call away, the husky Marlene Dietrich voice accentuating her Agony Sister advice.

In sum, my salaams go out to these altruistic friends and believers who have kept me alive and writing.